Dear Lord,
It Is My Prayer…

Dear Lord, It Is My Prayer...

GOD'S GRACE REVEALED THROUGH TIMELESS
DEVOTIONALS

A Woman's Devotional for all Times

UNITED CHRISTIAN WOMEN'S MINISTRIES

XULON PRESS

Xulon Press
2301 Lucien Way #415
Maitland, FL 32751
407.339.4217
www.xulonpress.com

Unless otherwise indicated, Scripture quotations taken from the King
James Version (KJV)–*public domain*

Printed in the United States of America.

ISBN-13: 978-1-54561-289-7

ACKNOWLEDGMENTS

Several years ago, the Lord impressed upon me to write, capturing His goodness on paper as an encouragement to others and as a reminder of His miraculous work. This compilation took a team effort to complete. A special thanks to all of the ladies across the United States who shared their story. Your willingness to be transparent with your life challenges speaks to your heart for women and their well-being. You have left your stories as a legacy for others as a glimpse of God's grace revealed. The name of each contributor is listed in the back of the book.

Thank you, Editing Teams. Your limitless dedication to reading and re-reading every submitted devotional made this project the best possible. Your time, gifts and talents used in this project will touch the hearts of many, as they see Jesus and His love in their daily reading. Thank you, Editing Team Members, (*their writings can be found in the book*):

Irene Aultman	Frances Christine Robinson
Deborah Bickhem	Elma R. Smith
JoAnn Hardy	Valarie Thomas
Mary Hooker	Verletta Myles Thompson
Theresa Mata	Portia Waynick
Jacqueline Moore	Pearl Wise

Other committee members who remained faithful to this project are Nedra V. Moore and Betty Brown. We extend our thanks for your faithfulness.

Also, we want to remember Sister Olvetta Mitchell, who went home to be with Lord before this book went to print. Her words of encouragement will live on in this publication.

Lastly, thank you to the United Christian Women's Ministries of the Church of Christ (Holiness) USA, under the leadership of National President Portia Waynick, for your continued support and prayers. God answered. As a result, you hold in your hands, *Dear Lord, It Is My Prayer... God's Grace Revealed Through Timeless Devotionals!*

Thank you for taking the journey!

Linda Coleman McDonald
Project Facilitator

TABLE OF CONTENTS

Dear Lord, It Is My Prayer... | ix

INTRODUCTION

Dear Lord, it is my prayer . . .

God's Grace Revealed Through Timeless Devotionals

WOW! *Dear Lord, it is my prayer* was written with you in mind! It took three years to complete with the help of over 150 women from across the country. These women prayed and thought about you the reader, as they crafted this seven-month devotional, which symbolically represents victory in our lives. In the Word of God, the number 7 is symbolic in the release of God's people from bondage. The Year of Jubilee occurred at the end of 7 years; the Israelites walked around the walls of Jericho 7 times; and God rested and called creation perfect on the 7th day. We pray that you experience a spiritual Year of Jubilee after completing this devotional along with us.

Dear Lord, it is my prayer is filled with real-life experiences penned by women who discerned God in their situation, and it is reflected in their "AHA" Moment. As you spend time with God each day, we pray that you find God in the midst of your situation. It is our hope that you grow closer to God as you venture through the pages of this devotional.

The goal of this devotional book is to encourage women to recognize that there is no such thing as hopelessness. Women can experience God's grace in the difficult areas of their lives. Some struggles may have been pushed to the back, or are more than we can handle, while others are too embarrassing to talk about. But know that another woman may have experienced the very same struggle that you have. To that end, the daily devotionals are listed topically in the Index. Feel free to study this devotional based on your circumstance, and as you receive victory, share your experience with others.

Dear Lord, it is my prayer is a tool that can be used to navigate through life's circumstances. As the title suggests, we pray that you take each devotional and allow it to minister to you where you are. We recognize the power of prayer, therefore, at the end of each devotional, you have space to meditate on your personal experiences and take them to God. We encourage you to write down the revelations you receive from God so that you can reflect on them at a later time.

"Let us then with confidence draw near to the throne of grace, that we may receive mercy and find grace to help in time of need" Hebrews 4:16 (ESV).

~ United Christian Women's Ministries ~
Church of Christ (Holiness) U.S.A.

AHA Moment

Accept yourself, God made you. Your weaknesses are not showstoppers

GET READY, IT'S TIME TO MOVE

"Call unto me, and I will answer thee, and shew thee great and mighty things, which thou knowest not." Jeremiah 33:3 (KJV)

The Lord has impressed me to write. The strange thing is that I have avoided this task because writing, in my opinion, is not something that I do well. I asked Him, "Are you sure?" He responded, "Write!"

One morning during my devotional time, God clearly said to me, "I made you Linda—I designed you just the way you are with weaknesses that will cause you to rely on me. **Accept the way I made you!**" These words resonated with me as I walked through the days that followed. I realized that in my personal walk with the Lord, fulfilling my destiny requires that I stop denying my weaknesses and allow God to bless me.

You may wonder what does this have to do with you. Has God ever given you a task that you could not fulfill? Before you start focusing on what you lack in skills, start with the knowledge that "I can do all things through Christ which strengtheneth me" (Philippians 4:13 KJV). God will provide whatever you need to ensure that His will is done. Accept the task, trust God, move forward, and He will show you great and mighty things.

Has God placed something on your heart to do? What's holding you back? Take a step of faith, and see what God does!

Dear Lord, it is my prayer _____
Linda C. McDonald
Decatur, Georgia

AHA Moment

Teach your children about God while they are young.

START THEM YOUNG

"Impress them on your children. Talk to them when you sit at home and when you walk along the road, when you lie down and when you get up."
Deuteronomy 6:7 (NIV)

The Scripture says impress the Word of God upon your children. Then, it gives instructions on how to do it. Speak to them about the goodness of God: 1) while sitting at home, 2) as you are out for a walk, 3) when praying at bedtime, and 4) when you arise each morning. As I look back over my life, some of these very instructions were used to teach me about God.

My AHA moment came after my first child was born. My husband was in the Marine Corp, and our daughter was a precocious four-year old. One day she asked, "How does the BIC ball point pen work when you click it?" Her question was answered, but her curiosity was not satisfied. She looked at the pen, proceeded to take it apart, looked it over, and put it back together again—click—it worked! At that moment, I realized the responsibility of teaching her about God had to begin at an early age. It was not just the Sunday school teacher's responsibility to teach her, but it was my responsibility, too. The Scripture says, "Start children off on the way they should go, and even when they are old they will not turn from it" (Proverbs 22:6 NIV).

I was blessed with nine children and each was like a delicate snowflake, all uniquely different. My responsibility, as a mother, was to teach and lead them. I watched them grow into adulthood, and they have not departed from the faith that was impressed upon them while young.

The challenge is more prevalent today than it was in the 1950's when the challenge for the child's young mind was not so daunting. Start teaching the children about God while they are young. It is your responsibility!

Dear Lord, it is my prayer _____
Olvetta Mitchell
Merrillville, Indiana

AHA Moment

Jesus feels our pain and sorrow.

JESUS CARES

"Jesus wept." John 11:35 (KJV)

We've heard and read this scripture for years, "Jesus wept," the shortest verse in the Bible. In John chapter 11, Mary and Martha's brother, Lazarus was sick unto death. Mary and Martha sent for their friend Jesus who was known as a healer. They sent for help, somewhat the way that we do when we cry out to God in prayer. While Mary, Martha and Lazarus were "going through", Jesus seemed to tarry. By the time Jesus arrived, Lazarus had passed.

Now wait a minute. Jesus is the Son of God; didn't He know what was going on? Martha said to Jesus, "If you would have been here, my brother would not have died." Then we have the words we have heard for years, JESUS WEPT.

Why did Jesus weep? This has never been very clear to me until this year. I, too, called on Jesus. I said, "Lord, my brother is sick and needs you right now!" Well, to my surprise, I thought Jesus didn't show up. I had a serious matter in this life! Jesus was late, and my brother died. Well, that short verse came to life for me. I learned through these words that Jesus knew it was not easy for our family. Jesus wept. He knew that we were hurting. He was not numb to what was happening, and as the saying goes, He was not caught by surprise. The scripture says it so well. We have not a high priest that cannot be touched with our infirmities and [grief] (Hebrews 4:15). I realized that Jesus wept with us even at the funeral.

So, what is the lesson? Jesus knows what is going on and is right there. He is a caring, compassionate God who does not leave us hanging. If you have experienced pain, suffering, or death, please know that Jesus cares.

Our prayer should be, Lord, help us to know that you are with us and that you care when we cry.

Dear Lord, it is my prayer _____
Mary Kennebrew
Little Rock, Arkansas

AHA Moment

It's okay to say "NO."

SEEK GOD BEFORE SAYING YES TO ANYTHING

"In all your ways acknowledge Him, And He shall direct your paths."
Proverbs 3:6 (NKJV)

When people ask you to do something and you are not sure about saying yes, don't be put on the spot to satisfy others. I understand now why I would hear Christians say, "Let me pray and hear what God or the Holy Spirit says," before giving an answer. Worldly people would say, "Let me think about it" before saying yes.

It is amazing how God will bring things to mind that we have done without Him. So, why would we think it is not necessary to always pray first and ask God to reveal what we should do? When we don't, we are pleasing other people and have forgotten to seek the Father first!

To keep myself out of trouble or regretting a decision I've made, I have learned to pray and wait on the Lord for guidance and directions. He has proven Himself in so many areas of my life. Even when I did not know what to do or which way to turn, He taught me how to pray and seek Him. We must wait on the Lord! Isaiah 40:31 (NKJV) says, "But those who wait on the Lord Shall renew their strength; They shall mount up with wings like eagles, They shall run and not be weary, They shall walk and not faint."

I challenge you, friend, to make sure you put Him first in every part of your life. It is okay to tell people no; they may not like it, but it will rest well with you. Seek and wait on the Lord so that you will make wise decisions. God must be glorified!

*"Wait on the Lord; Be of good courage, And He shall strengthen your heart;
Wait, I say on the Lord!" Psalm 27:14 (NKJV)*

Dear Lord, it is my prayer _____
Belinda Hubb
Washington, District of Columbia

AHA Moment

Blessed, and didn't know it!

GOD'S TRUTH IN COMMON WAYS

"In every thing give thanks: for this is the will of God in
Christ Jesus concerning you."
1 Thessalonians 5:18 (KJV)

When my mother passed away, I was devastated. She was *my mom*—the one I went to for counsel. Why would God take her from me? Didn't He know that I needed her?

Several years before I got married, my mother became very ill. I wanted my children to know their grandmother, so I brought my petition before God. My prayer was answered, and my children knew her well. The youngest was nine when she passed. Instead of thanking God for answering my prayer, I asked Him, "Why my mother, who loved and served you?" I repeatedly asked God, "Why?"

However, our Father is so good and loving, that I had to recognize His goodness, despite my sorrow. I needed to be thankful for Him blessing us with her.

God revealed His truth to me in a way that only He could! After returning to work, He sent a student to me saying that he was happy to see me and had wondered where I had been. With tears in my eyes and a broken heart, I said, "I lost my mom." He looked at me in wonderment and said, "Mothers must be wonderful people. I have heard such wonderful things about them. You see, I never knew my mother. She died when I was born; but I always said they must be wonderful people."

God showed me my selfishness. I knew my mother, and yes, they are wonderful people! I asked God to forgive me, and I thanked Him for opening my eyes to His truth: to be thankful in everything! He did not have to bless me with the experience of having a loving mother, but because He is love, He did!

Are you sensitive to the *common ways* God continually expresses His love for us?

Dear Lord, it is my prayer _____
Louvenia Wolfe
Florissant, Missouri

HEED THE WARNING SIGNALS!

"By faith Noah, when warned about things not yet seen, in holy fear built an ark to save his family. By his faith he condemned the world and became heir of the righteousness that is in keeping with faith."
Hebrews 11:7 (NIV)

It sounded like thunder! It was a loud cracking sound from a tree that had fallen in our back yard. The tree hit the ground with such force that our entire house shook from the impact. The tree was inches from crashing into our house; but our home was not damaged.

We knew, prior to the tree falling, that it was a hazard and a threat to our safety. Each time we had a storm with torrential rain and strong winds, branches from this tree would land on our roof. Yet, we ignored the warning signs. How many times have we received warning signals and ignored them? It never pays to disregard a warning issued for your protection or welfare.

God faithfully gives us warning signals. He purposely set up "warning" signs so that we can take precautionary measures. It is similar to road signs that tell us "Stop! Danger ahead!" Cautionary signs are placed along the road to warn of potential danger or to guide us safely to our destinations. Not only are these signs necessary on roadways, but they are needed in life to help us avoid danger and to move us in the right direction.

Noah listened to the warning from God and did exactly what God commanded him to do. He warned the people; however, they ignored him and were surprised when the flood came.

Sometimes the actual "whys" may not be revealed until later; however, rather than ignore the signs, pay attention, and make the necessary changes before it's too late.

Dear Lord, it is my prayer _____
June Bond
Houston, Texas

The line of communication is always open with God.

GOD ANSWERS OUR CALL

"Call unto me, and I will answer thee, and shew thee great and mighty things, which thou knowest not." Jeremiah 33:3 (KJV)

When I was growing up in the 60's and 70's and the phone would ring at the house, we usually had no idea who it was on the line before we answered. Thoughts would go through my head: Do I have time for this call? "I hope it's ___ calling." "Oh Lord, I hope it's not ___ calling." We did not know who it was on the line until the phone was answered.

Thank the Lord for the advancements in telephone technology. Praise God and bless the person who created *caller id*. Today, the phone rings and on our modern phones, in most cases, I know who is calling. I can quickly contemplate if I should answer the call or just let it go to voice mail. I realize this works both ways. When I make a phone call, it's not a sure thing that it will be answered. This is frustrating when I truly need to speak with someone.

I am so glad God is not like us when it comes to answering calls! He tells us in Isaiah 65:24," . . . *before they call, I will answer. . . .*" My favorite verse in the Bible is found in Jeremiah 33:3 (KJV), "Call unto me, and I will answer thee, and shew thee great and mighty things, which thou knowest not"—a very simple but profound verse, easy to understand. These words were spoken by God to the prophet Jeremiah to encourage him in his ministry.

Right now, whatever your lot may be, remember God's invitation to call on Him and His promise to answer and show you great and mighty things that you did know before. Have faith that His answer will allow you to overcome whatever situation you find yourself in. Call on Him; I guarantee you, He will answer your call.

Dear Lord, it is my prayer _____
Portia Waynick
Los Angeles, California

AHA Moment

Life is a race I must live to win.

ARE YOU IN IT TO WIN IT?

"Don't you realize that in a race everyone runs, but only one person gets the prize? So run to win! All athletes are disciplined in their training. They do it to win a prize that will fade away, but we do it for an eternal prize. So I run with purpose in every step. I am not just shadowboxing."
1 Corinthians 9:24-27 (NLT)

We are all competing in a race. I Corinthians 9:24-27 tells us there are those who are aimlessly strolling through life in this race, while others are preparing to win the prize. This prize is eternity with Christ and conditioning ourselves to win our race is a daily process.

There are many competitions that we prepare for, such as a beauty or running contest. In each contest, preparation is required. God sent His Son to be the Savior of the world, and He is reminding us that life is indeed a race for all eternity. Everyone is invited to participate. We are not to take our spiritual journey for granted. Get serious about the race, prepare and stay focused!

We should ask God, "What do you want me to do today? How do you want to use me? Whose life can I enrich?" To win the race we must first have a relationship with God. Before I married my husband, we developed a relationship. In order to win the prize with Christ, you must also develop a relationship.

We must commit to do two very important things: 1) spend time with God, and 2) focus on what is to come. We prepare by praying and studying God's Word. Also, it is crucial that we talk and listen to Him through the Word. We must concentrate on winning the prize daily. If we stay focused on the prize, He has promised that we will all be WINNERS!

ARE YOU IN IT TO WIN IT?

Dear Lord, it is my prayer _____
Pearl Lindsay
Los Angeles, California

CHANGE YOUR FOCUS

"I will behave myself wisely in a perfect way. O when wilt thou come unto me?
I will walk within my house with a perfect heart."
Psalm 101:2 (KJV)

Recently, I poured out my heart and soul to my friend about a person who upset me. It seemed the more I disclosed, the more she opposed. It became evident that she was not listening to me, and I did not understand. So, I got off the phone. Needless to say, I was very annoyed.

Seeking something to soothe my wounded pride, I opened my Bible and was led to Psalm 101.

I read it in its entirety. As I read, I was enlightened. David said, "I will behave myself wisely . . . I will walk within my house with a perfect heart. I will set no wicked thing before mine eyes: ... I will not know a wicked person. Whoso privily slandereth his neighbour, him will I cut off: him that hath an high look and a proud heart will not I suffer" Psalm 101:2-5 (KJV).
After reading this passage, I realized that my focus was on something I did not like that was making me angry and weakening my spirit. No wonder my friend was in agony over what I was disclosing. All she heard was complaining, discouragement, and self-pity. The Lord wants us to be victorious. We cannot do that if we focus on things that discourage us and makes us angry.

I challenge you to focus on the goodness of God and His faithfulness. When faced with a harmful situation, change your focus. Forgive quickly, and don't give life to any negative situation by discussing it others. "Set your minds on things above, not on earthly things" Colossians 3:2 (NIV). Help us Lord to focus on your goodness and faithfulness.

Dear Lord, it is my prayer _____
Natalie Smith
Farmington Hills, Michigan

ALWAYS BE GRATEFUL

"Enter into his gates with thanksgiving, and into his courts with praise:
be thankful unto him, and bless his name."
Psalm 100:4 (KJV)

God showed up in a miraculous way, and for that, I am eternally grateful.

In July 2013, my life had a major turn of events. My husband suffered a stroke, and I instantly became his caregiver. I began walking in unfamiliar territory stumbling and blundering with my husband's care. I was too busy to talk to God, or even pray for divine intervention. Although others prayed for us, I was careful to ask that they pray for none other than His perfect will. Being very tired and worn, I struggled with God. I endured moments of restlessness, sleeplessness, and anger. One morning before day, I recall crying out to God. What did He expect from me and where should I go? I wanted rest and I needed restoration — not just for my husband, but for me, too. He wanted my total submission to His perfect will. God ministered to me in so many ways that I now desire an even closer and more intimate relationship with Him. You see, sometimes God moves us in directions and positions us to receive His blessings because He wants us to embrace them.

God has smiled on me! He has delivered me, and therefore, my soul is grateful! He wants me to share and care for others as He cares for me. I endeavor to encourage others to diligently seek God and vow to serve Him in the midst of obstacles and challenges.

We should be thankful for the many blessings that God has bestowed upon us and for the miraculous way He has worked in our lives. We should ask that He transforms us into the vessel that can be used for His service and remove anything that is unlike Him.

Dear Lord, it is my prayer _____
Shenitha Pridgen
Jackson, Mississippi

AHA MOMENT
Though weak, He makes us strong.

SUFFERING IN SILENCE

"... My grace is sufficient for you, for my strength is made perfect in weakness."
II Corinthians 12:9 (NKJV)

There was a time in my life when I was angry with God because He would not save my husband, or at least, stop him from drinking. You see, my husband was an alcoholic. No matter what I said or did, I could not change him. I had to realize that was not my job! With each promise I would say "maybe this time" but that promise would quickly be broken. I had to trust the Lord to change his life; so, I just suffered in silence. He was not physically abusive to us, but we watched as he abused himself and, ultimately, destroyed his body.

When someone would ask how things were, I would smile broadly and say, "we're fine," although my spirit was screaming in pain. As I was learning to depend totally on the Lord, my role changed; I had become a caregiver. No matter how difficult situations would become or how many tears were shed, the Lord sustained me even in my weakest moments.

Often, we suffer due to the circumstances of our lives, but we have to trust the Lord to intercede. You have to remove the veil of frustration, pretense, and shame; seek His face, and spend time in His Word. Reach out to a friend, a prayer warrior, someone you trust; then talk and pray together. You do not have to suffer alone. The Lord promised Joshua that, "... I will never leave you nor forsake you" (Joshua 1:5 NIV) and that promise is still true for us.

My smiles became genuine as I learned I had the assurance of Galatians 6:9, "And let us not be weary in well doing: for in due season we shall reap, if we faint not." I have reaped joy, peace, and God's faithfulness as I have grown in Him. Rather than suffering in silence, you can lift your voice in praise. Incidentally, my husband *did* give his life to the Lord before he passed. HALLELUJAH!

Dear Lord, it is my prayer _____
Deborah Bickhem
Park Forest, Illinois

AHA Moment

Hold on and believe!

THE FAITHFULNESS OF GOD

"Faith is the confidence that what we hope for will actually happen; it gives us
assurance about things we cannot see."
Hebrews 11:1 (NLT)

God can change an impossible situation into one that is possible; however, it
takes faith. Faith is not obtained at the moment a storm hits. It comes through
studying the Word of God, praying continually, and believing that God can do
all things if we have mustard seed faith.

I am 61 years of age, and I know that God has kept me. Initially, I was introduced to faith through my mother and grandmother's faith in God. When I
was two, I experienced third-degree burns over my entire body except my face.
Although my parents had been told I would never have children due to the mag-
nitude of the burns, I gave birth to two children. This was done through prayer
and belief in Jesus Christ. My children are now adults, and I have six grandchildren—but God!

I have gone through many storms since that time. My father passed away
shortly after the birth of my son, my children's father was abusive and became
addicted to drugs, and I became a single parent. Finally, the person I relied on
most, my mother, passed away from breast cancer.

Prior to her death, I was hospitalized with stress-related chest pains that
the doctor said, "They will kill you, if you don't get it together." My mom said,
"Chile you don't have time to die because I am dying, and when I'm gone who
will take care of your children?" My mother's words reminded me that the Lord
had been holding me up, and I needed to hold on because my children were
depending on me.

"In the storms of life, you can survive by grace, faith, and hope." Lailah Gifty
Akita, *Think Great: Be Great!*

Dear Lord, it is my prayer _____
Marilyn Pitts
Los Angeles, California

AHA MOMENT

I realized in that moment, I wouldn't have time to get right;
I needed to already be right with the Lord.

HELP ME, JESUS!

"God is our refuge and strength, a very present help in trouble."
Psalm 46:1 (KJV)

It has happened every day since I have believed. I have been taken from faith-to-faith. I know He lives in me and cares about me each day. Travelling the highways and the byways can be grueling, tiresome, and even dangerous in Los Angeles, California. I am a Los Angeles commuter among the reported 1,494,895 commuters. One day as I travelled the freeway exceeding the speed limit, I encountered a flood of red lights. Hitting the brakes, the car spun out of control, I shouted, "Jesus!"

Had my moment come; would I die; would I hurt others? My Savior is an ever-present help (Psalm 46:1) in my time of need, and He cares enough to answer when I call (Isaiah 65:24). He loves me so much that He will catch me when I fall (Psalm 145:14). The power that is at work in me (Ephesians 1:19) raised Jesus Christ from the grave, and it is surely able to stop a spinning car in the midst of stopped traffic. As the car spun in its place, and finally came to a stop, I was an inch from the retaining wall. All I could do was thank Him as I quickly threw up my arms and shouted praises to Him.

Being assured by His Word to Joshua, ". . . as I was with Moses, so I will be with thee: I will not fail thee, nor forsake thee" (Joshua 1:5 KJV). His assurance each day calms me and gives me courage to stand in spite of the cars, drivers, and statistics. His correction will allow me to obey the speed limits.

Has your faith grown? Will you trust the Lord more to obey Him?

Dear Lord, it is my prayer _____
Theresa Mata
Los Angeles, California

SQUATTERS

"The snare is laid for him in the ground, and a trap for him in the way."
Job 18:10 (KJV)

Great preaching tells us to trust God and in a little while, everything will be all right. The truth is that if we do not go through the process of studying and applying the scriptures daily, things will not be all right.

I recently heard a news report about squatters in my community. The law forbids a citizen from using force to remove squatters from their property. The legal process of the judicial system is the only way to remove squatters. The property may be damaged, and possessions ruined; but squatters can only be removed lawfully. The owner jeopardizes recovery of property and protection if the legal process is avoided because squatters have rights.

I was livid when I learned that people could break into a house and take over! As I ranted and raved to my husband about how unfair this is, the Holy Spirit said to me, "Pam, I'm livid as well. People of God allow squatters to break into their hearts with: 'anger, rage, bad feeling toward others, curses and slander, and foul-mouthed abuse and shameful utterances from your lips" Colossians 3:8 (AMP)!

T. D. Jakes stated that the snare, referenced in Job 18:10, is a trap set to bring us down from the height of our potential into the grasp of the enemy. Squatters are like traps that bring spiritual wickedness, strategies, and deceitful practices hoping to ensnare us so that we give in to circumstances such as divorce or forsaking family. Get the squatters out with 5 smooth stones just like David:

1. Read the Scripture;
2. Practice what you read;
3. Write the vision;
4. Post it on the fridge; and
5. Carry it in your wallet or record your voice to hear the Word of God.

Those uncircumcised Philistines cannot squat in our house!

Dear Lord, it is my prayer _____
Pamela Lockett
Canton Township, Michigan

AHA Moment
The Holy Spirit was already inside!

CHANGED FOREVER

"For God so loved the world that he gave his only begotten Son, that whosoever believeth in him should not perish, but have everlasting life."
John 3:16 (KJV)

Raised in a strong Christian family, my parents and aunt set great examples as they modeled Christ-like behaviors. I understood God versus Satan as I witnessed many miracles and demonic actions. It should have been easy to stay on the right path, and I did what I thought was right. I believed I was saved, but I wasn't pleasing God. I began searching for the power of the Holy Spirit and whatever made "church people" shout. The more I searched, the thirstier I became. Yet, I did everything to feel satisfied.

Even though God spoke to me, I disobeyed and spent my time with people who were living in sin. However, it seemed okay since I didn't participate and still attended church. It surprised me when a lady said, "You know you can still go to hell!" The thirst was now unbearable. I cried out to God, "Help me! I'm a good person", but the Lord said, you don't even know me. "Not every one that saith unto me, Lord, Lord, shall enter into the kingdom of heaven; . . ." Matthew 7:21 (KJV).

God taught me through Bible study and prayer. While attending a conference where the praise and worship were phenomenal, I experienced the presence and power of the Holy Spirit from the inside out. Instantly, I was different and invited Him into my life to save me, forgive my sins, and to come into my heart to be my Lord and Savior. I had been searching for Him, but He was already there. God is real, and He gives us "an internal guide" —the Holy Spirit.

Please choose the God of heaven, and not the landlord of hell.

Dear Lord, it is my prayer _____
Julz Julemi White
Washington, District of Columbia

AHA Moment

Knee jerk reactions hinder our ability to truly follow God.

THE DANGER OF AN AUTOMATIC RESPONSE

"For as many as are led by the Spirit of God, they are the sons of God."
Romans 8:14 (KJV)

I was concerned. My friend's tendency to respond to unwanted, uncomfortable, or painful experiences with knee jerk reactions caused her to reject any possibility that God could be working in her discomfort. As Christians who are being conformed into the image of God's Son (Romans 8:29), we are to be led by the Spirit of God (Romans 8:14).

When we reject life's unpleasantness with automatic responses, there is a chance that we may be automatically rejecting the leading of the Holy Spirit without recognizing it. For too many, the idea of having a remote control that allowed fast-forwarding through unpleasant aspects of life sounds good. Like Adam Sandler's character in the 2006 movie, *Click,* when we don't want to deal with something or someone just—click!

Let me be clear. Not all automatic responses are to be avoided. In fact, we can develop some habitual reactions that are beneficial. For example, when we feel anxious we can choose to bring our concerns immediately to God in prayer with a thankful heart (Philippians 4:6-7 AMP). The result of this swift reaction to anxiety, God's Word promises, will yield incomprehensible peace standing guard like a garrison over our hearts and minds. On the other hand, if we react to life's discomforts with fretful imaginings, we risk going through life following our own way only to discover that we have missed real life with God altogether.

When we only engage in things that we are comfortable with, not only are we resisting God's desire to conform us into His Son's image, we also unwisely reject the Holy Spirit's direction and empowerment.

Dear Lord, it is my prayer _____
Christina Dixon
Detroit, Michigan

AHA MOMENT
Move by FAITH!

WHO NEEDS A MIRACLE?

"Now faith is the substance of things hoped for, the evidence of things not seen."
Hebrews 11:1 (KJV)

"And a certain woman, which had an issue of blood twelve years, And had suffered many things of many physicians, and had spent all that she had, and was nothing bettered, but rather grew worse,"
Mark 5:25-26 (KJV)

One day, a woman heard about the miracles that Jesus performed, so she decided to try Jesus. What a challenge, because a great multitude of people surrounded Jesus. The woman was very sick, weak and tired. The crowd was huge; no one was showing any courtesy. The woman knew that she had get to Jesus, but she could not see how to make it there. Now, her faith increased. She thought about how long she had been sick. So, she started saying, "Excuse me!" The crowd ignored her. She pushed and tried to squeeze her way, but the crowd pushed back. She did not move any closer. Every time her efforts failed, her faith grew stronger and stronger. The crowd yelled, "You need to wait! We are trying to reach Him too!"

Seeing Jesus move farther away, she thought, "I might not have another chance, because surely I'm dying!" She knew the only way to Him was to crawl on her knees on the ground. Oh, how she felt her little weak fingers being stepped on by the crowd's scandals and dirty feet! Then, she saw a long garment and said, "If I may touch but his clothes, I shall be whole. And straightway the fountain of her blood was dried up; and she felt in her body that she was healed of that plague" Mark 5:28-29 (KJV).

Jesus is a miracle worker. Your faith in Jesus makes you whole. When life becomes too difficult, we must put our faith in action to make it through!

Dear Lord, it is my prayer _____
Magdalene McNeil
Jackson, Mississippi

AHA MOMENT

Have faith, trust, pray, and thank God.

GOD WILL FIX IT

"Trust in the LORD with all thine heart; and lean
not unto thine own understanding."
Proverbs 3:5 (KJV)

I relocated to Georgia from Illinois twenty-four years ago with my sons, after deciding to accept a position there. I prepared between teaching summer school and working evenings as a Playground Teacher.

My first year seemed as if Murphy's Law applied, "Anything that can go wrong will go wrong." When renting a truck, I was assured that it was large enough to transport all of my possessions. All went well until the truck was halfway loaded. The professional movers *then* realized that it was too small. I followed the truck to Georgia, and then drove back for the remainder of my items.

After arriving, the truck was unpacked, but my car would not start. I returned the truck, and then rented a car to immediately drive back to Illinois, where I rented another truck, and drove back to Georgia. Not resting since the initial trip, I had to continue driving because orientation for the new job was mandatory for the next three days. I drove the truck, and my family followed me in the rental car. Upon completing orientation, I drove my mother to Illinois, and *again* returned to Georgia. Driving back-and-forth, five times during the week, was a total of 3,750 miles!

The first year in Georgia, had its share of unforeseen circumstances which were beyond my control. I thought, "Maybe God is trying to tell me something." My car had not been repaired satisfactorily, so I filed a claim, appeared on Court TV, and the judge ruled in my favor. I also had several new health challenges. Not having any local family support, my faith was tested, but I prayed, trusted, and focused on Him.

If you acknowledge Him in all your ways, "he shall direct thy paths." I thank God because, "I can do all things through Christ which strengtheneth me" Philippians 4:13 (KJV).

Dear Lord, it is my prayer _____
Verletta Thompson
Fayetteville, Georgia

AHA Moment

COMMIT YOUR WAYS

"Commit thy way unto the Lord; trust also in Him;
and He shall bring it to pass."
Psalm 37:5 (KJV)

Have you ever said, "Yes", to the Lord with a surrendered heart, and you had no idea where that promise would take you? I have experienced many blessings and difficult moments too — moments that only the Holy Spirit's comfort brought me through.

One such moment was when I was traveling to Honduras. We had boarded our flight, pulled onto the tarmac and then came to an abrupt stop. The pilot informed us there were some issues that required a mechanic. Turning on our phones while we waited, I received a text that my 81-year-old mom had just suffered a stroke and was paralyzed on her left side.

When we returned to the terminal to board a different airplane, I shared the news with the team and was asked if I needed to go and be with family. I must admit, I thought perhaps I should, but I clearly heard the Lord ask, "If I can't trust you now, then when?" I informed the team that I was going to continue to Honduras and that as I sought God's Kingdom first, He would take care of my mother.

We prayed for God to heal her, and I asked Him for confirmation. Immediately, I received a call that the paralysis had suddenly left her body. That was all I needed to hear! I left in peace to fulfill God's plan in Honduras.

God completely healed my mother. Her physicians are still amazed at her total and complete recovery. Not only did the Lord heal her, but He also performed miraculously in Honduras too! On my return flight, I stopped in Orlando to visit Mom and found her rejoicing in the God of her salvation!!!

Remember, He that calls you is faithful, and He will do just what He promised.

Dear Lord, it is my prayer _____
Lillian Brown
Jackson, Mississippi

AHA Moment
Look to the SON.

SONSHINE

"I will lift up mine eyes unto the hills, from whence cometh my help.
My help cometh from the LORD which made heaven and earth."
Psalm 121:1-2 (KJV)

Growing up on a farm, I learned a lot about plants. Many days I watched, and sometimes I helped my grandmother with her many flowers and plants that adorned our yard. It was one of the most beautiful yards in the community, once earning her the title "Garden of the Month"! During the spring and summer, my grandmother was constantly planting, potting, repotting, rooting, weeding, pruning, and watering to maintain her "title".

Often, she would come home from a visit with family or friends with sprigs of wilted plants wrapped in wet paper towels and put them in water. It was fascinating to see, just days later, vibrant leaves and tiny roots shooting from the once lifeless stems. Soon they would be ready to be potted.

In the fall, some of the potted plants would be brought inside. It was my chore to turn the plants. At first, I did not understand why, but I soon came to a realization that even with all of my grandmother's great care, the plants were lacking something. They missed being out in the sun. The plants would lean and face the window until the stems would start to bend with leaves like arms outstretched as if trying to reach the sun. Turning the pots around would cause the plants to straighten but soon they were facing the sun again!

I have learned that I am like the plants. In the **Son**, I thrive. I have everything I need. In times of adversity, when it seems as though walls are closing in around me trying to block out my life source, I know I must quickly "look to hills" where the **Son** is.

I challenge you to study all of nature. Look for signs of God's creations that are dependent on Him for existence.

Dear Lord, it is my prayer _____
Valarie Thomas
Sacramento, California

AHA MOMENT

God wants us to always give Him praise.

THE POWER OF PRAISE

"O Give thanks unto the LORD; for He is good: for His mercy endures forever."
Psalm 136:1 (KJV)

Have there been times in your life when you have felt defeated, discouraged, and afraid? Perhaps, you felt that God had forgotten about you although his word says that He will never leave not forsake you. In 2 Chronicles 20, King Jehoshaphat was advised that a great army was coming to attack the children of Israel. Fearfully, he questioned the Lord and reminded Him that He had rescued the children of Israel in the past, but the armies are coming against us now, and we don't know what to do.

The Spirit of the LORD said, "Do not be afraid nor dismayed . . ." for the battle is not yours, but God's" 2 Chronicles 20:15 (NKJV). "You will not need to fight this battle . . . stand still and see the salvation of the LORD, who is with you." (vs. 17) Jehoshaphat then bowed before the Lord and worshiped Him instructing the singers to go in front of the army singing, "Praise the LORD for his mercy endures forever." (vs. 21)

When trials come against us, we often forget how faithful God has been, how He has kept us, and how often He has rescued us. We wonder, "Why is this happening to me? What have I done to experience such hardship?" In spite of trouble, God continues to expect us to lift Him up in worship, praise, and acknowledgement of who He is, no matter how difficult the circumstances. "Give thanks in all circumstances, for this is God's will for you in Christ Jesus" 1 Thessalonians 5:18 (NIV).

During our most stressful hours, He reminds us, "that in all things God works for the good of those who love him, who have been called according to his purpose" Romans 8:28 (NIV). We should, therefore, give Him glory and sing as the Israelites, "Praise the LORD FOR His mercy endures forever." There is power in praise!

Dear Lord, it is my prayer _____
Deborah Bickhem
Park Forest, Illinois

AHA Moment

It takes time to pray.

KEEP PRAYING

"The effectual fervent prayer of a righteous man availeth much."
James 5:16b (KJV)

Prayer is one of the most precious and important aspects of my life because prayer does change things. There have been times when I have been troubled in my heart over various issues and prayer was my only resource for relief. The latter part of Luke 18:1 (KJV) says, ". . . that men ought always to pray, and not to faint." There have been times when I have prayed to God for a long period, pouring out my heart to Him. And after a while, I felt the burden lifted and relief over the situation.

One particular issue that troubled me for three years was the fact that my church did not have a permanent pastor. In all my years attending church, I have always had a pastor, a shepherd to lead the people and encourage us in our walk with God. During that time, I never stopped praying. My fervent prayer to God for three years was for Him to send our church a pastor — not just any pastor but one that truly loved God and had a love for God's people. Have you heard the saying, "He may not come when you want Him, but He's right on time"? Well, in God's time, He sent our church a very good pastor. I praise God for His goodness, mercy, love and answered prayer.

If the Almighty God who made heaven and earth takes time to hear our prayers, I encourage you to take the time to pray to Him. Whatever situation you find yourself in, do not hesitate to pray to Him. Keep praying effectively and fervently because your prayers matter to God.

Dear Lord, it is my prayer _____
Barbara Waynick
Long Beach, California

AHA Moment

Worship is about who GOD is and an opportunity to remember who we are.

AN AUDIENCE OF ONE

"Therefore, since we are receiving a kingdom that cannot be shaken,
let us be thankful, and so worship God acceptably with
reverence and awe. For our God is a devouring fire."
Hebrews 12:28-29 (NIV)

Worship, as we know it, is related to hand gestures, our eyes being opened or closed, our posture, and singing a slow song. It is simply to fulfill the original plan our Creator had when He decided to fill the world with people. We are selfish by nature, and we make requests and demands centered on our own position in life. Worship, in its true form, is about sacrifice because it is solely about glorifying and honoring God for who He is. How you view God is evident in how you worship Him.

If we consider God as our provider, our *worship* will be requests for blessings and thanks for those blessings. That form of *worship* is not true worship. It's actually praise or to speak well of God for what He's done and what He can do. Worship requires that we see God as more than simply a provider. When we reach the point that we are awestruck by who God is, all-powerful, all-knowing, our worship focus would shift. Then, we would realize that we are blessed, not because of the prayers God answers, but because we are able to serve an awesome, powerful, and loving Father.

Hebrews 12:28 (NIV) reads, ". . . and so worship God acceptably with reverence and awe." It is easy to believe that our supplications and requests deserve time in worship because in most worship experiences, we are making requests to God to do something for us. Hebrews Chapter 12 talks about discipline and obedience. Acceptable worship requires being disciplined and focused on acknowledging who God is, and not getting distracted by our own thoughts and concerns. We were created to worship Him.

Dear Lord, it is my prayer _____
Jessica Campbell Gant
Covington, Georgia

AHA Moment
YOU are the apple of God's Eye!

A LESSON FROM THE EYE

"For thus saith the Lord of hosts; After the glory hath he sent me unto the nations
which spoiled you: for he that toucheth you toucheth the apple of his eye."
Zechariah 2:8 (KJV)

We use our eyes constantly and, often, unawares, because we are accustomed
to *seeing* and usually not realizing the processes that are ongoing as we see.

When Scripture speaks of the apple of the eye, it references the pupil, which
is the center of sight. It *expands* when light is dim to let more light in. It *contracts*
when light is bright for regulating the light's intensity. This principle can aptly
be applied in our walk with God. When our way is dim, He *expands* our view
by sustaining us through our faith, "While we look not at the things which are
seen, but at the things which are not seen" 2 Corinthians 4:18 (KJV). When our
experiences are fair, He *extends* our focus in unspeakable joy.

Just as our eyesight (pupil) is the gateway to our minds and hearts, so we,
as God's "pupil", are the same to Him. He guides us whether the way is dark or
bright. He gives us light to see the pathway of life. Our part is to keep "Looking
unto Jesus the author and finisher of our faith" Hebrews 12:2 (KJV).
Remember, we are the *apple of His eye.*

Dear Lord, it is my prayer _____
Annie K. Bingham
Pearl, Mississippi

AHA Moment

God never fails.

MIRACULOUS BLESSING FROM GOD

"I will lift up mine eyes unto the hills, from whence cometh my help.
My help cometh from the LORD, which made heaven and earth." Psalm
121:1-2 (KJV)

In August of 2009, I suddenly became *extremely* ill. I went to the hospital's emergency room due to having excruciating abdominal pains. After checking into triage, a Magnetic Resonance Imaging (MRI) Test was administered, and that was the last thing I remembered until I awoke weeks later in a rehabilitation facility. I was unconscious and unaware of what happened during my hospitalization, so my daughters gave me a vivid description of what had transpired.

The day following the MRI, surgery was performed to repair an internal organ. While in the Recovery Room, my daughters were told that this procedure had gone well.

The next morning, I unfortunately took a turn for the worst. The physician thought that I may have had a stroke or was in a coma. Even worse, I had somehow gotten Septic Shock Infection which has a 95% mortality rate. I also had pneumonia, fluid on my lungs, two-heart valves blocked, and I was on a ventilator at 100% because I could not breathe on my own. The sclera or white part of my eyes was light brown with dark brown spots positioned like polka dots. Lastly, my kidneys stopped functioning for three days, because all of my organs were beginning to shut down.

I remained in the Intensive Care Unit for three weeks. Miraculously, and by the grace of God, I gradually got better. I had not walked since becoming ill in August, so I went to a rehabilitation facility for therapy where I remained until the end of November.

Although I have not been able to walk again, this experience has allowed me numerous opportunities to share this miracle with others and trust the Lord even more. Now, I enjoy spending my days praying, meditating, and watching the geese on the pond.

Dear Lord, it is my prayer _____
Barbara Wolfe Wardlow
Matteson, Illinois

AHA Moment
You have a responsibility to give.

A REWARD FOR YOU!

"Give, and it will be given to you: good measure, pressed down, shaken together, and running over will be put into your bosom. For with the same measure that you use, it will be measured back to you."
Luke 6:38 (NKJV)

A pastor once told me that my gift is a heart for giving to others. Whether it's your time, your talent, or your tithe, you have a responsibility to give. Being a caregiver has taught me so much about giving unconditionally, unselfishly and ungrudgingly. At times, I'm exhausted, but the good Lord gives me strength when I am weak. The smile, hug or kiss, that I get in return is so rewarding and worth the sacrifice.

The Word promises that when I give, it will be given back to me. How I give and how much I give will be the measure that is given back. The Lord is so gracious that I often feel I'm blessed more for the small things I do as a caregiver and for just being a friendly neighbor. You have something to give as well: your time as a caregiver, extra shoes in your car trunk to give to a homeless person, or an apple pie for your neighbor. Do as the Lord commands and be blessed in return for sharing the love of God!

As child of God, your prayer should be that you will give to others and share His love. Be ready to look for opportunities to bless others. In return, the Lord promises to give back a blessing that is running over and more than enough! That is so encouraging! I thank the Lord for using me to bless others and further His Kingdom.

Dear Lord, it is my prayer _____
Felissa Lynn Waynick
Los Angeles, California

AHA Moment

God cares about our whole bodies, not just our spirit.

HABITS THAT PREVENT HEALTHINESS

"But I discipline my body and keep it under control, lest after
preaching to others I myself should be disqualified."
1 Corinthians 9:27 ESV

Late one night, I was leaving my friend's house and stopped at a gas station to buy some candy. This was not the first time; and I knew my addiction to sugar had hit an all-time high. I had known about this addiction for some time. However, I did not know that it was bad enough to affect how I spent my money. I did not think I could stop eating candy. No fast that I tried worked. I asked God on many occasions to deliver me from my addiction to sugar. I even went to the altar asking for prayer. He broke the chains; and it was now my turn to walk in freedom.

Eating candy at the rate that I did was not healthy. I was not in control of my body. Living a healthy life not only has physical and mental benefits, but spiritual, as well. Eating well and exercising increase energy levels overall, which is associated with lower levels of depression and anxiety. When I eat better, I am more in tune with my ministry activities. I am more able to focus on other things when the focus is not my eating.

According to I Corinthians 6:19-20, God wants us to remember that our bodies are temples that should be used to edify Him. Therefore, we are required to improve our mental, physical and spiritual being.

Today, let us make a commitment to be healthier for the glory of God. Ask God what he wants you to do in order to improve your lifestyle.

Dear Lord, it is my prayer _____
Jasmine Wise
Monroe, Louisiana

AHA Moment

Real security is in God only.

ABIDING IN HIM

"He who dwells in the secret place of the Most High Shall
abide under the shadow of the Almighty."
Psalm 91:1 (NKJV)

I like traveling with my family and friends. We have traveled extensively by car throughout this country for vacations, conferences, and conventions. However, I was fearful of traveling alone out of town, even for short distances, and many times I would not go. This fear of traveling alone began to gain more and more control over me to the point that I missed many events.

The acknowledgement of my fear was the beginning of my journey of trusting God in every situation. His Word became real in my life. Fear is not of God, but a sign of disbelief in Him. 2 Timothy 1:7 (NKJV) reads, "God has not given us a spirit of fear, but of power and of love and of a sound mind." I believe in God, and knowing this, I have learned to accept God in a more personal way. He is everywhere, all-powerful, almighty, and He will never leave me. As the Psalmist says in Psalm 139:12 (NKJV), "Indeed, the darkness shall not hide from You, but the night shines as the day; the darkness and the light are both alike *to* You." The night is as day to Him. Nothing on earth can diminish His power and authority.

I found much needed courage and faith in knowing that God is with me and will sustain me daily. No matter where I go, He is God there, too! Regardless of where I am, He sees and knows all. Fear not because He is with us. I am abiding in His Word.

To live in His secret place and abide in the shadow of the Almighty is real security.

Dear Lord, it is my prayer _____
Betty C. Brown
Monroe, Louisiana

AHA Moment

If you want to experience who God is and all that
He is, you have to spend time in the secret place.

A SECRET PLACE

"He who dwells in the secret place of the Most High shall abide under the shadow of the Almighty. I will say of the LORD, 'He is my refuge and my fortress; My God in Him I will trust.'"
Psalm 91:1-2 (NKJV)

One thing I have come to recognize is that we often want to know what God requires of us, such as, what is His will for our lives and answers to our prayers. In order to know who God is, we need to develop a desire to draw closer to Him and increase our quiet time with Him.

We do not have to be ashamed in the secret place where we can be honest with Him. "But you, when you pray, go into your room, and when you have shut your door, pray to your Father who is in the secret place; and your Father who sees in secret will reward you openly" Matthew 6:6 (NKJV). In the secret place, I am able to pour my soul out to God. It does not matter what my situation is, I can let Him know what is going on with me—my struggles, emotional pain, or whatever it is, and God is always ready to hear and give me the reassurance that I can put my trust in Him. He has truly proven to be faithful to me.

As women of God, if we want to bear lasting fruit, the power to bear that fruit comes from time spent with Him in the secret place. "But the fruit of the spirit is love, joy, peace, longsuffering, kindness, goodness, faithfulness, gentleness, self-control" Galatians 5:22-23(NKJV). Our prayer should be that we draw closer to Him with our hearts fully committed to spending time in His presence, knowing that we will reap eternal benefits.

Dear Lord, it is my prayer _____
Dawn S. Cudjoe
Merrillville, Indiana

AHA Moment

Even during trials, He gives us joy and peace.

ATTITUDE CHECK

"Consider it all joy, my brethren, when you encounter various trials, knowing that the testing of your faith produces endurance. And let endurance have its perfect result, so that you may be perfect and complete, lacking in nothing."
James 1:2-4 (NASB)

Life's trials can impact us in ways that we could never imagine possible. The depth of pain that can be experienced from the betrayal of a friend, death of a loved one, breakup of a marriage, diagnosis of cancer, or the loss of a job has the ability to rob us of our joy and peace. The trials of life have the power to catapult us into a downward spiral of hopelessness, which can result in anger, resentment, bitterness, or depression. How is it possible for the Christ follower to maintain joy in the midst of trials?

I had a marriage break-up after 32 years. Yes, it was very hurtful spiritually and physically. BUT GOD was there to carry me through it all. I don't recall my attitude being hateful—just shocked!

James reminds us to do an attitude check when facing trials. He tells us to consider it pure joy. To "consider" means to think about. Having the proper attitude or perception, is necessary when confronted with adversities. How we think determines how we respond to life's difficulties. A wrong perspective can lead to cloudy thinking, selfpity, and doubt when facing trials. However, a clear perspective allows you to rest in God, knowing that He is perfecting your character and knowing this makes it more reasonable to "count it all joy." Having joy during our trials is not connected to an emotional feeling. Joy comes as we prayerfully appraise the situation from God's perspective. The trial does not serve to destroy us, but to produce godly character in us.

Paul said it best in Romans 5:3-4, ask yourself:
1. How has your trial affected your attitude?
2. How can you apply what you have learned when facing trials?

Dear Lord, it is my prayer _____
Sharon Johnson Cherry
Decatur, Georgia

AHA Moment

Maybe I'm the problem!

CHECK YOUR SETTINGS

"He shall call upon me, and I will answer him . . ."
Psalm 91:15a (KJV)

My husband and I got new cell phones! After 2-3 days, we realized that I was not receiving phone calls or text messages from him. He received my messages, but I didn't receive his. This situation was inconvenient and frustrating because our second car was out of commission, and we needed to communicate concerning rides, among other things. Several times I said to him, "Something is wrong with your phone." Since other people got his calls and messages, he suggested that we go back to the telephone store so that they could figure out why I didn't. Before that happened, a thought crossed my mind. What if my phone is the problem and not his? What if I had "blocked" my husband's number, making it impossible for him to get through to me?

I called and asked my daughter to tell me how I could determine whether or not my husband's number was blocked. She told me how to check my "settings". I did, and yes, his number was "blocked". I cannot tell you how, when, or why it happened, but my phone was set to refuse his calls.

How often do we think God is not listening and responding to us? He is trying to reach us, but we have inadvertently "blocked" His calls. We don't know how or when we did it, or may not be aware that we have done it. We may have blocked Him after experiencing a great disappointment. We may have blocked Him after experiencing some great success, subconsciously thinking that we don't need Him. We may have allowed our "busyness" to block out His voice.

If you ever feel that God is not responding to you, check your settings and make sure that you have not blocked Him. He has promised to answer us when we call Him.

Lord, please help me to keep my heart receptive to your voice.

Dear Lord, it is my prayer _____
Beverly Golden
Cleveland, Ohio

WORDS HAVE POWER

"Death and life are in the power of the tongue:
and they that love it shall eat the fruit thereof."
Proverbs 18:21 (KJV)

When was the last time you experienced the power of God through God's word? It may have been through healing, salvation, deliverance, or the filling of the Holy Spirit. The scripture tells us in Psalm 119:11, "Thy word have I hid in mine heart, that I might not sin against thee." God's word will keep us from sinning. Please take the time to also read the book James chapter 3 in the Bible which talks about the power of the tongue. James lets us know that bitter and sweet messages should not come from the same fountain and neither should words that bless and curse.

Have you ever stopped to examine the power of words and their everyday usage? Words can build up or they can tear down. Words can encourage or even discourage. Words can bless relationships or mess us friendships. The right words can speak life, or the wrong words can speak death. How often do we forget that once words are in the atmosphere they project a positive or a negative energy? It is impossible to retrieve words once they have been spoken. Many times, we try to say I am sorry, but it does not remove the hurt of words spoken in the wrong manner. Many friends have been misunderstood for a lifetime because of the wrong words exchanged in a conversation. Many family members have been divided because of words spoken at the wrong time.

My prayer is that the Lord makes us aware of the words we use every day as we walk with others. Let us ask God to teach us what to say in the right way today so that others will be blessed by our words.

Dear Lord, it is my prayer _____

Priscilla Fields
Prentiss, Mississippi

CHRISTIANS SHOULD ALWAYS FORGIVE

"For if you forgive men their trespasses, your heavenly Father
will also forgive you: But if ye forgive not men their trespasses,
neither will your Father forgive your trespasses."
Matthew 6:14-15 (KJV)

Has someone mistreated you? If so, how did you respond? Did you avoid
your transgressor, seek revenge, gossip, hold a grudge, or did you display Christian
love and pray for them? "Love is patient, love is kind. It does not envy, it does
not boast, it is not proud. It does not dishonor others, it is not self-seeking, it is
not easily angered, it keeps no record of wrongs. Love does not delight in evil
but rejoices with the truth. It always protects, always trusts, always hopes, always
perseveres. Love never fails" 1 Corinthians 13:4-9 (NIV).

The Parable of the Unforgiving Servant teaches us that we are *always* to forgive. "Then came Peter to him, and said, Lord, how oft shall my brother sin against
me, and I forgive him? till seven times? Jesus saith unto him, I say not unto thee,
Until seven times: but, Until seventy times seven" Matthew 18:21-22 (KJV).

As Christians, we must also follow the instructions given in Ephesians
4:31-32 (KJV), "Let all bitterness, and wrath, and anger, and clamour, and evil
speaking, be put away from you, with all malice: And be ye kind one to another,
tenderhearted, forgiving one another, even as God for Christ's sake hath forgiven
you." Jesus also demonstrated forgiveness as He hung on the cross: "Then said
Jesus, Father, forgive them; for they know not what they do" Luke 23:34 (KJV).

When we forgive, it may not be reciprocated, but we benefit by growing spiritually and are rewarded for our obedience and forgiving spirit.

"The first to apologize is the bravest. The first to forgive is the strongest.
The first to forget is the happiest." *Anonymous*

Dear Lord, it is my prayer _____
Verletta Thompson
Fayetteville, Georgia

Unlike earthly soldiers, a believer's armor is not seen by the natural eye.

CLOTHED AND READY TO FIGHT

"Therefore put on the full armor of God, so that when the day
of evil comes, you may be able to stand your ground,
and after you have done everything, to stand."
Ephesians 6: 13 (NIV)

We need the armor: girdle, shield, breastplate, sandals, helmet, and sword, which is the Word of God. We can suit up daily, but if we have not prayed or read our Bible, it is like having a cell phone with all its components without a cell provider. We must pray to stay ready for the battle. Each item of the armor protects our body during war. We must stay dressed to be protected from the schemes of Satan. God promised to give us the spiritual weapons we need to stand our ground when evil comes.

Prayer is extremely important in my life and as the issues arise, I naturally depend on Him daily. I know that He hears our prayers, and He answers! I have raised my children to call on God instead of taking life's circumstances into their own hands. Prayer must be the first priority and not the last resort.

God commands us to pray. Prayer should not be used only when we are under attack, but also, to keep in touch with Him in order to receive His power and strength. With your armor on, you can stand firm when your faith is challenged. When we are obedient, we are destined to win. To be victorious, we must put our lives in God's hands. His promises never expire, they are always redeemable, and are always true.

Dear Lord, it is my prayer _____
Valetta J. Ross,
Merrillville, Indiana

AHA Moment

*Even in the midst of chaos, I can still blossom like a rose
with the Lord on my side.*

THE ROSE THAT GREW IN CONCRETE

"For with God nothing will be impossible."
Luke 1:37 (NKJV)

If there were one simile that perfectly captures the essence of who I am, it would be that I am like the rose that grew in concrete. The emotional and physical traumas I faced were like weeds trying to choke the life out of me. Yet, because the Lord was my solid foundation, I still blossomed like a concrete rose in spite of my circumstances. "For with God nothing is impossible" (Luke 1:37).

I am the daughter of a mother and father who were stolen from me by mental illness. I am a survivor of abuse and neglect. I survived being ostracized and bullied mercilessly by my peers. The mere that fact all these traumas happened should have been my indicator to give up. I could have looked at my harsh circumstances and allowed the pain to smother my growth. Instead, I chose to look to the Father.

The Father began to create beauty in those ashes as He reminded me that even in the midst of pain, He is greater. The Word says there is nothing, absolutely nothing, impossible for God. Even the scars that I bear from past traumas are not greater than God. The Lord has been an everpresent help in the midst of my chaos and turmoil, and He used those circumstances to birth something so much greater in me than I could have ever imagined.

If you find yourself being smothered in the weight of pain, I challenge you to give it to the Lord of "possible". He knows the number of hairs on your head and placed every single star in the sky, so why not place your trust in Him? If you begin to look to the Father, I promise you will find all the peace you need in the midst of chaos.

Dear Lord, it is my prayer _____
Lynn Marie Brown
Decatur, Georgia

AHA Moment

What will God say. "Enter into my rest," or "Depart from me."

WHAT WILL YOUR ANSWER BE?

"Blessed are they which are persecuted for righteousness' sake: for theirs is the kingdom of heaven. Blessed are ye, when men shall revile you, and persecute you, and shall say all manner of evil against you falsely, for my sake."
Matthew 5:10-11 (KJV)

How do you respond to mistreatment, misunderstanding, being lied on, gossiped about when you are innocent? How do we respond when in stressful situations? Do you allow the Holy Spirit to respond on your behalf or are you overtaken by the situation? Sometimes, we forget that Satan is like a roaring lion, seeking whomever he may devour and we respond in our flesh. One would think that doing the ministry that God has given, would not include persecution and suffering. Ironically, that is when we suffer most because of our adversary is attempting to discourage us, and/or take us out. This is when the light of our salvation should shine brightest!

Have you wondered what God will say when you stand before His throne? Will He say because:

- Your neighbor offended you; did you still love your neighbor as yourself?
- Your husband did not obey the Word of God, did you still and honor and reverence him?
- Your pastor did not agree with your proposal for Vacation Bible School, did you still use your gifts for the edification of the body of Christ?"
- The board members disrespected you; did you still stay at the church?
- Your check was short this week; did you still pay your tithes?

And the list goes on.

The Christian walk is not based on anyone's behavior except yours! When you obey Him, the Word promises you can, "Rejoice, and be exceeding glad for great is your reward in heaven..." Matthew 5:12 (KJV). As Christians, we should be the light of the world and show the way to Christ.

Dear Lord, it is my prayer _____
Regina Washington
South Holland, Illinois

AHA Moment

It is better to give up and give in to God than to fight against your purpose.

GIVING UP AND GIVING IN

"For I know the plans I have for you," declares The Lord, "plans to prosper you
and not to harm you, plans to give you hope and a future."
Jeremiah 29:11 (NIV)

I am the product of a broken home. Both my maternal, as well as my paternal
family were broken. I witnessed firsthand the mental and physical abuse my
mother endured, in order to survive, at the hands of my stepfather. My grandmother, too, endured mental abuse from my grandfather. On the one hand, he
would bring me gifts, but on the other, he would destroy any dreams that I had of
having a grandfather to depend on. What I wanted most, as did most little girls,
was to have my dad around; but he was too busy to be a part of my life. Needless
to say, I, too, was broken. As a result of that brokenness, I erected walls to protect
me from any type of mental or physical abuse.

I never imagined I would find a man who would love me or treat me as a
queen. But God had a plan for me! I met and married my soul mate—a young
man who is God-fearing and positive. He encouraged me to develop a relationship with God, and I did. Is he flawed? Yes, just like all of God's children; however, unlike my stepfather, grandfather and dad, I can see God through his flaws.

When you give up and give in to God's plan, you will be able to find happi-
ness and joy with a man whose fundamental beliefs lay in HIM, and not man. Be
obedient to God's will, trust him and His blessings will be waiting for you. He
will release you from your pain and fill that space with His love. God is good!

Thank you Lord for giving me the strength to give up and give in to your will.

Dear Lord, it is my prayer _____
LaTonya Smith
Snellville, Georgia

AHA Moment

*The Bible is **written**, I can **read** it. If I say it, it can be **heard**.
If I show it, it can be **seen**.*

BE COURAGEOUS SOLDIERS FOR CHRIST

"Study to shew thyself approved unto God, a workman that needed
not to be ashamed, rightly dividing the word of truth."
2 Timothy 2:15 (KJV)

I accepted Jesus Christ as my personal Savior as a child, 63 years ago. My momma said if I didn't have Jesus in my heart, the devil would make me a BAD girl doing ugly things. I heard what she said, and I believed her. I felt the need of the Savior because I didn't want to be a bad girl.

By faith, I started my Christian journey. I didn't have biblical understanding of God's Word, but I knew I didn't want to be a hypocrite. I continued for about 35 years being satisfied with bits and pieces from the King James Version (KJV) Bible. Then one day, I realized that the instructions for Christian living had been **written** and I could **read it**. So, I started at Genesis 1:1 and ended with Revelation 22:21 that reads, "The grace of our Lord Jesus Christ be with you all. Amen." I've repeated that journey and will continue, so help me God.

After 35 years, how prepared was I to tell others what it means to be a Christian? Now as an aged woman, I teach the children; I teach the young women good things: ". . . to be sober, love their husbands, love their children, to be discreet, chaste, keepers at home, good, obedient to their own husbands, that the word of God be not blasphemed" Titus 2:4-5(KJV).

If I am offended, if my feelings are hurt, so what! There is nothing sacred about my feelings! I Peter 2:9 reads, "But ye are a chosen generation, a royal priesthood, an holy nation, a peculiar people . . ." So, I will speak, write, and demonstrate God's Word, in and out of season. I want to be a courageous soldier for Him. Be willing to serve Him at His command. Amen.

Dear Lord, it is my prayer _____
Jannie B. Johnson
Madison, Mississippi

AHA Moment

God gives new life to those who believe.

NEW LIFE

"For thou hast possessed my reins: thou hast covered me in my mother's womb.
I will praise thee; for I am fearfully and wonderfully made: marvellous are thy
works; and that my soul knoweth right well."
Psalm 139:13-14 (KJV)

Bringing new life into the world is a blessed experience filled with joy. My nearest sibling was eighteen years older than me, and I always wanted siblings my age that I could play with.

Prior to getting married, I wanted ten girls and ten boys. God, on the other hand, had another plan. I became the blessed mother of two wonderful daughters. I was twenty-eight years old when my first daughter was born and approaching my thirtieth birthday when my second daughter was born. I thank God daily for my daughters.

My youngest daughter had two miscarriages. Although the first miscarriage hurt, it seems that the second loss was even more painful. Specialists worked tirelessly, and we were certain that the little girl, whose name had already been chosen, was going to make it. We had such wonderful plans for her, but God had other plans. Two years later, my daughter and her husband tried again. We continued to pray daily and trust God. After several months, the doctors did not think my daughter would be able to carry this baby full-term. I thought about Job and continued to pray as he did.

My daughter was finally able to complete this pregnancy following a medical procedure. Praise God, for by His grace, a new life had been given! Just being given the gift of life was so overwhelming that I could hardly contain myself. I prayed for the health of both my daughter and granddaughter and, as Psalm 139:14 says, "You covered me in my mother's womb. I will praise you . . . for marvellous are thy works."

Dear Lord, it is my prayer _____
Georgette Davis
Gilbert, Louisiana

AHA MOMENT

Real Christians are visible.

WHAT KIND OF CHRISTIAN ARE YOU: VISIBLE OR INVISIBLE?

"What shall we then say to these things?
If God be for us, who can be against us?"
Romans 8:31 (KJV)

In my Christian walk over the years, I have learned and read that there are two kinds of Christians—the visible, and the invisible. The invisible are the ones whose hearts are far from God, and the visible are those after God's own heart.

If I have trust, I want to be assured that trust is reciprocated. Likewise, if I have love, I want love returned. Additionally, if I am being attacked, I want to know the reason why. Most importantly, I want to be a visible Christian by having faith that Jesus will keep me strong and cover my heart.

However, the invisible Christians manifest themselves by making bad choices that hurt others, destroy relationships, and bring about distrust. As Christians, we must be visible. We have to be mindful of other's feelings. We have forgotten how to "Love our brothers". Where is the love that we once embraced?

Which is easier: to trust what can be seen, or to trust what cannot be seen? Things which are real are easier to believe because they are visible. On the other hand, things that are not visible seem unreal. In order that we may become visible Christians, we must deny ourselves daily as Matthew 16:24 (KJV) reads, "Then said Jesus unto his disciples, If any man will come after me, let him deny himself, and take up his cross, and follow me."

We must connect, commune, and remain close in our walk with God. We must also be about our Father's business, forgetting about ourselves and staying focused on our Lord and Savior as we become more visible Christians.

Dear Lord, it is my prayer _____
Linda Campbell
Jackson, Mississippi

Distractions waste the blessings God gives us each day.

DISTRACTIONS

"I will meditate on your precepts and fix my eyes on your ways."
Psalm 119:15 (ESV)

After working both my jobs and attending school, at the end of the day, I realized nothing had been accomplished. I literally wasted my entire day. I felt badly because hours had been recorded for doing nothing. It was not as if there had been nothing to do, but I just could not focus long enough to complete any task. I laid in my bed and mentally went through my day. God showed me that I could not focus because I had not spent any time with Him. Reflecting and remembering, the time I spent with God was not as intentional or consistent as it had been previously. God led me to Psalm 119:33-37 (NIV). Purposely learning the ways of God, has caused a shift in my focus in all areas of my life.

If you were to take three minutes of silence to focus on God, chances are, your mind would drift to something you need to do, such as a problem at work, or the well-being of a sick loved one. Although all of these things are important, God wants all of your attention! We live in such a fast-paced world that it seems hard to focus on anything for three full minutes.

Ask God what is distracting you from Him, not only in the above exercise, but also in everyday life. What is stopping you from giving Him your full attention? Today, ask God what you can do to eliminate the distractions that are hindering you from totally focusing on Him.

God wants to be first in your life. He wants to delight in you as His daughter. Today, allow God to move in your life and free you from _all_ distractions.

Dear Lord, it is my prayer _____
Jasmine Wise
Monroe, Louisiana

AHA MOMENT

You can rely on God's guidance and protection.

DIVINE GUIDANCE

"The LORD will guide you always; he will satisfy your needs in a sun-scorched
land and will strengthen your frame. . .."
Isaiah 58:11 (NIV)

What do you do when you are in a desperate situation? Who do you call on
for help? Do you call on God? Some of the faithful people (Moses, Daniel and
Esther) throughout the scriptures bear witness to God's guidance to a successful
deliverance. If we ask God for guidance and rely on Him, He promises to lead
us in the direction we should go.

God is faithful to His promises. I still remember several years ago when
Hurricane Rita was heading toward Houston with the possibility of causing
extensive damage to the Gulf Coast area. After witnessing on television what
had happened in New Orleans during Hurricane Katrina, my husband and I
decided to head north to Dallas, Texas.

As we crawled along covering only 100 miles in 4 hours, we desperately
needed God to show us where to find gas. Many people were stranded on the
highway without gas, without water, and without lodging.

Praying for gas, we were led to pull into a gas station where there were only
a few cars. We thought no lines, then probably no gas. However, there was gas at
this station! **GOD provides!!**

Wondering where we should go from there, suddenly, a man with a white
beard approached us and said, "Take a different route to Dallas." Before we could
thank him, he disappeared as quickly as he appeared. We decided to follow his
directions to Dallas since the road we were previously traveling was so congested.
This was a better route to Dallas and a hotel. There was only one room available,
and we got that room! **GOD guides!!**

Not only did God hear our cry, He led us in the right path and provided
everything we needed. When you are facing uncertain situations, call on GOD!
He is your ever-present guide and provider in every circumstance.

Dear Lord, it is my prayer _____
June Bond
Houston, Texas

AHA MOMENT

Trust God no matter what the circumstances look like.

DON'T GIVE UP!

"I shall not die, but live, and declare the works of the LORD."
Psalm 118:17 (KJV)

We had one week to practice for the upcoming holiday event at the church. The youth were slowly learning their parts to the play; not to mention the memorizing of speeches. The cancellations and disappointments were flowing in by the minute. But we wouldn't give up. The person who had one of the leading roles had laryngitis and we had not prepared for a backup because this person was *never* sick. I can hear a tiny calming voice saying, "Don't fear, God's got a ram in the bush".

All of those sayings and words of comfort are nice, but this was the last week. What was I really going to do? Should I call everything off and just cancel the program? Again, I can hear that voice softly saying," Did you ask God?" I asked my sisters from the church to join me in prayer "for we know that all things work together for our good" as quoted in Romans 8:28.

I remembered my sister as she lay ill near death would quote, "I shall not die, but live, and declare the works of the LORD" Psalm 118:17. I didn't understand at the time that she knew her earthly hours were short but her determination to live for Christ was until the end. She was not going to give up no matter what the end result would be.

Whatever the situation is great, small, or even life threatening; we must press forward while trusting in God and the outcome will be for God's glory. Neither would I give up with my small holiday program dilemma. It turned out to be one of the best programs and souls were won for the Lord. Whether your discourse is large or small, don't give up and don't give in.

Dear Lord, it is my prayer _____
Frances Christine Robinson
Merced, California

AHA Moment

God is present with us everywhere we go, and we can trust Him.

A GOD YOU CAN TRUST

"In God I Have Put My Trust, I Shall Not Be Afraid.
What Can Man Do To Me?"
PSalm 56:11 (NASB)

Recently, I had a very sobering experience. My car was stolen; right in front of me!

At first, I felt helpless because I could not stop the thieves from taking my car. What made matters worse was that my purse, car keys, house keys and other belongings were still in the car.

I panicked. My personal information would be compromised! After overcoming the initial fear, I then became angry. Why me? I did not deserve this!

But then I realized I belonged to God and He was, then and is now, in control. He would protect me. God is everywhere, and He can be trusted! I know that God is always watching over me.

Then, I began to thank God that I was not harmed during the robbery. As a result of this harrowing experience, I began to pray more and genuinely seek the Lord through reading my bible more often.

My faith was strengthened, and my joy returned. I actually started praying for the young men who took my car. I prayed not only for their salvation, but that they would have a change of heart; a heart filled with love for others. I pray that they too would learn to trust God.

Dear Lord, it is my prayer _____
Linda Kennedy
Decatur, Georgia

A HOLY MOTHER — WHO IS SHE?

"She openeth her mouth with wisdom; and in her tongue is the law of kindness."
Proverbs 31:26 (KJV)

"Sanctify yourselves therefore, and be ye holy: for I am the LORD your God."
Leviticus 20:7 (KJV) "Because it is written, Be ye holy; for I am holy."
I Peter 1:16 (KJV)

A *holy mother* develops from a *holy woman*. Who is this *holy woman*? She is one who possesses the characteristics of a Proverbs 31 woman. She has wisdom, and loves the LORD.

While thinking about the term MOTHER for a special Mother's Day presentation, the Lord opened my heart to realize powerful words used to recognize some of the more significant qualities of a *holy woman*. She mothers to others (**mothers**). In my mind, the Holy Spirit showed me that the typical word "Mothers" could be a spiritual action verb "Mothers" as well.

When a woman mothers, she possesses many outstanding qualities and wears many hats well. Here are just a few of those Godly qualities:

M–Motivates, Mentors, Ministers to others
O–Obeys and Oversees with grace
T–Teaches and Trains followers as she leads
H–Helps, Honors, and Holds with Holy Hands
E–Energizes, Encourages, and Excels to Excellence
R–Respects, Responds, and Reinvents as needed
S–Serves and Stands with Spiritual Strength in the LORD!

Are you ready to take on those quality hats? Do you desire wisdom? According to Proverbs 8:11, "For wisdom is better than rubies; and all the things that may be desired are not to be compared to it." This incredible gem of wisdom is also presented in Proverbs 3:15 as, She (wisdom) is more precious than rubies: and all the things thou canst desire are not to be compared unto her.

Seek God for your spiritual hats and He will provide the wisdom!

Dear Lord, it is my prayer _____
Irene Aultman
Mitchellville, Maryland

AHA Moment

Love is caring for one another.

A PLACE TO LOVE ONE ANOTHER!

"A new commandment I give unto you, That ye love one another; as I have loved you, that ye also love one another. By this shall all men know that ye are my disciples, if ye have love one to another."
John 13:34-35 (KJV)

My mother was placed in a nursing home and it was an eye-opening experience for me. I realized that love does not happen automatically. In 2010, God inspired me to write a message of advice so that everyone will love and treat each other better.

Although my mother had the same routine, sometimes she did not receive the proper care she should have received in the nursing home. The facility was understaffed and therefore, sometimes she was neglected and mistreated. The condition was not readily detected. I felt so helpless and wondered why I did not see what was happening. In the darkest hour, God eased my burden and helped me to deal with the situation. It became clear that we all need to remember to treat each other like we would like to be treated; actually, love one another as God commanded us to do.

To keep the love commandment, have a Christ like heart, be caring, compassionate, and know your job when serving as a health care provider. Be careful not to treat people unfairly, you never know if one day you could end up there. We must be more like Jesus Christ each and every day, because we will not want to be in a place where we are neglected and mistreated! Remember to create a place in your hearts to always love one another!

Dear Lord, it is my prayer _____
Denise Henderson Thompson
Hyattsville, Maryland

AHA Moment

God equips us.

ACCEPTING THE CALL

"May he equip you with all you need for doing his will."
Hebrews 13:21a (NLT)

In 1976, at age thirty, my husband was asked to start a church in Toledo, Ohio. It was 45 miles away from our home, family, friends and jobs. The church's first congregation consisted of my husband, our 8-year-old son, 5-year-old daughter, and me pregnant with our third son and an occasional visitor. We faithfully commuted every Sunday for approximately one year.

We then decided to move our family of five to Toledo so that we could more effectively allow God to build the church. The move was exciting at first, but then it became more of a challenge than I could have ever imagined as a young mother and inexperienced young pastor's wife. As the church grew, I began to feel ill-equipped for the job of pastor's wife. It seemed I had no one to help me through this life changing experience.

I didn't know any other pastors' wives in their twenties that I could talk with and share what I was going through. My husband was committed to the call. No way, was I going to take him away from his calling. Who was going to teach me how to be an effective pastor's wife? How was I to learn to be the kind of help-mate a man of God truly needed?

I began to diligently cry out to the Lord; earnestly seeking His direction. His answer was, when He calls us to do something, He also equips us with whatever we need to perform the job. When God called my husband into the ministry, He equipped him. He also equipped and called me to be the wife my young pastor husband needed. He let me know that although I felt ill-equipped, He had already prepared me. I just needed to accept the call.

When God calls, just accept the call. He's already prepared you to do His work.

Dear Lord, it is my prayer _____
Lillian Johnson
Ypsilanti, Michigan

AHA Moment

Jesus wants us to be light in this dark world.

PLEASE TURN THE LIGHT ON

"... God is light; in him there is no darkness at all. If we claim to have fellowship with him and yet walk in darkness, we lie and do not live by the truth. But if we walk in the light, as he is in the light, we have fellowship with one another, and the blood of Jesus, his Son, purifies us from all sin."
1 John 1:5-7 (NIV)

"Turn the light on!" How many times have we heard these words from our children? There is something about darkness that causes fear in the heart of a child. When I was growing up, people would say the "Boogie man" would get us, whenever it was dark.

There are certain things done better in darkness just as certain things are done better in daylight. I witnessed this throughout my childhood. My mother loved gardening, and many mornings before we got out of bed, we could hear her pulling weeds, watering her flowers and singing in her garden. As believers, we are called to bring light into the world daily. Do we awake each day with anticipation of representing Christ? Do we get excited about showing the world that we are His and want to bring hope to the world?

Just as turning a light on in a dark room causes darkness to disappear, the light of Jesus in our lives also affects the darkness in this world. 1) REALIZE that we represent Christ and in him there is no darkness. 2) Ask God to SHOW you what areas are dim in your life and work to make them shine brighter. 3) DETERMINE each day to represent Christ wherever you go. 4) FELLOWSHIP with each other because of your walk with Christ. 5) CHRIST is the only one that purifies us. Remember to turn the light on daily, and let Christ be seen in you. Don't live a life steeped in darkness. Turn the Light on, and let it shine bright.

Dear Lord, it is my prayer _____
Pearl Lindsay
Los Angeles, California

AHA Moment
All means all

ALL THINGS – EVEN GRIEF

"And we know that all things work together for good to them that love God, to
them who are the called according to his purpose."
Romans 8:28 (KJV)

Nothing has the potential to shatter your faith like the death of your child.
Whether anticipated or unexpected, it is completely out of the "natural" order of
things. When my youngest son died suddenly no words could capture the depth
of my agony. For one thing, it was masked by a numbing disbelief. How could
this be God's will? He was only 34! He loved the Lord passionately. He was a
wonderful husband, amazing father, beloved son and he touched so many lives.

Grasping for some anchor of faith, I asked my pastor to help me confirm that
God had ordered my son's life from beginning to end; that his leaving wasn't a
random act; that God didn't wake up that morning saying "eenie meenie miney
mo" as if he was playing some cruel game.

With my pastor's support, God gently reminded me of many of my favorite
Bible verses. God's word confirmed that he knew my son fully, intimately, lovingly before he *was formed in my womb*. All his days were written in God's book
BEFORE I gave birth to him. That ALL things work together for good to those
who love God. That I could choose to give thanks in EVERTHING!

It is here in scripture that I find strength to seek God's perfect will when my
faith is weak. When total disbelief and total reality clash like noisy cymbals in
my head, it is a great mystery to mourn in gratitude. It is in the sacrifice of praise
that I exchange *beauty for ashes, joy for mourning, rejoicing for heaviness.*

Take your grief and lay it on God's shoulder. He is the ALL in ALL! Read
Psalm 139:13-16; 1 Thessalonians 5:18; 1 Peter 5:7 for comfort.

Dear Lord, it is my prayer _____
Iness Panni
St. Louis, Missouri

AHA Moment

We are blessed when we give.

AM I A GIVER?

"For God so loved the world, that he gave his only begotten Son,
that whosoever believeth in him should not perish,
but have everlasting life."
John 3:16 (KJV)

We live in a world where many people believe that they are owed something for nothing. Many students believe that they can sit in class and do nothing and get a good grade, because they were in class.

Sometimes we borrow money from family and friends, not intending to pay it back. We think, they have 'big bucks' and they won't miss the small amount we borrowed. Often, we are not thankful to and for our family and friends when they help us.

We treat Almighty God the same way. We think He owes us when we go to church every Sunday. We think that giving the Lord a dime out of each dollar we earn is asking a bit much. God's word says "... and prove me now herewith, saith the Lord of host, if I will not open you the windows of heaven, and pour you out a blessing that there shall not be room enough to receive it" Malachi 3:10 (KJV). Based on this scripture and others, we will be blessed when we give.

Give your time helping and sharing with others. Give of yourself by praying for them. Don't forget to give God His: money, time, worship and praise.

Once we become children of God, not only should we give to God and others, but be willing to SHARE the gospel to a lost world. After all, God *gave* His Son that all could be saved.

Dear Lord, it is my prayer _____
Pauline Thomas
Vallejo, California

AHA MOMENT
Removing Spiritual Distractions

GET THE CLUTTER OUT OF THE WAY

"... for ye shut up the kingdom of heaven against men: for ye neither go in yourselves, neither suffer ye them that are entering to go in."
Matthew 23:13 (KJV)

Removing spiritual distractions takes hearing and listening to God's word. It also takes recognizing that legalism and manmade traditions are in fact spiritual distractions. This can be a major challenge because we take for granted that everything that we grew up hearing is correct.

During a season in my life, I was seeking scripture interpretation on a particular subject. God began showing me how the Old Testament and the New Testament are parallel. The key to "rightly dividing" scriptures is understanding this. I struggled with what I had been taught versus what God's word states.

I was reading through the Bible, studying Old Testament and New Testament scriptures simultaneously. I came across Matthew: 23. It spoke to me like never before. Verses 23-28 jumped at me because it ate at the core of the legalism I had been saturated in. "Ye blind guides, which strain at a gnat, and swallow a camel. Woe unto you, scribes and Pharisees, hypocrites! for ye make clean the outside of the cup and of the platter, but within they are full of extortion and excess. Thou blind Pharisee, cleanse first that which is within the cup and platter that the outside of them may be clean also. Woe unto you, scribes and Pharisees, hypocrites! for ye are like unto whited sepulchers, which indeed appear beautiful outward, but are within full of dead men's bones, and of all uncleanness. Even so ye also outwardly appear righteous unto men, but within ye are full of hypocrisy and iniquity."

I asked myself, "What scriptures have these people been reading that the focus on outward appearance that legalism encourages, is acceptable?" The Spirit spoke to me and said, "We need to get the clutter out of the way so that people can enter in."

Dear Lord, it is my prayer _____
Monique H. May
Corona, California

AHA Moment

It takes faith to move all mountains in life.

BE A MOUNTAIN MOVER–MOVE THE MOUNTAINS!

"Truly I tell you, whoever says to this mountain,
Be lifted up and thrown into the sea! and does not doubt at all in his heart but
believes that what he says will take place, it will be done for him."
Mark 11:23 (AMPC)

From a biblical standpoint, mountains are symbols of obstacles or challenges in life.

"And Jesus said unto them, Because of your unbelief: for verily I say unto you, If ye have faith as a grain of mustard seed, ye shall say unto this mountain, Remove hence to yonder place; and it shall remove; and nothing shall be impossible unto you" (Matthew 17:20 KJV).

I have faced many challenges at work, church, and even in my family. My victory came only when I put my faith in God. I asked God to level the mountains of difficulty that came my way. He did just that. I thanked Him for the abundant supply of His Spiritual might and power in my life every day!

I have learned that faith is the required ingredient to be a mountain mover and faith is a prayer activator. Faith in God activates the hand of God and causes Him to move on our behalf. Jesus reminds us that "For this reason I am telling you, whatever you ask for in prayer, believe (trust and be confident) that it is granted to you, and you will [get it]" (Mark 11:24 AMPC).

Have faith in God and begin to move your mountains!

Dear Lord, it is my prayer _____
Vonn J. Jones
Washington, District of Columbia

AHA Moment
We are blessed to be a blessing.

BLESS ME LORD INDEED

"And Jabez called on the God of Israel, saying, Oh that thou wouldest bless me indeed, and enlarge my coast, and that thine hand might be with me, And that thou wouldest keep me from evil, that it may not grieve me! and God granted him that which he requested."
I Chronicles 4:10 (KJV)

As Christian women who are willing workers, we always find ourselves in a supporting role. We take care of everyone else until we literally become slack, falling short of caring for ourselves mentally, physically and spiritually.

While reading my daily devotional, I Chronicles, chapter 4, I stumbled through some names of the genealogy of a tribe. Jabez's name stood out. The bible passage says that he was more honorable and more glorious than his brethren. Jabez behaved himself in a manner such that he was able to ask God to grant him the desires of his heart; and God granted those things. It is also *my* desire to delight myself in the Lord as Jabez did so that I too can ask of God for the desires of my heart. Psalm 37:4 KJV

I tried to recall the last time that God worked through me in such a miraculous way that I knew beyond the shadow of a doubt that He had done it. It was then that I was lead to pray this prayer as often as I could remember to do so during every idle moment. This was the gift that I wanted from God; that I could be a blessing to someone else.

When was the last time that miracles happened on a regular basis with you? Our God is still in the miracle working business.

Dear Lord, it is my prayer _____
Frances Christine Robinson
Merced, California

LORD, OPEN OUR "SPIRITUAL" EYES

"And Elisha prayed, and said, LORD, I pray thee, open his eyes, that he may see.
And the LORD opened the eyes of the young man; and he saw."
II Kings 6:17 (KJV)

After petitioning the Lord for an inspirational Word to share, He showed me the words, "iBelieve". What instantly stood out to me was the "i" in iBelieve, which represents the spiritual eye.

When we look with our "natural" eyes at our circumstances, we cannot see beyond what the natural eye sees. Fear and hopelessness grips us and doubt enters in. But when we look at the same circumstances with our "spiritual" eye—the eyes of faith—we see what God sees.

I was having problems with my knee. The pain was unbearable at times. I found it difficult to go up and down stairs, and it was painful to stand up after sitting down.

My pastor called for a prayer shut-in one Friday night, and I remember praying and asking God to heal my knee. I laid face down on the altar crying out to God for deliverance from the pain and for healing. I was determined to stay on the altar until God healed my knee. By faith, I believed that God was going to heal my knee that night, and I would leave church rejoicing for my healing. God did just that! More than two years later that knee is pain free.

As believers, God wants us to open our "spiritual" eyes and believe His promises so that we may see faith in action. I often say, "Faith is holding onto nothing until it becomes something."

The Lord desires that every believer's "spiritual" eyes be opened so that we may see in His Word what He wants us to see.

Dear Lord, it is my prayer _____
Orelia A. W. Nicholson
Richmond, Virginia

AHA Moment
Real power is possible.

CONNECT TO POWER

"He giveth power to the faint; and to them that have no might
he increaseth strength."
Isaiah 40:29 (KJV)

Living intentionally, not just existing and living joyfully because you feel the sheltering embrace of God's power can be a reality if you just keep giving your pains, sorrows, situations, and circumstances to Him.

Perhaps it seems small and trite for me to talk about the sadness and loss I felt when my beloved family members died, after all death is inevitable. Besides that, I had experienced the death of other family members. I also knew that God's word gives precious promises about those who die in the LORD. Add to God's promises the normal stages of "grieving" and any Christian should be just great. Well I'm here to tell you that when my mom died and then my sister died just three months later I became dysfunctional. The pain seemed unbearable. We all say, "Life goes on", but it is probably better to say, "Time passes". Sadness can become a dark curtain that remains drawn daring any light to enter. I had no energy, no strength. I woke up tired and went to bed tired. I went through the motions of daily life as if I was actually in gear, but every day was dark. I was thankful for the love and care of a spouse, but I still felt completely lost.

I began an aggressive campaign of self-talk. I audibly spoke God's word. I engaged in an inner dialogue with God's word. I wrote God's word as if copying standards for misbehavior. The power available through God's word is restorative. The greatest pain or sorrow is unable to stand when met with the greatness of God's power.

The chorus of a familiar hymn by Annie J. Flint says, "His love has no limit, His grace has no measure, His power has no boundary known unto men. For out of His infinite riches in Jesus, He giveth, and giveth, and giveth again."

Dear Lord, it is my prayer _____
Janice Harper
Long Beach, California

AHA MOMENT

Trusting God takes faith, confidence, and strength!

DEMONSTRATED FAITH

"For with God nothing shall be impossible."
Luke 1:37 (KJV)

I was a secretary for 7 years and decided to leave the federal government to become a firefighter. Although I did not realize the struggles it would take to become a firefighter, I was determined to make a huge change in my life. Courage to make the change did not come easily. I learned swiftly and discovered that I was going to have to apply God's Word and step out on faith. I meditated on His Word and quickly learned that I had to increase my faith. It took studying and believing God's Word, trusting and depending on His promises, and basically taking Him at His Word.

To become a professional firefighter, I had to complete several difficult tests including a physical strength and endurance test just to achieve acceptance into the fire training program. The endurance test was hard. I was afraid because I had no prior experience as a firefighter and never volunteered as a firefighter before. I doubted myself. However, the Lord said to me, "Apply your faith and remember My scripture, Philippians 4:13, I can do all things through Christ which strengtheneth me." The Lord carried me through the entire training process to become a professional firefighter. I successfully remained in that position for 21 years, and now today, I am a professional Fire Inspector.

The point that I want everyone to know is that no matter how difficult your circumstances appear just trust God anyway, seek His promises, and stand on His Word regardless. Let go of your fears. Believe in Him. He will not disappoint you, and He cannot fail. He is a God of the impossible who made my firefighting experience possible. He will do the same for you. Be strong in the Lord and be encouraged. Apply God's Word and demonstrate your faith!

Dear Lord, it is my prayer _____
Natalie D. Bell
Washington, District of Columbia

EVERY EVENT IS AT HIS COMMAND

*"He shall call upon me, and I will answer him: I will be with him in trouble;
I will deliver him, and honour him."*
Psalm 91:5 (KJV)

When our trust in Jesus is tested with what we hold most precious, we must hold fast to his promises and the understanding that God is God all by Himself!

It was Thanksgiving. I lifted my hands in prayer and praise as the rising sun ushered in a new day at Lake Gaston. "Every event is at His command." That was the quote from my devotional. What did that mean? Less than fifteen minutes later, Jesus began to teach me. Our daughters were in a terrible accident while traveling to the lake house. I froze in shock. "Every event is at His command", resounded in my spirit. The natural man screamed, "This cannot be God. God what did you do?" The spirit whispered again. "Every event . . .." He will give his angels charge over you" Psalm 91:11. Now, I had to choose to trust him.

As we traveled to the hospital, we didn't know what we would find. Those who saw the mangled car asked the same questions, "How many died? Those who saw two young ladies sitting on the side of the highway marveled, "No one died and no bones broken?" Both walked away from a car that had rolled three times, was crushed, windows imploded; without a speck of glass on them. The doctor called it luck. I said it was the hand of Jesus commanding the event.

Both daughters said, "As the car rolled, we cried, "Jesus! Jesus! Jesus!" He was in control of the event even before I knew it was happening. Although the appearance of the car spoke loss and defeat, every event is not as it appears. We serve the omnipotent God!

What looks devastatingly impossible isn't. We can trust Him; even beyond what we know and see.

Dear Lord, it is my prayer _____
Geraldine Boddie Meredith
Washington, District of Columbia

AHA Moment

Your light should always reflect Christ.

IS YOUR LIGHT OUT?

"Let your light so shine before men that they may see your good works,
and glorify your Father which is in heaven."
Matthew 5:16 (KJV)

This morning during my devotional reading, suddenly the lights blinked, came back on, blinked again- came back on, then blinked again and stayed out! This was all due to high winds the previous night. Although, it was an overcast morning, I could still see how to safely move about my house. I immediately went to look for an oil lamp and candles that we keep for such emergencies. My house and the entire neighborhood were without power!

The spiritual analogy came to my mind immediately. How bright is my light? Am I blinking in this dark world for others to see? Am I a 100-watt bulb on Sunday and a 40-watt bulb on Monday? Is it so dim that I can barely see my way? Is my light completely out? God forbid! Is it on a candlestick or partially hidden somewhere? Am I like a foolish virgin as mentioned in Matthew chapter 25, trying to wait for Christ to return? Do I have sufficient power or spiritual light to complete my life's journey?

Jesus is "the light of the world." As Christians, we should always have our light burning bright. When our spiritual light grows dim gradually, we may not notice it; but others will. Our loving heavenly Father can use an ordinary life event like a power outage to shake us up and get our attention. It may be time for a spiritual check up to remind us to always reflect Christ.

Dear Lord, it is my prayer _____
Linda Martin
Memphis, Tennessee

CONQUERING THE HIDDEN SPIRIT OF BITTERNESS

"Hatred stirs up strife, But love covers all sins."
Proverbs 10:12 (NKJV)

Being the eldest of four children, it is easy to become annoyed by my younger siblings. Early one Sunday morning, I was aggravated with my brother for hogging the bathroom. With only a few minutes remaining before leaving for church, I could no longer contain my impatience. "You always do this!" I irritably declared. As the day progressed, I realized that I was blindly hosting a spirit of bitterness towards my brother. Had anyone asked me if I was bitter towards my brother, I would have denied it.

Oftentimes we are unaware that we are hosting a spirit of bitterness. We must always test ourselves by examining if we are easily angered when individuals offend us or if we recall past offences of bitterness.

Love helps us to conquer any hidden spirit of bitterness. Love covers all sins. It keeps no record of past wrongs or offenses! It is unconditional love "agape love" which is God's supernatural love where one gives most, even when the least is deserved.

It is imperative to forgive others the moment an offense occurs! Jesus teaches that we must pray for those who mistreat us, but more importantly we must pray for the condition of our heart. The heart allows us to easily discern a speck in the eyes of another without perceiving the plank within our own eyes. Jesus died on the cross for us while we were yet sinners. He died for our sins because He is love, and He loved us! That is why He is not satisfied when we will not forgive or have any bitterness in our heart towards others.

Stop to ask the Lord to reveal any bitterness, hatred or unforgiveness that is hiding in your heart. He will expose it, but then we must humble ourselves, repent and ask the Lord to take it away and give us a clean heart.

Dear Lord, it is my prayer _____
Nikkia Fletcher
Germantown, Maryland

I KNOW YOU!

"O LORD, you have searched me and known me . . .
you are acquainted with all my ways."
Psalm 139:1, 3b (NKJV)

Many people have something they might try to hide. It may be some fear, shameful situation; some weakness, or embarrassing decision they wish they could undo. Regardless of what it is, God knows and He is with us.

As a young believer, I witnessed (shared the Gospel) to many women on the street; going door to door in neighborhoods. As we witnessed, we reassured them of Gods omnipresence and omnipotence. In church, I worshipped with women who needed the same reassurance. Life presents us with so many challenges! As wives, mothers, caregivers, sisters, and breadwinners, we face life situations that make us want to hide. We hide our frustrations, fears and inadequacies. We wear a mask. At one time, I did.

Being an educator in the private sector is challenging. Demands of the job left me with emotions of failure as a wife and mother. Life was moving so fast! I traveled daily throughout the city when the D.C. Sniper was at large. This left my head spinning. I felt so vulnerable and no one knew. Psalm 139 reassured me. It was consoling to know that Jesus knew what was on my mind and there isn't any place that His hand cannot reach. I don't have to hide my weaknesses; they are already exposed.

We need to embrace the fact that we are exposed. He knows what we think. That's a good thing! His eyes are always on us. What a relief! Wherever we are in our lives, God is there. He knows about our feelings of inadequacies in our homes, jobs, and relationships. He sees behind the mask we put on each day when we face the world. God has the power to heal us. No more mask! We are exposed.

Dear Lord, it is my prayer _____

Geraldine Boddie Meredith
Washington, District of Columbia

AHA MOMENT

Seek the Lord for your purpose. He is eager to reveal it to you!

DO YOU KNOW YOUR PURPOSE?

"Come now therefore, and I will send thee unto Pharaoh, that thou mayest
bring forth my people the children of Israel out of Egypt."
Exodus 3:10 (KJV)

Moses knew his purpose. It was to lead the children of Israel out of Egypt.
Pharaoh's daughter also had a purpose; to keep Moses alive. In Exodus Chapter
2, the Word speaks of how she had compassion on baby Moses when she found
him floating down the river in an ark; even finding a way for him to be cared for
and nurtured. She cared for him as her own son. God put compassion in her heart
for the Hebrew baby, and she protected his life. (Exodus 2:5-10 KJV)

So, why are you here? Do you ever wonder why? I wondered for some time.
I prayed fervently and earnestly in faith for His revelation and finally it came. For
years, I had so much compassion for the lost. I read all I could about the areas in
the world where most of the population did not serve the living God. I became
very passionate about people knowing my God. I soon realized that my purpose
in life was to win souls for Christ!

Soon afterwards, I became part of the outreach ministry at my church where
my passion and purpose are being fulfilled. As part of this ministry, I am able to
witness to the homeless with spiritual nourishment as we provide them physical
nourishment. As part of this team, we also minister to those who are ill and visit
nursing homes to serve the elderly and disabled persons.

Do you wonder what your purpose is? Spend time with the Lord in prayer,
study His Word, and in His own time, He will reveal your purpose for being here
and help you fulfill it.

Dear Lord, it is my prayer _____
Linda Kennedy
Decatur, Georgia

AHA MOMENT

Accept Jesus Christ to live forever in Heaven!

FAREWELL!

"And God shall wipe away all tears from their eyes; and there shall be no more death, neither sorrow, nor crying, neither shall there be any more pain: for the former things are passed away."
Revelation 21:4 (KJV)

Until recently, I was so sad to see the New Year come and say farewell to the old one. I don't know why it was so hard for me. I guess another year older and things like that. But, I thought and said to myself, "Who knows what God has in store for the New Year?" We may experience more blessings, more prayers answered, and a chance to do better where we've fallen short compared to the prior year. There's another day coming; probably sooner than we think. That day will be when we say goodbye or "farewell" to this life, as we know it, and live again.

"In a moment, in the twinkling of an eye, . . . the dead shall be raised incorruptible, and we shall be changed." I Corinthians 15:52 (KJV)
Likewise, according to I Thessalonians 4:16-17 (KJV), "For the Lord himself shall descend from heaven with a shout, with the voice of the archangel, and with the trump of God: and the dead in Christ shall rise first: Then we which are alive and remain shall be caught up together with them in the clouds, to meet the Lord in the air: and so shall we ever be with the Lord."
A change is coming based on Revelation 21:1 (KJV). "And I saw a new heaven and a new earth: for the first heaven and the first earth were passed away. . . ."

According to the scriptures, there won't be time to fret or look back at what's being left behind. There will be no more pain, tears, and sorrow. I'm looking forward to that day.

Today, if you accept Jesus as your Savior, Lord and King, you too can look forward to that great day.

Dear Lord, it is my prayer _____
Prissie Jenkins
Los Angeles, California

AHA Moment

Fasting is not about manipulating God.

FASTING FOR A HUSBAND

"Why have we fasted, they say, and you have not seen it?
Why have we humbled ourselves and you have not noticed?"
Isaiah 58:3 (NIV)

Several years ago, when I was single and living in Hawaii, my friend and I decided to embark on a fast for our future husbands. I decided to go on the Daniel fast for three weeks. While fasting and praying, I waited anxiously on GOD to reveal my husband to me. I pictured myself running into a beautiful muscular Samoan man on the beach. We would fall in love and would live happily ever after.

After three weeks of fasting, that beautiful Samoan never appeared. Fatigued and tired from not eating anything but fruit and vegetables for three weeks, I felt hurt and disappointed. I called my father and asked, 'How is this possible that I have fasted for three weeks and nothing, nada, has happened to my love life?!"

My father graciously explained to me that you can fast and pray for things in life, but it is not until GOD is ready to answer that prayer request that you will experience the fruit of your sacrifice. This was a tough pill to swallow. I realized that I looked at GOD as a genie in a bottle. I thought if I do this then He should reward me with this. Unfortunately, that is not how GOD works.

The next time you decide to fast, ask GOD "not my will but your will be done" Luke 22:42b (NIV). Fasting is to humble us before an all-powerful and all-knowing God who will answer in His perfect timing and perfect way. I thank God for loving me enough to teach me the importance of fasting.

Dear Lord, it is my prayer _____
Erica Lindsay
Los Angeles, California

AHA Moment

God wants us to obey him so that he can protect us from emotional and spiritual trouble.

OBEDIENCE FOR PROTECTION

"But Samuel replied: 'Does the LORD delight in burnt offerings and sacrifices as much as in obeying the LORD? To obey is better than sacrifice, and to heed is better than the fat of rams. . ..'"
1 Samuel 15:22 (NIV)

There were two times in my life when obedience to God was especially important. The first time, God told me to stay at a four-way stop a little while longer before pulling off. I obeyed! A car ran the stop sign to my right and would have run straight into me. The second time, He told me to stop following someone on social media. This time, I did not obey. I saw something that hurt my heart so badly it almost brought me to tears.

These moments together showed me that obedience at all times is key. I cannot be obedient when it's convenient for me. God had a plan in both situations, but I only followed Him in one of them. Afterwards, I had to repent for not obeying which was my sacrifice. Obeying 100% of the time is now my goal.

John 14:15 (ESV) reads, "If you love me, you will keep my commandments." Ask God to help you obey His commandments for life, not only for today, but also in the years to come. You can be assured of God's protection when you obey His Word and listen to the Holy Spirit.

Dear Lord, it is my prayer _____
Jasmine Wise
Monroe, Louisiana

AHA MOMENT

By God's grace and mercy with faith, I am here today!

GOD IS ALWAYS THERE

"For the law was given by Moses, but grace and truth came by Jesus Christ."
John 1:17 (KJV)

God has seen my family and me through many trials. My Jesus has the power over life and death. I was near death and not being fair to my Lord and Savior Jesus Christ. While going through sickness, I prayed that the Lord would touch my body and pleaded with Him to give me another chance. The Lord is just as true as His Word. By God's grace and mercy and my faith in Jesus Christ, I am here today. He is as faithful yesterday as He is today. He gave me a second chance!

I am a witness; Jesus Christ is the only way. He is always there to give you another chance. I am thankful for what my God has done in my life; and that reminds me not to take my God for granted. I thank God for being God! I thank God for being my Lord and my Savior Jesus Christ.

Jesus Christ can be seen everywhere. Most of all, others should be able to see my Lord in me and you. We should be praising God and giving Him all the glory for his faithfulness shown to us. We should take the time to be His hands and feet for those who need His help.

Dear Lord, it is my prayer _____
Linda Lacey
Portsmouth, Virginia

AHA Moment

To God, you are priceless!

GOD'S CHOICE

"The LORD has appeared of old to me, *saying*: Yes, I have loved you with an everlasting love; Therefore with loving kindness I have drawn you." Jeremiah 31:3 (NKJV)

Travel back to your elementary school days. You're on the playground for a game of kickball, sock ball, or whatever the activity was. The teacher tells the team captains to choose team members from among their classmates. Captains survey the group for the best players. One by one, individuals are chosen and the teams are selected. Standing there remains one lonely child, still waiting. By default, the child is placed on a team, perhaps feeling rejected.

Our tendency is to gravitate to those who are the strongest, brightest, prettiest, most affluent or influential. However, when we focus solely on these things, our choices are usually shallow and void of God's wisdom. Aren't you glad God does not operate the same bias way? Remember 1 Corinthians 1:26-27 reminds us that God doesn't always call those who the world thinks is wise, mighty, prestigious or have high social standing. Often, He chooses just the opposite to honor His name. When selecting Israel's next king, Samuel was impressed with the physical attributes of Jesse's older sons. While Samuel was impressed with the outward, God was impressed with the heart of Jesse's youngest son, the shepherd boy David. God reminded Samuel that man looks on the outward appearance, He looks at the heart. (1 Samuel 16:6-13)

The next time you feel like the rejected child on the playground, insignificant, unimportant, and without value, remember that you are precious in God's sight. The God who stood on the vastness of nothing, and called the worlds into existence, overseeing every detail, is the same God who created you and called you by name. He sees you, chooses to love you, and highly values you. You are that "pearl" of great price and He gave everything for you. Meditate on that!

Dear Lord, it is my prayer _____
Sheila Bingham Jones
Los Angeles, California

AHA MOMENT

When I greeted my ex and nothing jumped in my chest,
I knew I was healed.

HEALED AND WHOLE

"The Lord is close to the broken hearted and saves those
who are crushed in spirit."
Psalm 34:18 (NIV)

As I lay in my bed with tears flowing past my ears, all I could think was will I ever smile again? Rejection, anger, bitterness and fear were just a few of the emotions that consumed me. I'd been in church all my life and never heard anyone testify how God had healed or carried them through a divorce. There was an ache in my soul, a pain in my heart, and an emptiness that I knew would take a miracle to heal. I told God, "You have to help me, I cannot afford to lose my mind, and I don't have the money for professional help." Weeks and months went by and I maintained my sanity. No one really knew my pain. I wanted my heart healed.

My prayer request was Lord heal my heart. My sister was reading a book and one of the chapters dealt with letting go of past hurts. When I finished reading the chapter, I felt something physically flow from me and I said, "Thank You God!" I felt a release that Saturday night.

The following Monday, I attended a Martin Luther King Holiday celebration where my daughter was performing. My ex-husband was there with his family. I greeted them and him and nothing jumped in my chest. The following month, I attended my son's senior sermon at seminary. While his dad was there, I greeted him and nothing jumped in my chest. On my way back to work, the tears flowed and I gave God praise for healing my heart, restoring and making me WHOLE. Today, we can share and fellowship with our children in peace and harmony without anger and bitterness.

When you feel hurt, turn the pain over to God and receive the healing!

Dear Lord, it is my prayer _____
Connie J. Tate
Pearl, Mississippi

AHA Moment

Prayer changes a dilemma to miracle.

HEAVENLY INTERVENTION

"Be careful for nothing; but in every thing by prayer and supplication with thanksgiving let your requests be made known unto God."
Philippians 4:6 (KJV)

"The effectual fervent prayer of a righteous man availeth much."
James 5:16b (KJV)

Driving home one afternoon, I was about to change lanes to turn left. Suddenly, a car came from out of nowhere and rushed by to my left just before I was about to turn. God held out His hand of protection and prevented me from a crossover accident just in the nick of time! I stopped immediately, and by God's help, calmed myself. What a close call!

Then, the car that had rushed by me flipped over. It was a police vehicle which was fleeing to be someplace very quickly. Trembling in my car, I prayed for the driver. What a predicament to be in – going so fast until the car flips upside down.

Still in shock and awe that God had protected me, I could do nothing but pray and say, Thank You JESUS, Thank You Lord for keeping me out of harm's way! In a few minutes, the ambulance arrived, people gathered to help and the driver emerged and walked to the ambulance. His life was spared and he didn't appear to be seriously injured.

The Lord shielded that driver that day and I believe that he even prayed as the car was flipping over. Let us remember that a faithful prayer overturns dilemma and brings about a miracle. God received all the credit for the miracle that day and every day. He keeps us from seen and unseen dangers every hour. For that protection and unconditional love, we are grateful.

Trusting in prayer will overturn any situation, if we have faith and believe. Prayer can overturn a dilemma and bring about a miracle.

Dear Lord, it is my prayer _____
Irene Aultman
Mitchellville, Maryland

AHA Moment

God is forever with us.

NEVER FORGOTTEN

"For he himself has said, 'I will never desert you, nor will I ever forsake you.'"
Hebrews 13:5c (CEV)

Have you ever wondered where God is when you need him? Certainly, he heard your cry. Your situation requires God's immediate attention and intervention. You have cried silently, prayed fervently, and recited the right scriptures. God should have been here for you by now! You begin to doubt whether He even heard your distress call for help.

Where is God? Has He forgotten about you? Maybe you have felt this way.

When my son was 8 years old, he was anxiously waiting for me to pick him up from the after-school program. I was running late because of a last-minute work request and slow traffic. I should have already been there. As I drove up to the school, I saw my son anticipating my arrival. With tears in his eyes, he ran and hugged me. He said, "Where were you? I thought you had forgotten about me". I told him that I could never forget about him because I loved him.

Just like we love our children and would never forget about them, God feels the same way towards us. He loves and cares about us. He would never forget about us. Psalm 34:17 (KJV) reminds us, "The righteous cry and the Lord hears and delivers them out of all their troubles."

God sees. God hears. God knows. God is always on time.

In Exodus 3:7, God saw the affliction of the Israelites; He heard their cry. He knew their sorrows. He remembered his promise. It appeared that God had forgotten about them, however, God was purposely working out a deliverance plan. God miraculously delivered the Israelites out of bondage to a better place.

God always keeps His promises! Whenever we call on God, He is faithful in keeping His word. He will always be there for us.

Dear Lord, it is my prayer _____
June Bond
Houston, Texas

AHA Moment

Knowing that God has all power.

HIDDEN UNDER HIS WINGS

"The LORD is good, a strong hold in the day of trouble;
and he knoweth them that trust in him."
Nahum 1:7 (KJV)

I grew up in a Christian home where I was taught to fear God, obey the Ten Commandments and never forget the Golden Rule; among other scriptures. At age twenty-four, my childhood dreams were becoming a reality until I discovered a lump in my left breast. I prayed to God that I didn't have cancer because of my husband and our five-month-old daughter.

The doctor confirmed an abnormality and stated bluntly, "You need to find a doctor **to** have that thing removed." I was crushed. However, it gave me the opportunity to trust, pray and seek God's guidance. In November of 1969, a benign cyst, the size of a golf ball was removed from my left breast. I was informed of the importance of annual checkups because of the possibility of recurrence. For the next thirty-five years my trust was put to the test again and again as I underwent many needle biopsies, aspirations and ultrasounds due to cysts in each breast.

In January of 2005, hidden behind scar tissue was a small lump. In February, I had a lumpectomy. A one-centimeter malignant tumor was removed from my left breast. From that April through mid-May, I had thirty radiation treatments. I no longer have cysts. I can attest; God is good.

In 2015, I celebrated being cancer free for over 10 years. I can never thank God enough for healing me. I thank Him for giving me an additional forty-six years to work in His vineyard. I appreciate how He uses me as a support system for other cancer victims.

I remember the life lessons my parents taught and passed them on to family and others.

During the journey of life, we are confronted with many obstacles but God is in control and we should always trust in Him.

Dear Lord, it is my prayer _____
Sarah Beechem Daily
Jackson, Mississippi

AHA Moment

God is the God of comfort and peace.

I AM HEALED

"Blessed be the God and Father of our Lord Jesus Christ,
the Father of mercies and God of all comfort."
II Corinthians 1:3 (KJV)

I watched my widowed daughter suffer from cancer for about a year. She endured doctors, steroids, radiation, chemotherapy, cancer centers, and rehabilitation nursing homes. She wanted me to be with her most of the time to pray and hold her head in my arms. Her young adult children were working, but stayed with her when they could. Her last Christmas with the family was beautiful. She played games and reminisced about the past with her siblings. She did repent and became a new believer!! God relieved her from her suffering and took her home to be with Him in April 2014.

Several months later, my other daughter asked me to take her to the doctor. She insisted he give her a MRI, which showed she had cancer. She had recently married and had gone on her honeymoon shortly after her sister passed.

She was a seasoned Christian and a prayer warrior. In 2014, she and I went to Hawaii for a week; a place she always wanted to visit. We enjoyed the time together. Every morning, she sang "Blessed Assurance" in the shower. She loved to pray and thank God. At a bible study, she was so adamant saying, "*I am healed*", that I believed she had a revelation from God.

But as the weeks passed, she began to have horrific headaches. While her husband was at work, I would stay with her. She also liked to lay her head in my lap and ask me to lay with her in the bed. I cradled her like a baby, just as I had done with my other daughter. God took her home to be with Him in February 2015. Both were 57 years old. They are both healed!

Believe that God will give you peace after you experience more grief than you think you can.

Dear Lord, it is my prayer _____
Aldoria Gilbert
Kansas City, Kansas

AHA Moment

It's a spiritual thing; the victory is in Jesus.

THE FIGHT FOR MY MIND

"Casting down imaginations, and every high thing that exalteth itself
against the knowledge of God, and bringing into captivity
every thought to the obedience of Christ."
II Corinthians 10:5 (KJV)

Having been reared in a Christian home, from childhood I understood that sex was created by God and reserved for marriage. I had my crushes and there were guys who were interested in me. A few times those interests were mutual, but I was never really tempted to transgress in this area.

I was probably a young adult when I heard the expression, "You have to have sex, or you'll go crazy." As a Christian, during multiple seasons, I experienced what I termed "spiritual oppression." Said spiritual oppression was a force that seemed to seize control of my mind, with the objective to cause me to sin via inappropriate sexual behavior or relationships. My body, without rhyme or reason, craved touch. Impulses prodded me to initiate pursuit of several Christian bachelors. Although I was never attracted to women, this season of spiritual oppression even suggested this as an option. I would feel strange around, or suspect of some women. When I described this oppression to my mother, I told her that now I understood what it meant to be under extreme pressure to fulfill a genuine or counterfeit desire or longing.

As I prayed, I could truthfully say, "God, this is not me, these are not my thoughts or desires. I know it's not of You. Help me, please." The way of escape (I Corinthians 10:13) was to cast down imaginations and bring all thoughts captive to Christ and the truth about God. Praise the Lord, I was freed!

The hymn writer Charles Wesley penned, "He breaks the power of canceled sin, He sets the prisoner free."

For believers who are experiencing spiritual oppression, the Lord is able to keep the sanctified from falling.

Dear Lord, it is my prayer _____
Nedra V. Moore
East Cleveland, Ohio

AHA Moment

Be careful how you judge others.

RIGHTEOUS JUDGMENT

"Judge not according to the appearance, but judge righteous judgment."
John 7:24 (KJV)

My husband and I enjoyed taking our children on road trips across country when they were younger. On one of our many trips, we were headed back home to California after traveling for over five thousand miles. While on the freeway about a hundred miles from home, we began to hear a noise. When the noise got louder, my husband asked me, "What is that noise?" I was of the opinion that it was another vehicle on the road, so I began to look around for the culprit. I spotted an old beat up truck that was coming up fast behind us. I told my husband that the noise was coming from that old truck. I thought to myself that it shouldn't even be on the road. After that beat-up old truck came up and sped right past us, we noticed that we could still hear the noise. My husband decided to pull over onto the shoulder of the road to make sure that there was nothing wrong with our car. We were both surprised to find that we had a flat on one of our rear tires. That flat tire was what was making the noise. After my husband changed the tire, we were on our way again. Thankfully we made it home safely.

Whenever I think of that incident, I realize how I had totally misjudged the situation. I had made up in my mind that the truck was the cause of the problem, simply because of how that truck looked. Have you ever misjudged a situation? Have you ever been totally wrong about what you were thinking or saying about someone? Often times, with very little or no information at all, we jump to the wrong conclusion.

Jesus reminds us in Matthew 7:1-2 (KJV), "Judge not that ye be not judged. For with what judgment ye judge, ye shall be judged: and with what measure ye mete, it shall be measured to you again."

Dear Lord, it is my prayer _____
Jo Ann Hardy
Lakewood, California

AHA Moment

If it matters to you, it matters to God. Pray!

DON'T FORGET TO PRAY

"Be careful for nothing; but in everything by prayer and supplication with
thanksgiving let your requests be made known unto God."
Philippians 4:6 (KJV)

I have often heard my pastor preach, "If it matters to you, it matters to God.
If it's a concern of yours, it's a concern of God's." Some things seem so small, yet I
can still pray to God regarding them. For example, a lost earring, misplaced keys
or a "good" parking spot. Oh, they seem so small yet they were not so extremely
small that I couldn't forfeit the privilege to pray about them. This particular
time, it was my house keys and car keys that I was unable to locate. Searching for
them proved futile. I reminded myself that I had done everything except pray.
I then prayed to my Heavenly Father who knows everything! "Lord, you know
where my keys are. Please just put my hand on them." That was the turning point
to my dilemma. The Lord revealed to me the location of many keys and within
moments my keys were in my hand. God heard and answered my prayer. Thank
you Lord for your faithfulness towards me!

Although a request may appear to be insignificant, God reminded me that I
can cast all of my cares upon Him because He cares for me. Whether it is humon-
gous hardships or pea-sized problems, I can take them all to God in prayer.

God is omniscient, He knows everything and He loves you. He is your
Heavenly Father and longs to hear about whatever matters to you. Go ahead
and talk to Him. Remember, He is just a prayer away!

Dear Lord, it is my prayer _____
Betty A. Avery
Detroit, Michigan

AHA MOMENT

There is only one true and living God; with whom nothing is impossible.

POSSIBILITIES

"For nothing will be impossible with God."
Luke 1:37 (NASB)

As a little girl growing up in rural southern Louisiana, I looked forward to the annual showing of Rodger's and Hammerstein's version of Cinderella. Usually on a Sunday night, I could not wait to sit in front of the black and white RCA television set. As I watched Cinderella's fairy godmother, I would sing the words "Impossible, for a plain yellow pumpkin to become a golden carriage? Impossible, things are happening every day." I knew that song word for word and sang it as loud as I could, with all of the enthusiasm I could muster.

Since that time, the true resolver of possibilities has made Himself known to me. Later, He would allow me to know that He is an omnipotent, merciful, faithful God with whom nothing is impossible. Over the years, our family experienced serious bouts of illness and long periods of hospitalization. In some cases the doctors offered no medical hope, but we remembered and even reminded the physicians that we believed in the God of possibilities. We often referred to the passage, which reads . . . "And Jesus said to him, 'If you can?' All things are possible to him who believes" (Mark 9:23 NASB).

In many of the trials and circumstances that our family faced, the impossible became possible. The Lord provided strength to bear the burden or grace and mercy where the burden was removed.

Will you surrender all your cares today to the God of all possibilities?

Nothing is Impossible (Words and Music by Eugene L. Clark)
Nothing is impossible when you put your trust in God;
Nothing is impossible when you're trusting in His Word.
Hearken to the voice of God to thee;
"Is there anything too hard to Me?"
Then put your trust in God alone and rest upon His Word;
For ev'rything, O, ev'rything, yes ev'rything is possible with God.

Dear Lord, it is my prayer _____
Mary Hooker
Houston, Texas

AHA Moment

Patience is part of the process.

EAGLE'S NEST

"But those who wait on the Lord Shall renew their strength;
They shall mount up with wings like eagles,
They shall run and not be weary, They shall walk and not faint."
Isaiah 40:31 (NKJV)

For the past several months, I have been fascinated with an eagle's nest that I have been following on the internet. I have learned that two eagles, "Ozzie" & "Harriet", have occupied this nest for nearly 10 years. This particular nest in Florida, serves as their home from October through May of each year. Thanks to the technology of video cameras, I observed Harriet lay eggs in the winter. I was able to watch this family until the anticipated eaglets hatched, grew and eventually emptied the nest. Through this experience, I have personally seen Isaiah 40:31 in this nest of eagles and it is amazing!

The baby eaglets, dependent on the parents, wait in the nest a minimum of three months and build great strength. As they develop into fledglings, they exercise their wings until they are strong enough to lift them to a branch just a few inches away. When they become eagles, they attempt to "branch out" on their own. For the first time, they take flight from the nest, as if they have been doing so all of their lives. They fly with an energy that does not seem to perish.

I am grateful to know that this is what waiting for the Lord looks like; I may not see the process at the time. He is taking me through as clearly as I can view the eagle, and the outcome is just the same. I am also grateful this occurs each fall through the spring as it also aids as a visual of what seasonal changes look like in our lives.

If you are in need of strength, learn from the eagles. Be patient and wait on God for your strength.

Dear Lord, it is my prayer _____
Datrice Vanzant-Weathers
Chicago, Illinois

AHA Moment

There is no room for self as a servant of God!

THE BIGGER PICTURE!

"Let this mind be in you which was also in Christ Jesus, who, being in the form
of God, did not consider it robbery to be equal with God, but made Himself
of no reputation, taking on the form of a bondservant,
and coming in the likeness of men."
Philippians 2:5-7 (NKJV)

There is a great temptation in life to desire self-sufficiency. We say things like,
"I got myself into this mess, so I will get myself out." "If you get in trouble, pull
yourself up by your bootstraps." These statements speak to self-sufficiency. This
is such a small, limiting view of life.

To complete His assignment on earth, Jesus, the all-powerful Messiah, completely "emptied Himself" and became an obedient servant of God. What does
that mean? He threw away all His ambitions and positional authority for one
purpose — to please God! He saw the bigger picture!

In the Christian life, all of us must make the transition from serving God to
becoming servants of God. It seems like a play on words, but it is far more than
that! It is all about seeing the bigger picture. For example:

When you simply serve God:
- You choose what you want to do.
- You do things that are convenient to you.
- You decide what you are going to deal with.

But, as a servant of God:
- You simply say, "Here am I, send me!"
- Your time is His time.
- You allow Him to direct your steps.

Your entire attitude, demeanor, and outlook are different. God is looking for
servants—people who are willing to give of themselves for the cause of Christ no
matter what the cost. He desires those that are prepared to go whenever, wherever and do whatever it takes to please and obey Him. He wants people who see
the bigger picture. Do you?

Dear Lord, it is my prayer _____
Tavia Patterson
Houston, Texas

AHA Moment

Worry paralyzes our faith!

DON'T YOU WORRY!

"But seek first the kingdom of God and His righteousness,
and all these things shall be added to you."
Matthew 6:25-33 (NKJV)

In 1989, I married the love of my life. I quickly became a stay at home mom with 3 children under age 4, relying on my husband's salary and God blessing what we had. Yes, there were things that we had to sacrifice, but we were never hungry or homeless.

Today I am working at the local high school, and trusting God to grow my cosmetology business, while our 3 children are in college at the same time. Everyone needs something, and not knowing how we can make it happen, causes life to be frustrating at times.

Worrying can eat away at your body but does not change the outcome—I know. It can cause you to doubt yourself, as well as doubt God's Word. When we worry, fear and doubt prevail. Matthew 6:27 (NLT) says, "Can all your worries add a single moment to your life?" The answer is "No!" Although I may not know how all of my family's needs will be met, Matthew 19:26 (NLT) reminds me that Jesus said, "Humanly speaking, it is impossible. But with God everything is possible." Two of our children have graduated college, and it is because of God. Hallelujah!

We need to turn our worrying into praying. Seeking God early every day will allow Him to talk to us throughout the day, as we are focused on Him. God will give us grace in our hour of need when we trust Him. He knows what we need before we ask, and there is nothing too hard for Him. All power belongs to God so "Don't worry, Pray!" You cannot fight this battle alone. While waiting for God to answer, praise Him! Thank Him for what He's going to do in your situation. Then encourage yourself to be obedient to the Word.

Dear Lord, it is my prayer _____
Valetta J. Ross
Merrillville, Indiana

AHA Moment
God's servants are faithful in little or much.

A FAITHFUL SERVANT

"His lord said unto him, well done, thou good and faithful servant: thou hast
been faithful over a few things, I will make thee ruler over many things:
enter thou into the joy of thy lord."
Matthew 25: 21 (KJV)

A co-worker of mine shared this incident that happened at her church. There
was a deacon who went down to the church every Sunday morning. He checked
the church from front to the back, making sure everything was ready for services
that day. If the heating system or air conditioner needed to be turned on or
adjusted—he did it. For over forty years he quietly performed these and other
duties. One day the Lord surely whispered, "well done, thou good and faithful
servant . . . enter thou into the joy of thy lord" Matthew 25:21.

The following Sunday as church members entered the sanctuary that winter
morning something was different. Why is it so cold in here? Did someone forget
to turn on the heat? Suddenly, they remembered the old faithful deacon was no
longer there and nobody had been appointed to replace him.

Some of God's best servants are quietly working in the shadows for Him.
They lovingly perform seemingly menial tasks with no praise and ask for none.
They receive no pay and ask for none. They receive no certificates or plaques and
ask for none. Their reward awaits them in heaven.

I ask myself a few questions: When my journey on earth ends, will anybody
miss me? Will the Lord recognize me as a good and faithful servant? Have I
lovingly rendered services to others? Have I been faithful in using my talents and
abilities to God's glory? Each one of us needs to take an honest look at our lives.
Consider the activities in your day or week that might be unprofitable toward
building God's kingdom. Get rid of them! Redeem the time!

Dear Lord, it is my prayer _____
Linda L. Martin
Memphis, Tennessee

AHA Moment

Just ask Him, He's listening.

GOD IS ALWAYS NEAR

"... I will never leave you nor forsake you."
Hebrews 13: 5c (KJV)

Our lives have become more and more dependent on computers, but when they crash, we crash. But lost data is never *really* lost; it is still there; it is retrievable. We depend on God; although we don't see Him, and sometimes we can't feel Him, He is always there for us.

I had spent weeks working furiously to update my files when, one day, it happened—my computer crashed! Oh, I had been responsible and made backup discs, but I soon discovered that the outdated information on them was useless. I panicked. "Lord, help me," I cried. "I *have* to have my files." I frantically tried to bring the old computer back to life, but it was dead as a doornail. My files were lost forever.

That same day I bought a new computer, but it was just an empty can without my files. I believe God whispered in my mind, "Check your email," He said. Sure enough, in my Sent Folder and in my Trash Folder, I found *everything* I needed, and then some. I was able to retrieve years-old, even deleted files. How wonderful! The files were there all the time. Now, thank God, my life is back to normal, computer dependent, and running smoothly again.

God calms our spirits in crisis moments, and helps us in our times of need. He cannot be lost; He is Omnipresent. Like the lost files, He has been there all the time since Genesis 1.

Whatever we need, we can ask God. He will never leave us nor forsake us. He is a very *present* help in times of trouble.

I pray that we will remember that God is always near, whispering to us how to find what is lost and how to restore what is broken. Give us listening ears, O God, for you make *"every thing beautiful"* in your time. (Ecclesiastes 3:10)

Dear Lord, it is my prayer _____
Cheryl Bibb
Pearl, Mississippi

AHA MOMENT

Forgive me God as I forgive others.

MY PRAYER FOR FORGIVENESS

"And forgive us our sins; for we also forgive every one that is indebted to us.
And lead us not into temptation; but deliver us from evil."
Luke 11:4 (KJV)

To God:

Forgive me God for my lack of appreciation to you for all you do for me in spite of my complaining and being ungrateful. Forgive me for not walking in faith and trusting you to take charge of all the situations in my life. I pray that you give me a new attitude of joy for your love. You suffered and sacrificed your life on that wretched cross just for me, for us. Thank you, Lord for saving my soul and making me mentally and spiritually whole. Thank you Lord that all I have needed, you have provided. Praise ye the Lord!

Forgive me God as I forgive others. Forgive me for any feelings of anger, bitterness, hatred, envy, jealousy, animosity, hurt or strife. I forgive others that have hurt me, talked about me, lied to me or on me, wronged me, ignored me and failed to treat me the same as others.

As I remember how they treated you and how you forgave them, help me to do the same. All these unholy feelings I have in my heart against anyone, forgive me I pray. I pray this in the name of Jesus. "Then said Jesus, Father, forgive them; for they know not what they do." Luke 23:34a

Dear Lord, it is my prayer _____
Mary E. Crute
Los Angeles, California

AHA Moment

Totally surrender "it" to God.

SET FREE FROM THE BONDAGE OF ABUSE

"Be careful for nothing; but in every thing by prayer and supplication with thanksgiving let your requests be made known unto God. And the peace of God, which passeth all understanding, shall keep your hearts and minds through Christ Jesus."
Philippians 4:6-7 (KJV)

Years ago, I fell in love with a man who blessed me with two wonderful sons. What I didn't know was that he would become abusive. Many days and nights he would fight me even when I was pregnant. I bore this abuse and neglect for sixteen years. One might ask, "Why did you stay?" As a young woman I thought I was "in love." There were many times I thought I was going to lose my mind. On one occasion I wanted to take my sons and change my identity. He was a stalker and crack cocaine addict. I never knew the mood he would be in when he came home. Once he tried to kill me by hitting me with a bottle between my eyes. I will wear a scar on my face forever, but God kept my eyes. It was then when I really woke up and realized that God had a better plan for my life.

This testimony is to let women know you can get delivered from an abusive relationship. First of all, you must have a sincere heart and totally surrender it to God and wait on him to deliver and set you free.

After years of healing and getting my life together, God sent me a great man and now I can truly say I am happy and living a life God designed. I have learned when you are happy, you will not tolerate being around people who make you feel anything less.

Dear Lord, it is my prayer _____
Terri Hill
Wilmington, Delaware

AHA Moment

His presence brings healing.

THE PRESENCE OF GOD

"For I know the thoughts that I think toward you, saith the LORD, thoughts of peace, and not of evil, to give you an expected end. Then shall ye call upon me, and ye shall go and pray unto me, and I will hearken unto you. And ye shall seek me, and find me, when ye shall search for me with all your heart."
Jeremiah 29:11-13 (KJV)

I have seen God in the transformation of lives, including my own. I have seen God with His healing power and saving grace in 2002 in the healing of my son. My son was diagnosed with pneumonia, heart failure (fluid around the heart) and an enlarged heart. His feet and legs were so full of fluid at one point that they were twice their size. Our family and friends were praying for him and God heard their prayers. His heart doctor was so impressed with his healing that he showed us x-rays of his heart before and afterwards; revealing his heart was back to normal, his lungs were clear and there was no swelling in his feet and legs. What was even rarer, his heart was no longer enlarged. Praise the Lord, Hallelujah! I won't stop praying now. Prayer changes things!

The Holy Spirit comes into the believer's life and manifests His presence. He comes to bless, to empower, to exalt Christ and bring heaven into us. There is a new vision, a different view of God's kingdom and the importance of life. The blood of Christ is magnified, and the cross is always before us. The later part of Isaiah 53:5 says, "And by His strips we are healed." Gods healing brought life to my son. His presence transforms lives.

Dear Lord, it is my prayer _____
Mary E. Crute
Los Angeles, California

The Lord is the Creator God, and He rewards us with children to raise for His glory.

THE GIFT

"Lo, children are an heritage from the LORD,
and the fruit of the womb is His reward."
Psalm 127:3 (KJV)

In May 1973, my husband acknowledged the call to preach the Gospel. As a young married couple with a pretty little girl and an active boy, eleven months apart, the Lord surprised us with the news that we would have another baby. The thought of having another child by midsummer overwhelmed me; however, I cried tears of joy while my husband was excited about his call to preach.

The Lord had faithfully provided everything we needed. My husband was gainfully employed, and we had been blessed to purchase our first home. Having two little ones in diapers, I wondered how I would manage another baby and my husband's call to ministry. Would he be a pastor, an evangelist? Would we have to move from our comfortable home? How in the world would I care for three toddlers under 3? My prayer was often, "Lord help me!"

One morning, as my husband left for work and the babies were sleeping soundly, a rare moment of quiet, I began to pray and read the Scriptures and share my burden with the Lord where I always found comfort. I read Psalm 127 which opens, "Except the Lord builds the house, they labor in vain that build it". My eyes then focused on verse 3, "Lo, children are an heritage of the LORD: and the fruit of the womb is his reward . . . ." It was as if the Lord had highlighted this Psalm just for me! I had never thought of these little ones as a gift or a reward. Somehow a song of praise welled up in my soul. The weariness that I had felt disappeared, and I knew this was not just another baby, but a gift from my Creator God. From that moment on, the complaining ceased, and gratefulness and joy replaced my anxiety.

Dear Lord, it is my prayer _____
Mattie Winn
Vallejo, California

AHA MOMENT

Procrastination is not always slothfulness; sometimes it's divine interference.

TIMING IS EVERYTHING

"To every thing there is a season, and a time to every purpose
under the heaven: A time to get, and a time to lose;"
Ecclesiastes 3:1, 6a (KJV)

Have you ever had one of those seasons when everything in your life is going smoothly? You can't wait to get up and start a day of productivity and success. Have you ever had one of those seasons when everything in your life is just a bit off? Your To-Do list items seem to get extended and not accomplished. You anticipate tomorrow for its promised hope, new mercies, and second chances. I've experienced both, especially the latter circumstance. I am learning to discern between slothfulness—with which I am well acquainted—and God's divine purpose.

I rarely miss my church's annual National Convention. One year, my lodging was covered, and I had money for food and offerings; however, the location was 2,500 miles from home and I did not have money for transportation. Months ahead, I began checking fares for planes, trains, and busses. Weeks out, I was thrilled to see a budget-friendly 7-day advance rate on the bus, but I still continued to monitor airfares. The airfares kept increasing so I decided to order my bus tickets before the advance timeframe expired. Shockingly, those rates had spiked significantly. I had hesitated and lost. What now? I was so sure I was supposed to attend the convention. Would I be home alone instead?

God had a provision. A friend of mine who works for an airline offered me a Buddy Plan ticket that cost less than the initial bus fare! Previously, she didn't have any more employee discounts available. Subsequently, a relative cancelled a trip: that became my opportunity. Shortly after that convention this friend retired. Timing is everything.

Not to sanction negligence or a "*que sera sera*" approach toward responsibility, but, ladies, let's give ourselves grace rather than grief.

Dear Lord, it is my prayer _____
Nedra V. Moore
East Cleveland, Ohio

AHA Moment

Life is about learning how to wait well.

I DON'T MIND WAITING

"For I know the plans I have for you, "declares the Lord, "plans to prosper you
and not to harm you, plans to give you hope and a future."
Jeremiah 29:11 (NIV)

Joyce Meyer says, "Patience is not simply the ability to wait—it's how we behave while we're waiting." 2014 was my year of promised blessings. Three years prior, I graduated with a Master's Degree in Education, specializing in school counseling. When I first started interviewing, I was turned down for many positions that I wanted. I kept hearing things like, "we are looking for someone with experience." I guess 700 non-paid internship hours didn't count as experience. I was beyond discouraged and I felt like my education was useless. I was wondering when I was going to begin my career in education. It was very discouraging to graduate from college and be unemployed, underemployed, or working a job that I despised."

My family continued to encourage me, "Let us not be weary in doing will, for at the proper time we will reap a harvest if we do not give up," Galatians 6:9 (NIV).

In August 2014, I finally began my career as a Special Education School Counselor. I received the promised blessing. Everything that I had experienced prepared me for this position. In my waiting season, God placed me in situations and people in my life that were preparing me for the next step. In my waiting season, I learned how to completely trust God and understand that He has a plan for my life.

In your season of waiting, I encourage you to wait well, trust God, and have patience. Waiting well is having an attitude of worship, obedience, joy, service, and praise. As you wait, have a spirit like the disciples when they received their final assignment to fulfill the Great Commission: to listen, obey, and trust God's plan. "Then they worshipped him, and returned to Jerusalem with great joy. And they stayed continually at the temple, praising God" Luke 24:52-53 (NIV).

Dear Lord, it is my prayer _____
Dana Cudjoe
Merrilville, Indiana

AHA MOMENT

Mom, I remember when you used to smile.

SMILE

"O taste and see that the Lord is good: blessed is the man that trusteth in him."
Psalm 34:8 (KJV)

God, I am so glad my joy comes from you. I want my light to shine so others may see the joy in me and know that it comes from you.

While attending graduate school, my husband's job required him to be out of town quite a bit. I often ended up dragging my children to classes with me at the university. They would have to sit quietly in the college library while I completed last minute assignments. I would sometimes come out of class sessions to see them sleep or I would have to discipline them for not having completed their homework assignments. One day while finishing up an assignment, I had to give my children a stern look of chastisement as they sat impatiently waiting for me. My nine-year-old looked up at me with a sad but serious face and whispered "Mom, I remember when you used to smile." I had to hold back my crushed expression and tears to get through my class assignment.

So many times, we forget to smile especially when we are stressed. We serve a God who ". . . is able to do exceeding abundantly above all that we ask or think, according to the power that worked in us" Ephesians 3:20. Many times we forget the power we have, we become so wound up in circumstances that we forget God's goodness which allows us to have joy within.

Psalm 34:8 says "O taste and see that the Lord is good: blessed is the man that trusteth in him."

Always remember to smile and to praise God in whatever assignment you are tasked to complete.

It is my prayer that I keep a smile on my face so that others may see the beauty and love that God has given me even in stressful situations.

Dear Lord, it is my prayer _____
Verneice Wise
St. Louis, Missouri

AHA MOMENT

God's protection and provision brings rays of light.

BEGINNING AT THE END

"The LORD shall preserve thee from all evil: he shall preserve thy soul. The LORD shall preserve thy going out and thy coming in from this time forth, and even for evermore."
Psalm 121:7-8 (KJV)

It has now been over ten years since my husband passed away. During the ambulance ride to the hospital, God clearly spoke these words to me, "I've got you!" I was not sure what those words, "I've got you" really meant. I went along believing those words, but sometimes I was in a fog. I was assured that God promises are true. During the last ten years, I have seen God supply all of my needs. He supplied not just my needs but also the needs of my four young sons. He went above and beyond, not just supplying our necessities of food, clothing and shelter but also granting us some of our wants.

I have truly found that God is faithful. God's mercies are renewed every morning. I must take each day and each challenge knowing that God knows what is ahead. I do not need to know everything; I only need to know that God is working in my favor.

I challenge you to dig in and anchor into God because in God you will find all that you need.

It is my prayer to speak of His faithfulness at all times. I pray that He helps me to see in good times and bad times. I know that He is always in control during and beyond times of emotional and physical leanness.

Dear Lord, it is my prayer _____
Annette Richardson
St. Louis, Missouri

AHA Moment

When reflecting on life's journey, you will be amazed.

EMBRACING THE LOVE OF GOD

"For I am persuaded that neither death nor life, nor angels nor principalities nor powers, nor things present nor things to come, nor height nor depth, nor any other creature, shall be able to separate us from the love of God which is in Christ Jesus our Lord."
Romans 8:38-39 (NKJV)

I have always felt God's presence in my life especially when I gave my life to Him. I believed that faith connected me to Him. However, I failed to wholeheartedly embrace God's love during the good, the bad, and the ugly. It was not until my only child had a serious accident that I reflected on my life and my relationship with God. You see, I believed and felt guilty that my sins caused this to happen to him. He was young, enthusiastic about serving God, obedient, and was genuinely a good person.

So, one night in his hospital room while watching him sleep, I asked God to heal him and show me what I had done. God opened His book to me! My answer became real through Romans 8:38 and 39. The word persuaded (convinced) means to move by evidence to belief. God revealed that, "Things are going to happen"; powers are going to come against us and cause us to doubt His presence and His love. But, that meditation caused me to be fully convinced of the Blessed Assurance of God. His word in Romans 8:38-39 assured me that it is His nature to love us. We are secure that He will never separate His love from us. He will not let anything come between us and Him.

So, I am persuaded of these three things: first, God loves us; next, God has shown His love to us by the gift of His Son Jesus Christ; and then, His divine love is with us in all things because we are in Christ and are loved for his sake. Are you persuaded?

Dear Lord, it is my prayer _____
Monocia Connors
Jackson, Mississippi

AHA MOMENT
Keep your focus on Jesus.

FOCUS

"You will keep in perfect peace him whose mind is
stayed on you, because he trusts in You."
Isaiah 26:3 (ESV)

July 3rd was always one of the best days of the year for me as a young child growing up in Chicago. It was the day my family and I would get together and spend the entire day at The Taste of Chicago. My mother, three of her sisters, all my cousins and Grandma would eat until we could stand no more. Then we would relax by the lake and enjoy the fireworks show at the end of the night as the Chicago Symphony Orchestra played patriotic music in the background.

Our last year as an entourage in attendance came to an abrupt halt when the evening festivities ended with one of my aunts having a severe panic attack. As the crowd of hundreds of thousands stood to depart, my aunt standing not taller than 4'10" was suddenly overwhelmed. She began screaming and hollering like a mad woman before she broke down in frantic tears. My cousins and I were outdone and embarrassed; this was the feistiest family member in the entire family. We could not believe the scene playing out before us. My eldest aunt stepped directly in front of her hysterical sister, grabbed and held her hands and commanded, "Don't look at anything or anybody except me." The panicking aunt obeyed and began to calm down. Meanwhile, the rest of us were locking arms in a circle around them. We kept a barrier around them as we slowly eased toward a tree where my aunt recovered as the crowd dissipated.

When I read Isaiah 26:3, I think of that situation that occurred over three decades ago as a visual of what it looks like for me to remain attentive to Christ as opposed to the chaos of this world around me. When I focus on the world, I become panic stricken.

What are you focusing on? Are you in a place of panic or peace?

Dear Lord, it is my prayer _____
Datrice Vanzant-Weathers
Chicago, Illinois

AHA MOMENT
God sends His angels to bring comfort.

MINISTERING ANGELS

"My God hath sent his angel, and hath shut the lions' mouths, that they have not hurt me: forasmuch as before him innocency was found in me; and also before thee, O king, have I done no hurt."
Daniel 6:22 (KJV)

I love to remember how God ministered to me through my Mother. She was diagnosed with a terminal illness. Right before her death, I woke up and went into her bedroom to give her medicine. She was on her bed and she told me," I did not sleep at all last night, the angels kept me up." My mother told me that they were all over the room; up in corners, in the ceiling and everywhere. She said that they didn't bother her, they just kept moving. As she talked about the angels there was a smile and such a peace on her face. I knew she was ready to be with the Lord and I was able to accept what was coming.

Weeks later when she departed this world she had that same peaceful expression on her face. I will cherish that morning always, remembering that peaceful smile and the story of the ministering Angels. I often read Daniel 6 where it says God sent an angel to Daniel and I believe He sent angels to my Mom." Our God is Awesome.

I thank Him for the peace he gives that passes all understanding.

Dear Lord, it is my prayer _____
Jerri Bell-Yarbrough
Bogalusa, Louisiana

AHA Moment

Patience, experience, and hope are great faith builders.

GOD WILL MAKE A WAY

"But seek ye first the kingdom of God, and his righteousness;
and all these things shall be added unto you."
Matthew 6:33 (KJV)

When I was elected to the National Missionary Board of my church I felt it was a great honor, but I also felt unworthy to be included among such devout women. My sense of inadequacy intensified when I couldn't locate a position description. Not knowing the responsibilities of my new role, I began sending e-mails and making phone calls to inquire, "What does this mean? What do I do?" It was gratifying to be informed that the officers of my Board were scheduling a set of meetings in Jackson, Mississippi to draft a description of my role.

Due to a previous commitment in Michigan the weekend before the meeting, I could not take advantage of a shared road trip to Jackson. I would now have to fly. It's usually difficult to find affordable flights from Ohio to Jackson, and this occasion was typical. I thought I had a reasonable budget, but I could not afford the prices.

While in Michigan, I continued to check for flights that matched my money and my travel window. I arrived home from Michigan late in the evening. My dad handed me a stuffed manila envelope that had been dropped off that afternoon by a missionary friend. She told my dad that a deacon at church gave her some money and told her that the Lord told him she needed it. Other members of the congregation also generously contributed. She concluded, "This must be Nedra's money." I immediately booked my flight to Mississippi.

My plans, priorities, and purposes were to glorify God. To that end I persevered, did the next right thing, and expected Him to make away (Romans 5:3-5). I learned anew the verity of God's Word. Church-ese says, "He may not come when you want Him, but He's right on time!"

Dear Lord, it is my prayer _____
Nedra V. Moore
East Cleveland, Ohio

AHA MOMENT
We Have No Control!

TRUST GOD

"The Lord is my shepherd; I shall not want. He maketh me to lie down in green pastures: he leadeth me beside the still waters. He restoreth my soul: he leadeth me in the paths of righteousness for his name's sake. Yea, though I walk through the valley of the shadow of death, I will fear no evil: for thou art with me; thy rod and thy staff they comfort me."
Psalm 23:1-4 (KJV)

On February 29, 1988, my life, as I knew it, changed forever. My husband was involved in a fatal car accident. This loss sent shock waves through me. I fell to the floor in a prostrate position and began to beg the Lord for strength that I knew only He could provide. It was then that I had to rely on everything that I had been taught about our Lord and Savior. As I was preparing for his home going, the 23rd Psalm began to resonate in my spirit. I heard the Lord encourage me to be like David when he said he walked through the valley of the shadow of death. I am certain that David was dealing with several emotions at the time; but he continued to "walk through."

As women of God, we must learn that we are subject to the will of God for our lives. We are not our own. I had to alter my five-year plan that included my husband, and just live the life that God had in store for me. No matter what we face, God is bigger than any problem we may have. We must put our complete faith and trust in His promises to us. We know that no matter what obstacles we may face, the hand of the Lord is upon us. As we learn to put our trust in Him, we will see him move us out of "the valley" just as He did for David.

Dear Lord, it is my prayer _____
Brenda Newsome
Prentiss, Mississippi

AHA Moment
Trust in God's healing!

GOD'S HEALING POWER

"And Jesus saith unto him, I will come and heal him."
Matthew 8:7 (KJV)

In the year of 2015, I was battling a disease called Depression. This debilitating and devastating disease was really breaking me down. I tried to hide this disease behind my smiles whenever I went to church or when I was just being around people. I prayed to God to help me overcome this disease that was negatively impacting millions of people's lives every day. I also trusted and believed in God's word that he would heal me from this disease.

One Sunday morning when I went to church, my brother was the preacher for the day and his sermon was about Depression. He spoke on how he had suffered through depression and how God had delivered him from the disease. Through this message, I knew God was speaking to me. From that point on I started fervently praying and asking God to heal me from this depression. Every day I started listening to gospel music, praying, reading, and meditating on His word. As the months went by I started feeling better and there was no need now for any medication. I no longer hide behind my smiles. My smiles were now genuine. I have been giving God the praise for how he came and healed me just as he did for the servant in Matthew 8:7.

God will do it! Just have faith and trust Him!

Dear Lord, it is my prayer _____
Loretta Jackson
Wilmington, Delaware

HOW BRIGHT IS YOUR LIGHT?

"Let your light so shine before men, that they may see your good works, and glorify your Father which is in heaven."
Matthew 5:16 (KJV)

A few years ago, some of my co-workers and I were scheduled to attend a seminar. The seminar was to take place at a hotel that was located only a few blocks down the street from the building where we worked. Most of us decided to simply walk down the street to the hotel. After arriving there, we were all given name tags to put on and a packet containing the material that would be used during the meeting. After the seminar was over, I gathered my belongings and began to walk back down the street to the building where I worked. As I passed by a group of people standing near the sidewalk, a young man that was in this group turned around and said to me, "Hello Jo Ann." I looked at the person addressing me but I drew a total blank. I did not remember ever seeing him before and wondered how in the world he knew my name. He saw the perplexity on my face and smiled. He then pointed to my jacket and said, "Your name tag." I had forgotten to remove my name tag before leaving the hotel. After walking past him, I couldn't snatch that tag off of my jacket fast enough.

What do people see when they look at those who profess Christianity? Are we representing Christ in a positive light? In 1 Peter 2:9 we read, "But ye are a chosen generation, a royal priesthood, a holy nation, a peculiar people; that ye should shew forth the praises of him who hath called you out of darkness into his marvelous light." If we display behavior that is contrary to God's word, the negative impression that we make on others, is not as easily removed as taking a name tag off your jacket.

Dear Lord, it is my prayer _____
Jo Ann Hardy
Lakewood, California

AHA MOMENT
Singles are significant to God.

SINGLES

"But I would have you without carefulness. He that is unmarried careth for the things that belong to the Lord, how he may please the Lord: But he that is married careth for the things that are of the world, how he may please his wife. There is difference also between a wife and a virgin. The unmarried woman careth for the things of the Lord, that she may be holy both in body and in spirit: but she that is married careth for the things of the world, how she may please her husband. And this I speak for your own profit; not that I may cast a snare upon you, but for that which is comely, and that ye may attend upon the Lord without distraction.
I Corinthians 7:32-35

As usual, I was anticipating, with pleasure, the national holiday of Thanksgiving. My household gathers with extended family members to share two days of food, fellowship, and fun. I made a mental rundown of who we could expect to be in attendance this year. For the first time, it struck me on how many adults in the family are in some state of singleness. Some, including me, have never been married. Some have been engaged. Some are widowed. Some have been divorced...once or twice and some are separated.

Reflecting on the life situations of these family members; a scriptural truth came to mind found in Psalm 68:6a, "God setteth the solitary in families." I share the significant savor that this Thanksgiving gathering holds for each member of our family, the singles in particular. Singleness too has an honorable status as it pertains to the availability of a Christian's time for the advancing of God's kingdom. Notable singles of the Bible include Daniel, Ezekiel (became widowed), Jeremiah (told not to wed), Mary & Martha.

Are you in some state of singleness? Whether or not you have "the gift of singleness," are you content enough for your life to glorify God? (I Timothy 6:6; Philippians 4:11)

Dear Lord, it is my prayer _____
Nedra V. Moore
East Cleveland, Ohio

AHA Moment

Stability comes from the Son.

SALVATION COMMITMENT

"How shall we escape if we neglect so great a salvation, which at the first began to be spoken by the Lord, and was confirmed to us by those who heard Him."
Hebrews 2:3 (NKJV)

I moved 18 times before I turned 40 years old and "NO", I am not from a military family. I did not grow up going to church. To tell you the truth, the only Bible I remember opening was that of my aunt, a Jehovah's Witness. Her home was the fourth one I recall living in for one year; this is when I frequented the Kingdom Hall three times a week. I am extremely grateful for that time in my life because it helped me to accept the "real truth" when it presented itself, and it did not come in the form of The *Watchtower* or *Awake* magazines. The Truth is The Holy Bible.

I saw the true gospel in action while moving several more times. In other words, I began to see God moving in my mother. She was a new creature for sure. Old things had passed away and I tell you, she was new! The slow but steady changes in her life were so evident that I went to her church in Chicago to investigate! What happened to my Momma? I wanted to know-many wanted to know! Well, my research paid off. I learned that Jesus Christ died for my sins. During the revival at my mother's church, on August 14, 1992, I accepted Salvation, believing that Christ died and rose again for me.

However, it would not be until ten years later that I would commit my life whole heartily to God and that has made all the difference in the world. This is when I was able to stop desiring what God was doing in other people's lives because the movement I received was undeniable Him! I have not seen Him ease up since.

When you accepted Salvation did you also make a full commitment to Christ? If not, why not do so today.

Dear Lord, it is my prayer _____
Datrice Vanzant-Weathers
Chicago, Illinois

AHA MOMENT
You can resist the Devil; he will flee from you.

VICTORY OVER STEALING

"Submit yourselves therefore to God. Resist the devil, and he will flee from you."
James 4:7 (KJV)

My mother related the following story of struggle and victory to her children numerous times. She also shared it with others as a witness and for their edification.

My mother accepted Jesus Christ as her personal Savior at the age of nine. As scared as she was of water and of getting her hair wet, she overcame both because she intensely wanted to be baptized. She was baptized in a river in Mississippi. As a child, she was drawn to the hymns of the church; she would run and skip about, singing her favorites. However, as is the experience of many young believers, she encountered several challenging situations. One episode had a definitive impact upon her spiritual maturation. At sixteen years of age, she began stealing money from her mother. No one suspected her. One of her brothers was accused of being the thief; which, of course, he denied. She knew that she was wrong and wanted to quit. Finally, one day she determined to break that sinful habit. She purposed that she would not take any money that day. She clearly heard the devil say, "If you don't steal today, you'll steal tomorrow." She answered back, "That may be, but I'm not going to do it today." From that moment, the bondage was broken. She never stole again.

Remember, Jesus himself as an impoverished man, a compassionate, charismatic, controversial rabbi, a single adult, etc. – "was in all points tempted like as we are, [of the devil] yet without sin" (Hebrews 4:15). His overcoming power and victory are ours. Even if, God forbid, we should sin; Jesus is our advocate with God (I John 2:1).

Dear Lord, it is my prayer _____
Nedra V. Moore
East Cleveland, Ohio

AHA MOMENT

Regardless of the challenges today, with our Savior, this is a good life!

THIS IS A GOOD AND JOYOUS WAY

"But let all those that put their trust in thee rejoice:
let them ever shout for joy, because thou defendest them:
let them also that love thy name be joyful in thee."
Psalm 5:11 (KJV)

Life will come after you. Even as a Christian, we are not immune to life's challenges. We have not been promised flowery beds of ease. In the troubled times of today, how can we escape? Where is peace? How can we make it?

If you are a child of God, you have been promised by the Savior, "...lo, I am with you alway, even unto the end of the world" (Matthew 28:20 KJV). We have the King of glory and a Father in heaven with us. He is our peace and our rest. Wow! So let's regroup, rethink, smile, and rest along life's way. Psalm 16:11 (KJV) says, "Thou wilt shew me the path of life: in thy presence is fullness of joy; at thy right hand there are pleasures for evermore."

I must remember that:

- in trouble, He is a Redeemer;
- in sickness, He is a Healer;
- in decision-making, He is a Director;
- when in need, He is a Provider;
- when overwhelmed, He is a Deliverer;
- when broken, He is a Comforter;
- when weak, He is a Refuge;
- when afraid, He is a Shelter; and
- when feeling alone, He is always there!

"All I Need," a hymn written by Charles P. Jones states, "All I need, all I need, He alone is all my plea, He is all I need." Another song declares, "Perfect submission, all is at rest, I in my Savior am happy and blest; Watching and waiting, looking above, Filled with His goodness, lost in His love." ("Blessed Assurance" by Fanny Crosby) We have joy and all that we need because of Him!

Dear Lord, it is my prayer _____
Mary Kennebrew
Little Rock, Arkansas

AHA Moment

Love your spouse as Christ loves the church.

HOW IS YOUR RELATIONSHIP WITH YOUR SAVIOR?

"For I am persuaded, that neither death, nor life, nor angels, nor principalities,
nor powers, nor things present, nor things to come, Nor height, nor depth, nor
any other creature, shall be able to separate us from the love of God,
which is in Christ Jesus our Lord."
Romans 8:38-39 (KJV)

As a seasoned married couple was preparing to celebrate their Golden
Wedding Anniversary, a young reporter was preparing to wed the love of
his life. He was ecstatic to be assigned the job of interviewing the renowned
Christian couple about what had been their best kept secret of having such a
loving life together. They stated that the key ingredients were to: "Love, and forsake all others." They also said, "If you remember to love your spouse as Christ
loves the church; you are more than half way there." They made the following
commitments:

- Love, respect, and honor each other as stated in the wedding vows.
- Let everyone know that no one is more important than each other.
- Never knowingly do anything that will hurt, disrespect, or make the
  other one feel uncomfortable in any situation.
- Never allow anyone else to come between your relationship with
  each other.
- Never give anyone the impression that you would secretively do some-
  thing for someone else to satisfy their needs.
- Never support someone else in disrespecting the other.

We can take this same advice and apply it to our relationship with our Savior.
As Christians, we are married to Jesus Christ our Savior. The world should see
that we will not knowingly do anything to disrespect our commitment to Christ,
nor will we support others in breaking the vows we made to serve Christ. They
should also see that Jesus Christ is most important in our lives, and we will not
allow anything to separate us from His love.

Dear Lord, it is my prayer _____
O'ka Duren
Jackson, Mississippi

AHA Moment

"God sightings" come when you walk and talk with Jesus daily.

GOD IS LOVE

"He who does not love does not know God, for God is love."
I John 4:8 (NKJV)

Some years ago, my family would travel to conventions and other church events and stay in the homes of fellow church members. It was customary that we each recite a Bible verse before the breakfast meal. My 4-year-old brother proudly said, "God is love." The daughter of our host, who was also 4, immediately began to cry. When asked why the tears, she replied, "He took my verse!" The more I know God and have "God sightings," I have learned that the Bible verses are true and not restricted to one person.

An example of a "God sighting" was when I prayed for God to wholly save my husband. God said, "Get out of the way, love him and show him My love. Every time I bless your family, share that blessing verbally with your husband." Being obedient, I reminded him of a trip we had taken with no problems; how he got a promotion at work; how our children were blessed; and how health issues were overcome; and I credited it all to God. I stopped nagging and started loving. After a "soul-saving sermon," my husband dedicated his life to Christ. It was a "Peter's at the door" surprise to me—a "God sighting!"

Wherever God reigns, there is love, the very first Fruit of the Spirit (Galatians 5:22-23). You cannot have one without the other. Through some of my darkest days, God reminded me of I Corinthians 13:4-7 (NIV, paraphrased): *Love is patient, kind, does not envy, does not boast, is not proud, does not dishonor others, is not self-seeking, is not easily angered, keeps no record of wrong, does not delight in evil, and rejoices in the truth. Love protects, trusts, hopes, perseveres, and never fails.*

I challenge you to become a God watcher; share your "sightings" with others, and love as He loves us.

Dear Lord, it is my prayer _____
Elizabeth Izard
Conyers, Georgia

AHA Moment

Your words can kill or build!

USE WORDS TO HONOR GOD

"Death and life are in the power of the tongue:
and they that love it shall eat the fruit thereof."
Proverbs 18:21 (KJV)

An old adage that resulted as a response from playground bullying states, "Sticks and stones may break my bones, but words will never hurt me!" It implied that physical force—not insults, hurt. On the contrary, words *are* extremely powerful. When used in a positive manner, they can be encouraging, motivating, and build one's self-esteem. However, if used in a negative demeanor, they are detrimental, discouraging, hurtful, and may consequently leave permanent scaring.

Thumper, in the animated movie, "<u>Bambi</u>" stated, "If you can't say something nice, don't say nothing at all."

God holds us accountable for what we say, so we must choose our words wisely. Matthew 12:36-37 reads, ". . . every idle word that men shall speak, they shall give account thereof in the day of judgment. For by thy words thou shalt be justified, and by thy words thou shalt be condemned." We must, therefore:

1. **Speak kindly:** ". . . Love your enemies, bless them that curse you, do good to them that hate you. . ." Matthew 5:44 (KJV);
2. **Avoid gossip:** "He that goeth about as a talebearer revealeth secrets. . ." Proverbs 20:19 (KJV);
3. **Avoid profanity:** "Let no corrupt communication proceed out of your mouth. . ." Ephesians 4:29 (KJV);
4. **Speak the truth:** "Let no corrupt communication proceed out of your mouth. . ." Ephesians 4:29 (KJV);
5. **Think before speaking:** "Let every man be swift to hear, slow to speak, slow to wrath. . ." James 1:19-20 (KJV).

God, enable me to use my words to show Your love to all. "Let the words of my mouth, and the meditation of my heart, be acceptable in thy sight, O LORD, my strength, and my redeemer" Psalm 19:14 (KJV).

Dear Lord, it is my prayer _____
Verletta Thompson
Fayetteville, Georgia

AHA Moment

On your mark, Get set, Go!

WORK OUT TO LIVE ETERNALLY

"I press toward the mark for the prize of the high calling of God in Christ Jesus."
Philippians 3:14 (KJV)

During a particular season in my life, working out was on my daily agenda. While vacationing in Niagara Falls, I visited the hotel's gym to work out. These words were on the wall: Endurance, Train, Commitment, Performance, Push Through, Consistent, Work It Out, Run and Walk. Immediately my thoughts went to how my Christian walk should be:

Enduring hardship as a good soldier (II Timothy 2:3); *Training, bringing every thought into captivity to the obedience of Christ* (II Corinthians 10:5); *Committing our ways unto the Lord;* (Psalm 37:5); *Pushing through: Praying until something happens; Work out your own salvation* (Philippians 2:12).

It is good to work out to be healthy, but God wants his children to develop a consistent attitude of prayer and fellowship with him. Pray without ceasing (1 Thessalonians 5:17). Prayer is building my strength and stamina to endure hardships. I still work out physically on occasion; I need to be fit to run this race. Romans 12:1 (NIV) reads, "Therefore, I urge you, brothers and sisters, in view of God's mercy, to offer your bodies as a living sacrifice, holy and pleasing to God—this is your true and proper worship."

I'm truly committed to running this spiritual race daily. When my eyes open every morning I give thanks to God, pray and read my Bible. Now I am equipped and ready to press forward.

Do your best to present yourself to God, striving to achieve that imperishable crown.

Dear Lord, it is my prayer _____
Constance J. Garner
Novi, Missouri

AHA Moment

I had a debt I could not pay.

JESUS PAID IT ALL

"God made him who had no sin to be sin for us, so that in him we might
become the righteousness of God."
II Corinthians 5:21 (NIV)

One evening while out of town, I had dinner at a restaurant. At the end of
the meal, I summoned the server for the bill. When she got to my table, she told
me that a stranger had already paid my bill and wanted to remain anonymous. I
know that I should have been grateful, but that was not the response I felt. Why
should somebody pay my bill? Did I appear to be a poor, decrepit, or needy
person? I think not! I had my own money. I could pay for my own meal. In case
that stranger was watching me, I composed my thoughts as I did not want to
appear ungrateful and offend their generosity. I smiled and told the server what
a nice gesture that was. I left her a nice tip (since I now had extra money) and
proceeded to my car.

I got in my car, and all of a sudden, I knew that the presence of the Lord was
with me. The message was so clear. *I had a debt I could not pay.* I was poor; I was
decrepit; and I was in dire need. My payment according to Romans 6:23 would
be death and could not be paid by a stranger because John 15:13 (KJV) tells me,
"Greater love hath no man than this, that a man lay down his life for his friends."

God made this spotless lamb who had no sin to become sin for me. He took
my place on that cross. He became like me so that I could belong to God. I would
not just be righteous but would become God's righteousness!

I challenge you to be grateful for the debt that was paid for you by our Lord
Jesus Christ.

JESUS PAID IT ALL!

Dear Lord, it is my prayer _____
Portia Waynick
Los Angeles, California

AHA Moment

God has a perfect gift for me.

YOUR PERFECT GIFT

"For I would that all men were even as I myself. But every man hath his proper
gift of God, one after this manner, and another after that."
I Corinthians 7:7 (KJV)

It is so often that we find ourselves wanting for this and asking for something
and hoping for whatever it may be. But how often do we want to *share* what we
call that 'perfect gift'?

We are so consumed by wanting some trinket or treasured item; or holding
the winning ticket; or even being the hundredth customer to walk in a department store and have bells and whistles go off and win a grand prize. Yet, how often
do we seek God to reveal to us the gift He's given to each of us? That perfect gift
that can be used to exalt Him.

I work on a job where packages are received, sorted, distributed and delivered to various recipients. One can only imagine the expression on their faces
when the package is received and opened. There is added excitement since it
appears they have received the perfect gift.

I think of the awesomeness of the God that we serve and how He has a special gift for us. He has given each of us a special perfect gift to use to glorify Him.
Do you know what your gift is? Claim it and glorify God!

Dear Lord, it is my prayer _____
Frances Christine Robinson
Merced, California

AHA Moment

Never put God in a box!

GOD IS AN EXTRAORDINARY HEALER, SO NEVER PUT HIM IN A BOX!

"In whom we have boldness and access with confidence by the faith of him."
Ephesians 3:12 (KJV)

One Saturday, after a spirit-filled program at church had ended and refreshments were served, two ladies and I finished cleaning the church kitchen and went home. After arriving home, I began to prepare for Sunday service. Because of the diligent work in the kitchen that night, I was extremely tired. After taking a shower, I applied some soothing cream to my feet, that I had never used before, said my prayers, and went to bed. I had a restful night's sleep.

As I woke up the next morning, feeling refreshed, I noticed that my feet and right side were tingling. The Holy Spirit told me that the tingling was not only in my feet and the right side of my body, but from the top of my head to the bottom of my feet. I had a stroke during the night as I slept. I was shocked, but He calmed me down.

I had to make a decision to go to the emergency room or go to my church! Church won out! By faithful confidence, I know that my Lord Jesus Christ blessed me for this action of faith. I trusted God for His extraordinary healing and did not put Him in a box. However, I felt the need for a medical checkup, and the doctor confirmed what the Holy Spirit had already told me, GLORY HALLELUJAH! According to II Corinthians 7:16 (KJV), "I rejoice therefore that I have confidence in you in all things."

As we trust God for our healing, never put Him in a box.

Dear Lord, it is my prayer _____
Monique O. Jones
Bladensburg, Maryland

AHA Moment

God heals our brokenness.

WILT THOU BE MADE WHOLE

"... He said to him, 'Do you want to be made well?"
John 5:6 (NKJV)

"Wilt thou be made whole?" is a question that applies to us and the relevance of our ministry in God's kingdom. We all have broken places that need God's healing and restoration. However, do we really want deliverance from the things that prevent us from fully devoting ourselves to God's plan? It seems easier to remain in the shadows and claim inadequacy, rather than seek God's healing. He has not called His people to exist in mediocrity; making excuses for not engaging in kingdom work.

How do we get to a place where our brokenness is "fixed", and we are free to meet the needs of others through ministry? In John 5:6, Jesus asked the man at the pool of Bethesda, "Do you want to be made well?" The man's healing was dependent upon his decision. God's divine mercy does not act independently of human confession, faith, and desire.

We must decide that we want to be made whole. Without that decision, the highest blessings are unattainable. A simple "yes" is all that is needed. We operate at our greatest capacity when we say "yes" to wholeness. Whoever accepts the Deliverer will be made whole by the power of God.

We often give Jesus a litany of excuses why we remain in our brokenness. He does not want our excuses but an affirmative decision to be healed. We have to yield to the Sovereignty of God. For many years, I could not figure out why I repeatedly suffered from many of the same hurts. I did not become completely whole until I fully surrendered to God's control.

The man at the pool was to get up and walk, as we must. When we become whole, saying "yes" to emotional wholeness, our behavior changes. We can then move to the next level and walk with power in the plan that God has for our lives.

Dear Lord, it is my prayer _____
Bettye Willis
Atlanta, Georgia

AHA Moment

A Godly heart is required, rather than a "better than you" image.

REFLECTIONS OF A GODLY HEART

"Just as water mirrors your face, so your face mirrors your heart."
Proverbs 27:19 (MSG)

When you look into water, you see a likeness of your face. The face is reflected in the water. When you look into your heart, you see what you are really like. The heart reflects the real person.

Jeremiah 17:9 (KJV) tells us that, "The heart is deceitful above all things, and desperately wicked: who can know it?" I recall during our early days of salvation, how we criticized and judged others, as though we were born righteous, pure, and had never committed a sin. News flash: This is not true. We have been there and done it too. Our hearts have been deceitful and desperately wicked. We wanted others to operate in our image and not the image of God.

Proverbs 4:23-27 (MSG) warns to, "Keep vigilant watch over your heart; that's where life starts. . . leave evil in the dust." ". . . I have something to say to each one of you. Don't think that you are better than you really are..." (Romans 12:3 ERV).

I have learned that Jesus Christ is morally perfect and yet He identified with us in our needs and temptations. That unselfish identity makes Him superior to any other person, past or present.

Be mindful of your images displayed. Be sure to reflect a Godly heart based on Christlike values. Do not think you are better, more highly, or more important than you really are. Avoid a false sense of superiority in your heart thinking.

Dear Lord, it is my prayer _____
Vonn J. Jones
Washington, District of Columbia

AHA Moment

God wants you to trust Him.

SEEK GOD'S GUIDANCE

"Trust in the Lord with all your heart and lean not on your own understanding;
in all your ways submit to him, and he will make your paths straight."
Proverbs 3:5-6 (NIV)

Have you ever felt a sense of confusion, or been in a state of delirium? God is waiting on your behalf to intervene and help. I can recall a time in my life when I was extremely ill. I was going about my daily routines as a school teacher, but found myself nauseated and vomiting for a period of weeks.

I was confused and tried to take matters into my own hands. When I went to work, two of my colleagues told me that I needed to see a physician. I didn't want to. Eventually, I went to the doctor and after numerous tests, I was diagnosed with hyperthyroidism.

I was afraid. I had never heard of this disease before and did not want to have surgery. I prayed and asked God for His guidance. The doctors decided that I did not require surgery, but instead a nuclear medicine test would help diagnose any malignancy. Thank God, a diagnosis was achieved without invasive surgery.

God always wants the best for us. He has given us free will, and sometimes we just want to do things our way. We must submit and allow Him to direct our paths.

When you need guidance and direction, ask God to help you and He will never fail you.

Dear Lord, it is my prayer _____
Yvonne Bayne
Jackson, Mississippi

AHA Moment

Operate in a spirit of unity.

POINTS OF CONTENTION

"With all lowliness and meekness, with longsuffering, forbearing one another in love; Endeavouring to keep the unity of the Spirit in the bond of peace."
Ephesians 4:2-3 (KJV)

Operating in a spirit of unity can be challenging at times, especially when the flesh causes us to want to throw lowliness and meekness out of the window in exchange for pride and aggressiveness. Zealousness, often confused with the leading of the Holy Spirit, often drives one to look for points of contention in everything.

Many of you may have grown up in similar churches as I did, where the subtext of sermons or the conversations of more seasoned "saints" were peppered with attacks on every new fad, occurrence, or activity, etc. Divisions often arose because of differences in opinions on a lot of these subject matters. A lot of time and energy was often wasted addressing these matters as opposed to truly being about our Father's business.

During the early years of my walk with God, I probably was in a constant state of frustration because I looked for points of contention in everything. I don't know if I consciously looked for them, but they were there. After some years of this, I began to seek God for true guidance. God revealed to me that the things He wants us to take a stand on are clear in His Word. We do not need to "make mountains out of molehills." Satan distracted Eve from the command that God had given Adam, by getting her focused on the fruit itself and questioning God's motive for giving the command.

We need to stop allowing the devil to distract us with things that don't even matter in the big picture. This is, in fact, a tactic of Satan.

Dear Lord, it is my prayer _____
Monique H. May
Corona, California

AHA Moment

Use PURPLE to defeat the enemy!

THERE IS PURPOSE IN THE PURPLE!

"And the soldiers platted a crown of thorns, and put it on his head,
and they put on him a purple robe."
John 19:2 (KJV)

"The soldiers made [wove; twisted together] a crown from some thorny
branches [of thorns] and put it on Jesus' head and put a purple robe [purple
was the color of royalty] around him."
John 19:2 (EXB)

Have you ever thought about the significance of the various colors that God made? What about the color purple? One day, God showed me that there was a purpose in the purple beyond what is seen with our natural eyes. Why purple, you may ask. Well, in the Bible, the color purple is seen as a symbol of royalty. For example, in John 19:2, the soldiers put a purple robe on Jesus to mock His supposed royalty, not realizing that Jesus was in fact, royalty. Also Proverbs 31:22 (KJV) reads, "She maketh herself coverings of tapestry; her clothing is silk and purple." Purple symbolizes royalty in the Proverbs Woman who is in the royal family of Christ. As I have read, purple is also associated with wisdom, dignity, creativity, spirituality, and peace.

The enemy is in the earth to make us feel perplexed, powerless, and poor in spirit. These feelings lead to disappointments, distractions, doubts, and discouragements. I have learned to pray and not allow negative devices to consume me. The purpose is in the PURPLE. We must:

P–Pray and know that our price is far above rubies.

U–Understand and fear the LORD.

R–Rise to the occasion, reach out to others, and rejoice.

P–Perceive goodness.

L–Love others and be kind.

E–Exercise wisdom.

We are fearfully and wonderfully made (Psalm 139:14b). Are we precious in God's eyes? Yes, we are! When the second guessing, mockery, or doubts come, remember that you are a Child of the Most High God. There is purpose in the purple. Use it well!

Dear Lord, it is my prayer _____

Irene Aultman

Mitchellville, Maryland

AHA Moment

Waiting pays off.

WAITING

"But they that wait upon the LORD shall renew their strength; they shall mount
up with wings as eagles; they shall run, and not be weary; and they shall walk
and not faint."
Isaiah 40:31 (KJV)

Waiting on the Lord requires patience. On December 18, 2013, I took my
husband for his dialysis treatment. I returned home and waited for his phone call
to let me know that I could pick him up. When the phone rang, a nurse from
the kidney clinic told me that my husband had gotten sick. I cannot remember
exactly all that she said, but I knew that I needed to get there right away. The
nurse, in as calm a manner as possible, told me that he was being transported to
the hospital, but for me not to drive myself there.

My daughter had been contacted at her job about the situation, and she was
on the way to get me. I was extremely upset, but I took heed to the suggestion of
not driving myself. We got to the hospital and found out that my husband had
suffered a heart attack. He was later diagnosed with double pneumonia. He had
been medically sedated so that his heart and lungs could rest, and he was not
able to communicate with us.

There are times in our lives, when even though we want to move hastily, the
best thing for us to do is just wait. My husband recovered, with therapy and all,
and I am so glad that I waited for my ride to the hospital that day and did not
jeopardize having an accident.

Dear Lord, it is my prayer _____
Shirley Duncan Dillon
McComb, Mississippi

AHA MOMENT

Trusting in God and His purpose for you will bring you inner peace.

LONGING FOR MORE

"And Jesus said unto them, I am the bread of life: he that cometh to me shall
never hunger; and he that believeth on me shall never thirst."
John 6:35 (KJV)

Have you ever had doubt, insecurity, or just felt you were missing out on
something in life? We all do, or at some point, we will. I can recall feeling inade-
quate. I felt as if I wasn't doing enough in my life. I would look around and see the
great accomplishments of others and how God had blessed their lives. I wanted
those same things to happen in mine. I was longing and thirsting for something
more in my life.

After a while, I started paying attention to that tiny voice, called the Holy
Spirit that convicts you ever so often and He relayed to me that I was acting out
of character as a Christian. I was focused on what others had, instead of asking
for the desires of my heart. God was telling me that He longed to give me those
things. He is Jehovah Jireh; our provider. Instead of focusing on what I didn't
have, I needed to focus on how big God is and what He is capable of doing.

I've had the desire to be in health care administration; which involves public
speaking. Sure, I love talking; but there are key concepts that you should develop
in order to speak effectively. I prayed and God used one of my mentors as a
messenger.

My mentor began sending emails encouraging me to join Toastmasters, Inc.
Initially, I was hesitant, but then realized that God was using those emails to
prepare me. It's amazing how God works! We just have to pray, reflect, trust,
and obey Him.

Whenever you get that feeling of insecurity, doubt, and deficiency; feeling
like you desire more; ask God to help you discern if your desires are in His will.

Dear Lord, it is my prayer _____
Roxanna "Roxy" Bayne
Jackson, Mississippi

AHA MOMENT

Through the tears, the pain, and the unexplained, resolve to trust God!

IT IS NECESSARY

"For my thoughts are not your thoughts, neither are
your ways my ways, saith the LORD."
Isaiah 55:8 (KJV)

If your heart is breaking beyond a pain that you cannot describe and unexpected circumstances have forever altered the course of your life, I understand.

In one moment, my life changed dramatically. On January 25, 2015, my husband and I walked into a prominent hospital anticipating a successful transplant surgery. Two months later, after a series of unexpected complications, peaks and valleys, I walked out a widow. I am now beginning a new life. Not one that I asked for, but one that God, the Great Orchestrator of my life, has chosen for me.

However, He can turn tragedy into triumph and use our heartbreaking circumstances as wonderful ministry opportunities. Because of our time in the hospital and my husband's subsequent death, the Gospel was shared with the medical staff. There were also opportunities to encourage and pray for other patients and their families. After performing one of those midnight surgeries on my husband, the surgeon sat down and talked with me. As I shared my faith, I watched him break down in tears realizing that he needed a renewed walk with God.

After His resurrection, Jesus met with His distraught disciples in the upper room. They desired a Deliverer from Roman oppression, but God desired a Deliverer from Satan's oppression. Jesus explained to them that "it was necessary" for Him to die to fulfill God's greater purpose; one that exceeded their immediate expectations (Luke 24:13-47 NKJV).

This may be your "necessary" moment. Your vision may be blurred right now, but God has a purpose for all that has happened, even this. He may use circumstances to redirect your steps. He may use your pain so that something greater is born in you for His glory. My story is not over and neither is yours. Trust God to resolve any pain.

Dear Lord, it is my prayer _____
Sheila Bingham Jones
Los Angeles, California

AHA Moment

I am a friend of God.

MY BEST FRIEND FOREVER

"And the scripture was fulfilled which saith, Abraham believed God, and it was imputed unto him for righteousness: and he was called the Friend of God."
James 2:23 (KJV)

We live in a world where there is so much technology surrounding us. We have TVs, cell phones, iPods, tablets, laptops, and let's not forget to mention the various types of social media. These are all considered to be some type of companion that we have learned to accept as a virtual friend.

I can remember my kindergarten days and having best friends named Shirley and Joyce. We were the fearless trio fearing nothing and no one; so we thought. And then, moving to another school, we made new friends named Stacy and Dianne. And again, changing schools and graduating into junior high school, we made even more friends and being a part of the so-called elite group. In high school we were introduced to the boyfriend syndrome while initiating the "Best Friends Forever" or BFF code amongst our little group.

The rainy and dreary days seemed so long and cold when my BFFs were not around. It was not so easy trying to substitute a partner for playing sports when my BFFs were absent from school.

At our church, all of the young girls were part of a group called the Sunbeams. It was during one of our Saturday Sunbeam meetings that my friends and I were introduced to the Lord Jesus Christ. At a summertime vacation bible school, we were led to accept Christ as Savior and we were baptized. On a Friday night during a small church revival, I met my true 'Best Friend Forever.' He is my Lord and Savior Jesus Christ, and He will never leave me nor forsake me. (Romans 10:9-10 KJV)

Once you have accepted Jesus as your Lord, you will always have a friend.

Dear Lord, it is my prayer _____
Frances Christine Robinson
Merced, California

AHA Moment

God's grace, mercy, and unconditional love saves us from the shadow of death.

SHADOW OF DEATH

"Yea, though I walk through the valley of the shadow of death, I will fear no evil: for thou art with me; thy rod and thy staff they comfort me."
Psalm 23:4 (KJV)

In 2009, my 5-year-old nephew and I went for a walk through the neighborhood. We heard dogs barking. As we begin to pass a gate, two pit bulls came running out toward us.

One jumped on my nephew knocking him to the ground. The other dog charged toward me. When I heard my nephew screaming, I fought off the dog that was attacking me; and turned to reach for the other dog that was chewing on my nephew's face.

I pulled the ninety-pound pit bull away as she was gnawing for my nephew's throat. The female pit bull caught hold of my foot, I begin kicking her away and the male pit bull knocked my nephew and me to the ground. As I was pulling myself and my nephew up and kicking at the dog, I shouted for help. I saw a man in a car, calling out to us. My nephew was able to get in the man's car safely.

Still fighting with the dog, I was given strength to put him in a head-lock. We fell to the ground. A woman passed me a stick. I released the dog and stood to my feet and struck the dog with the stick. Then I begin falling toward the ground and the man and a lady blocked my fall. The man who took my nephew into his car stated again and again that he watched for over thirty minutes, and he could not believe what he saw.

When faced with danger, God will give you the strength to be victorious. Among scripture to reflect on, consider Psalm 34:4, 2 Timothy 1:7, Psalm 34:7, Isaiah 54:17 and Romans 8:28.

Dear Lord, it is my prayer _____
Mary Harris
Los Angeles, California

AHA Moment

I must do HIS work today.

WHAT MUST I DO TODAY?

"I must work the works of him that sent me, while it is day: the night cometh,
when no man can work."
John 9:4 (KJV)

Being a busy professional and a single woman, I often make plans with friends and loved ones. Balancing my job, social invitations, church, and other options, I often find myself reluctant to make a commitment. Instead, I reply with hesitation. "I would like to. . ." or "I might. . ." and "maybe."

And then a series of four family deaths in less than one year reminded me, night is coming and opportunities fade away. What *must* I do? How do I set priorities in my life when so much of the world calls on me?

Jesus answered this question with power. He said, "I must work the works of him that sent me while it is day."

"Must" meant His priorities were clear. There were guiding principles in His life that directed His choices. He took action. Jesus calls our attention to His service today. Now is the accepted time.

Jesus had what every supervisor in the business world craves; a sense of urgency. John 9:4 reveals for me two excellent questions. What are the musts in my life? If Jesus had a sense of urgency, as His follower, shouldn't I also have one? The Christian life calls us to believe; also to do the work while it is day.

With the help of my prayer circle, my priorities are clearer now. Our occupation does not matter: a plumber, a professor, a cleaning lady, or a cleric. We all share the work of spreading the gospel.

Each of us has a practical mission that is divinely sent. It is an urgent mission that matches our talents, skills and experiences. We pray to allow nothing to stop us, distract us, deceive us, or make us hesitate to do the work.

We do it because WE MUST.

Dear Lord, it is my prayer _____
Valora Washington
Chevy Chase, Maryland

AHA Moment

God keeps His promises even in difficult times.

REMEMBER WHAT GOD TOLD YOU

"So do not throw away your confidence; it will be richly rewarded.
You need to persevere so that when you have done the will of God,
you will receive what he has promised."
Hebrews 10:35-36 (NIV)

Our God is the God of promise. He prepares us for His promises and keeps His word to fulfill them. We can hold onto His promises in spite of what the circumstances look like around us.

I'm reminded of the time in 2002, when I was living outside of my home state and God told me it was time to move back home. I had no desire to do so, but I reluctantly made my way back to Mississippi. After working on my new job for a few months, I had strange medical symptoms that led me to the doctor. A cancer diagnosis soon followed.

I remember the great peace I had that day in 2003, sitting in the doctor's office hearing his diagnosis. My mom and I were to go shopping after that appointment, not realizing I was about to be diagnosed with cancer. The doctor was very grave, and I could see my mom was heartbroken. Yet I remained cheerful. My mom said to me, "What do we do now?" I told her, "We're going shopping."

I could keep my cheerfulness at that time, because I remember what God told me before I moved back to Mississippi. He told me I would have a familiar illness, but it wouldn't kill me. There are many other things he told me and they came to pass. Although I am still waiting for some of the other promises, I can keep my confidence when I remember what God told me.

I have learned to keep my confidence in God and His Word.

Regardless of what circumstances look like, remember what God has told you, "He will never leave you nor forsake you" (Hebrews 13:5c, KJV).

Dear Lord, it is my prayer _____

Sondra Arthur
Terry, Mississippi

AHA Moment

Recognize the season you are in and use it to grow spiritually!

SEASONS CHANGE

"To everything there is a season, a time for every purpose under heaven:"
Ecclesiastes 3:1 (NKJV)

Every moment in life is not going to be all tulips, hugs and kisses 24/7. When I first heard this as a new Christian, I thought to myself, "How could this be, when we serve such an awesome God?" I was, to say the least, confused and discouraged. Then, the Lord led me to read Ecclesiastes 3:1-8.

There was a season in my life when I was jobless, heartbroken and honestly hopeless. I had just graduated from college and was finishing up my graduate studies. Life seemed full of great "worldly" accomplishments (including my education, for which I am truly grateful. HALLELUJAH!). However, I still felt under accomplished. "How could this be, Lord? I am being obedient, reading Your Word and even involved in ministry in my church." It wasn't until I read those first 8 verses in Ecclesiastes chapter 3, that my blinded eyes were open to the Holy Spirit.

Our sovereign God through our Lord and Savior Jesus Christ is so intentional! He knows exactly what He is doing in our lives, and He places us exactly where He wants us. I later realized that I was in a season of "rest" because the Lord was setting me up for my next appointed position. Sometimes, we place ourselves in situations as well, because of our disobedience.

Speak to our Lord, read Ecclesiastes for yourself, and let the Holy Spirit give you the discernment to understand what season you are experiencing. Recognize where He has you. Is it in a place of healing? Are you in a season of shedding people and sinful habits? Use the lessons from that season, and watch yourself grow in the Holy Spirit.

Holy Father, I ask you on this day to reveal to me what season you have me in. I want to learn from it and grow spiritually. In Jesus' Name, Amen!

Dear Lord, it is my prayer _____
Janay Brinkley
Bowie, Maryland

AHA Moment

All things are working for your good.

MINOR SETBACK + SETUP = MAJOR COMEBACK

"And we know that all things work together for good to them that love God, to
them who are the called according to his purpose."
Romans 8:28 (KJV)

The year 2015, began an uphill battle for me. I had just lost my job and I was
unsure about any future income. I had two children in private school, a mortgage,
a new vehicle, and all the other obligations that come with life. Although a sense
of doubt touched the pit of stomach, I didn't allow it to consume the plans that I
knew God had for me. The Holy Spirit reminded me that my minor setback was
a set-up for a major comeback.

I did not lose faith and I never stopped believing. I didn't miss the opportunity to submit my tithes, I kept in contact with my pastor, began to grow a deeper
relationship with my Bible and with God through our weekly Bible classes. I got
up and started making opportunities for myself. Once I started relying on the
grace of God instead of focusing on what man had done to me, doors began to
open at every turn. I realized all things were working together for my good. I got
my first large-sum contract, was appointed to an elected county position and I
even got married and had a baby.

When things seem dim or disappointing, I challenge you to cry, scream, lay
on the couch and do nothing—do whatever it is you have to do to let your frustration out. Then get up! Know that God has a higher purpose for you. When
one door closes, another door opens with God's grace and mercy along with daily
opportunities to live the purpose that He has determined for you.

Dear Lord, it is my prayer _____
Zakiya Summers
Jackson, Mississippi

AHA Moment

God does not need our help!

WAIT

"But without faith it is impossible to please him: for he
that cometh to God must believe that he is, and that he is a
rewarder of them that diligently seek him."
Hebrews 11:6 (KJV)

I learned the principle of tithing early in my Christian walk, and I purposed in my heart to always give my tithes before paying my bills. If I stepped out on faith, I believed that God would provide. My faith was tested.

One particular month, my mortgage and tithes were due at the same time, and there was not enough money to pay both. If I paid the mortgage, I could not pay my tithes. I said, "Lord, I'm going to pay my tithes, and YOU take care of the mortgage." I know that God is sovereign and that He can do the impossible if I wait on Him! The mortgage due date was drawing near and nothing had happened. Thinking I could help God out by using money that had been earmarked for something else to pay the mortgage, the Holy Spirit said, "I thought you asked GOD to take care of it?" I replied, "Yes I did!" Immediately, I asked God to forgive me!

Here's how God worked it all out. Since I had not yet received the monthly mortgage statement, I decided to call the mortgage company. I was informed that my mortgage was being transferred to a new servicing company, not to make any payments until the new statement arrived, and that no late fees would be applied. "Thank you, Lord!" He is a rewarder of them that diligently seek Him!

As women, we can maneuver and make things happen. However, we must learn to wait patiently on the Lord to answer our prayers. Wait on God with confidence that He will work all things together for the good.

God really doesn't need our help. "Wait patiently on the Lord," and while you wait, thank Him in advance for the victory.

Dear Lord, it is my prayer _____
Viola Purry
Detroit, Michigan

AHA MOMENT

Maintain faith in the midst of your storm.

WEATHERING MY STORMS

"And He arose, and rebuked the wind, and said unto the sea, Peace, be still.
And the wind ceased, and there was a great calm."
Mark 4:39 (KJV)

In the South, thunderstorms are common. I travel to work each day on Interstate 55 North. It's during those times that I have seen many changes in weather. The meteorologist made it clear that the weather would be getting worse as the day progressed. Listening intently to the forecast, I left work early to get ahead of the changing weather and traffic.

I ran into the worst storm I had *ever* seen. In times past, I prayed and watched God move in a miraculous way. However, this time nothing happened. Fear overcame me. I continued into the dark clouds with the wind and rain beating heavily upon my vehicle. I could barely see or hold my vehicle on the road. Frantically asking God *why not* as in times past, a still small voice said, "Sometimes we must go through storms in order to gain deeper faith and trust in God."

Upon hearing this, my fear subsided. I dropped my speed and kept moving through the storm. Many vehicles had pulled over. I kept driving; knowing that I would either arrive home soon or run out of the storm.

In Mark 4:35-41, the disciples were in the midst of their storm with Jesus aboard the ship. While He was soundly asleep, the disciples challenged Him to wake up asking, "...Master, carest thou not that we perish?" Jesus arises from sleep and simply responds, "...Peace, be still." The storm obeyed His voice and there was immediate calm. Jesus could have done the same for me. However, just as he did with the disciples, He allowed the winds to come so that I could see the salvation of the Lord.

He allows storms to come in our lives so that He may calm them; all in an effort to strengthen our faith.

Dear Lord, it is my prayer _____
Lillie Earlene Smith
Hazlehurst, Mississippi

Fasting makes me draw closer to God.

WHAT SHALL I GIVE THEE?

"I can do all things through Christ which strengtheneth me."
Philippians 4:13 (KJV)

Fasting had always been a struggle for me because I love to eat; but I realized that fasting is necessary in order to draw closer to Jesus. I must be alone with God to hear His voice. Fasting is a form of worship, and it requires sacrifice.

I often have intentions of fasting. My day may have begun well; however, I did not successfully complete the fast. Any excuse would do! I would pray, "Lord, please help me to fast, pray, and not allow excuses defeat me. Please direct my path!"

During a Sunday morning worship service, my pastor extended a challenge to the congregation to join him in fasting, ". . . to seek of Him a right way for us, and for our little ones, and for all our substance" Ezra 8:21(KJV). We were to have no food from dawn to dusk for six days. He also invited us to join him on a 6:00 am prayer conference call.

Now, I had the desire to fast, and here's my opportunity! When desire and opportunity become married to one another, God's will is done. Determined to fast, I signed the pledge form.

It was not easy; I allowed myself to surrender to Him. The first day, prayer was constantly flowing from my heart, but the second day, I failed. At that point, I asked the Lord not to give up on me and strengthen me to complete the fast — and *HE did!*

Fasting causes us to humble ourselves before God. It gives us the strength to resist temptation. When fasting becomes a part of our personal worship, we become more focused on Him and are more aware of His presence.

What will you sacrifice to worship HIM?

Dear Lord, it is my prayer _____
Denice Johnson
Chicago, Illinois

AHA MOMENT

Everything looks better with a different point of view.

WHAT'S YOUR POINT OF VIEW?

"Looking unto Jesus the author and finisher of our faith."
Hebrews 12:2a (KJV)

One day I was talking with a close friend, and as she was braiding my hair, we discussed my wedding. She commented how beautiful everything was decorated and how delicious was the food; but I had a different point of view. I was beginning to complain about how the music system did not work and the stove had only working eye. Her joyful expression started to turn sour. Without realizing, I had changed her point of view.

As a newlywed, my husband and I go through many situations. It seems like there's always a new issue that arises. From differing opinions of acceptable times to come home, to negotiating holiday schedules, there is so much to learn and work out. Sometimes it seems like too much to handle! But then, I hear about the experiences of other married couples, including newlyweds. One such couple experienced infidelity resulting in a child within 6 months of saying "I do". Another couple of 15 years is going through a horrible separation. When I hear about these stories, I suddenly realize whose turn is it to replace the trash bags doesn't seem like such a big deal. Their stories changed my point of view.

As a believer, it is important where we focus our point of view. The Bible tells us exactly where to look. Hebrews 12:2 tell us, "Looking unto Jesus the author and finisher of our faith; who for the joy that was set before him endured the cross, despising the shame, and is set down at the right hand of the throne of God." Jesus is where our hope and trust should lie, in good and bad situations. He endured so much to give us that hope. So when you find yourself feeling down, check your point of view.

Dear Lord, it is my prayer _____
Jandrea Brown Sims
Monroe, Louisiana

AHA Moment

There is no confusion. Sin's the problem—Christ's transfusion.

TRANSFUSION

"But now in Christ Jesus ye who sometimes were far off
are made nigh by the blood of Christ."
Ephesians 2:13 (KJV)

"We have a 9-1-1 emergency. Individual is down. We are going to need some blood.... No, we can't move the patient. Is it any way you can get the blood here – to us! This is an emergency! I need you to act fast."

Simply identified by his first name, Thomas, I recalled an article I read about him having a rare blood type, RH–null. It was noted that his blood type was so rare that it had been dubbed as being the most precious blood on earth, "Golden Blood" because it can be given to anyone with negative RH blood type. This Thomas could save countless lives. However, if he ever needed blood himself, he can only receive RH-null blood. It almost seems a pity, wouldn't you agree? Who is going to "save" poor Thomas? Well, the very One who is going to save poor you and poor me. . .Jesus the Christ.

How thankful we are that Christ readily came to us! Our sinfulness created a chasm between a Holy God and us. Christ's blood, shed upon the cross of Calvary, addresses our need for forgiveness, and it serves as our transfusion—the act of pouring or transferring blood from one vessel to another.

"There is a fountain filled with blood drawn from Emmanuel's veins; and sinners plunged beneath that flood lose all their guilty stains...lose ALL their guilty stain...." The words of this glorious hymn published in 1772, by William Cowper transcends centuries with its truth.

Dear Lord, it is my prayer _____
Gwendolyn Hudson
Dolton, Illinois

Stuck in traffic, I realized that I need to rely more on God's guidance.

WHICH WAY?

"I will instruct you and teach you in the way you should go. . ."
Psalm 32:8 (NIV)

Traffic congestion is an all too familiar occurrence in Houston. There are times when I try to find a better route to avoid the traffic jam. I wonder which direction is the best or quickest way to get to my destination.

A few days ago, I was leaving work at 5:00 p.m. so that I could get to the gym for my 6:30 p.m. exercise class. I walked briskly to my car and drove out of the parking garage towards the street. As I approached the street, I noticed the traffic congestion near my office building. I came to a complete stop and wondered "which way" I should go to avoid being stuck in traffic. I decided to turn right because the traffic was moving at a steady speed; seemingly, I had made the right choice. Two blocks later, I was amidst cars and buses going nowhere. How did I get into this traffic jam?

Often times, we move in the wrong direction and need guidance to point us in the right way. When driving in our vehicles, we rely on a Global Positioning System (GPS) or the street signs to direct us. When we are traveling the road of life, God is our roadmap to guide and teach us. God led the children of Israel during their wilderness experience. God was before them in a pillar of cloud by day and in a pillar of fire by night to guide them along the way (Exodus 13:21). God is a constant guide on whom we can depend.

Do you trust God to lead you where you should go? Do you get upset when your plans are delayed and you are running into one obstacle after another? You can trust God as your guide for He knows "which way" is the best way.

Dear Lord, it is my prayer _____
June Bond
Houston, Texas

AHA Moment

I am who God says I am!

WHO AM I?

"How precious are your thoughts about me, O God."
Psalm 139:17 (NLT)

Sometimes in life, we are given names—labels that seem to follow us for a lifetime. As we travel the road of life, these "labels" speak to us at every turn. They say:
- You are too big.
- You are not smart enough.
- You are not pretty enough.
- You are not good enough for that.
- You are too stubborn.
- You know you can't do that.
- You will never be anything . . . and the list goes on.

Without even realizing it, we start to agree with the opinions of others. We tell ourselves:
- No one will love me like I am because_____ .
- I can't get that job because _____ .
- I will never be able to do that because _____ .

We have been programmed to think that we are not worthy of the love or the blessings of God. However, this is contrary to what God says about His children.

He knows us inside and out. God says in Psalm 139:1-2 (NLT), "O LORD, you have examined my heart and know everything about me. You know when I sit down or stand up. You know my thoughts even when I'm far away." He knows me in a very special way and understands my character. He knew me before I was formed in my mother's womb. He knows my thoughts before I think them, yet His thoughts about me are good!

I am God's chosen, and He loved me so much that He purchased me with the Blood of Jesus Christ, His Son.

Who am I? God's special creation and I am everything that God says that I am!

Dear Lord, it is my prayer _____
Carolyn Moore
College Park, Georgia

AHA Moment
Worship is a heart overflowing with praise to God.

WORSHIP AND PRAISE OR MURMURING AND COMPLAINING – THE CHOICE IS YOURS

"About midnight Paul and Silas were praying and singing hymns to God, and
the other prisoners were listening to them."
Acts 16:25 (NIV)

Paul and Silas in Acts 16:16-25 had a big choice to make. They were falsely accused, unjustly arrested, severely beaten and then thrown into prison. The jailer was ordered to make sure they did not escape, so he took no chances and placed them in the inner prison. Besides the trauma of the severe beating, they were fastened in stocks immobilizing their arms and legs resulting in severe cramps and loss of circulation. The atmosphere there was depressing. According to the standards of that day, a prison was like a dungeon—a dark, damp, stench-ridden place, with no facility for waste or comfort of any kind.

Would they murmur and complain about their bad situation, or would they choose to worship their God who could do something about it? If they had chosen to murmur and complain, their testimony would have been ineffective to the other prisoners and to their faith in God. However, they knew and remembered that when you seek God in your dreadful situation, He will change it or see you through it. Because their godly response was to worship and praise and not complain, they were freed from the prison, ministered to by the jailer, and he and his entire household were saved. This choice allowed God to be glorified in their lives even in their dire circumstances.

So, the next time you find yourself in a bad situation that you, the devil, or others may have caused, instead of complaining, ask yourself, "How can I glorify God even in this?" Proverbs 24:10 (KJV) says, "If thou faint in the day of adversity, thy strength is small." In those times when you feel overwhelmed, worship Him instead of worrying.

Dear Lord, it is my prayer _____
Darlene Hancock
Detroit, Michigan

AHA Moment
You do not have to struggle alone.

YOU ARE NOT ALONE

"Call to me and I will answer you and tell you great
and unsearchable things you do not know."
Jeremiah 33:3 (NIV)

Christ never said it would be easy, but on the other hand, He said it is possible. From 2009 until 2010, I went through one of the greatest struggles in my life. I lost my job, was losing my properties, and wondered what I was going to do with my family. I needed a huge financial blessing immediately. It seemed that everywhere I turned, the door slammed shut. I remember going to a prayer breakfast early one Saturday morning. The facilitators said to all of whom were there on time, "God wants you to ask Him for what you want, and He will provide."

My first thought was to ask for a financial breakthrough. Then, I remembered Solomon's prayer to God in the Bible. I immediately asked God to help me to pray for others, so I prayed the following:

Dear Heavenly Father,
I pray right now for my dear sister. You know the pain she's endured,
and she needs you now. Father, I know you love her unconditionally.
Please hear my prayer and bless her with what she's in need of today.
In Jesus' name, Amen.

Afterwards, I saw Him answer. This has been surreal! God had done just as I asked. He has truly told and shown me great and unsearchable things that I did not know. My family has also remained stable throughout this transition and the blessings continue to flow.

Perhaps, you are going through a challenge in life today, and are wondering, "Who can I call on for help?" Look no further. Jesus is waiting on your call.

Dear Lord, it is my prayer _____
Renay Allen
Decatur, Georgia

AHA Moment

He knows what is best.

UNSHAKEABLE FAITH

"But without faith it is impossible to please Him: for he that
cometh to God must believe that He is, and that
He is a rewarder of them that diligently seek Him."
Hebrews 11:6 (KJV)

Picture yourself in a hospital bed and the doctor walks into your room. He says to you, "you have cancer." I can witness that it is not an easy thing to hear. You must have the mindset that God always knows what is best. You must have an assurance that God will see you through. The Word of God states that, "And we know that in all things God works for the good of those who love him, who have been called according to his purpose" Romans 8:28 (NIV).

God is our Father, and we must have faith to believe that He loves us, and that He is well able to provide for all of our needs. So, the next time you find yourself waiting for deliverance in a particular situation, try reminding yourself that you must put your faith in the Deliverer not the deliverance. You must put your faith in the Healer, not the healing. Faith is a fruit of the Spirit that God wants to develop in our lives. Essentially, faithfulness to God is loyalty to Him.

I give thanks to my Heavenly Father for planting an unshakeable faith in my spirit. Through Him, I can react properly to any situation.

Dear Lord, it is my prayer _____
Ernestine Jones
Clinton, Maryland

AHA MOMENT

Wait on the Lord for a Godly spouse!

A SEASON TO BE HIDDEN

"Keep your heart with all diligence, For out of it spring the issues of life."
Proverbs 4:23 (NKJV)

Sometimes the Lord intentionally hides us for a season. He places us in a season of singleness to bring us closer to Him. If this is your current season, nothing is wrong with you! Understand that the Lord is preparing you for His purpose.

Ladies, we must stop trying to be seen, especially by all the wrong men! Until the Lord is done working on our heart, we will not be found by our God-ordained spouse. Sometimes, as women, we become pressured by society's standards and rush into a relationship with the wrong man. During our hidden season, Satan will attempt to distract us by sending a counterfeit man who appears to be a God-ordained husband. However, through God's discernment, the man's wicked heart and false intentions are exposed.

To resist the temptation of Satan, it is vital to remain in the Word of God and be led by the Holy Spirit. Do not rush the process! Marriage is not two halves coming together as one. It is two whole individuals joining as one! Only a genuine relationship with Jesus Christ can make one completely whole in the Lord. Let the Lord guard your heart and teach you how to be a God-ordained wife. Obey the Word of God, surrender to His will, and He will send your God-ordained spouse in His own timing. In the meantime, be encouraged, guard your heart with the Lord's leading, and wait on Him for a Godly spouse.

Dear Lord, it is my prayer _____
Nikkia Fletcher
Germantown, Maryland

VICTORY IN JESUS–TRUSTING JESUS BRINGS VICTORY

"These things I have spoken unto you, that in me ye might have peace. In the world ye shall have tribulation: but be of good cheer; I have overcome the world."
John 16:33 (KJV)

". . . greater is he that is in you, than he that is in the world."
I John 4:4b (KJV)

Who do you put your trust in when you have tribulations, disappointments, or illnesses? Jesus Christ is the answer. Trusting God is vitally important in conquering all types of exams or tests that we encounter.

While attending graduate school, I became very ill and had to miss classes for several weeks. Using the power of prayer to address my situation, God restored my health and, subsequently, the doctor released me. Make no mistake; God healed my body! Critical exams were coming up and study time was very limited due to the time I had missed as a result of my severe illness.

Knowing that prayer can work things out for good; I continued to lift my prayers to my Heavenly Father. My faith would be tested. God wanted me to trust Him for this specific purpose. He guided my studying time and provided the focus I needed to refresh and learn a lot of facts and problem-solving techniques with resolutions in a short time span.

All glory goes to God and I thank Him for His grace and mercy. I not only passed the exams, but exceeded those who spent the entire time in class. Yet, there were with no penalties against me for class time missed. God came to my rescue and prepared my mind to have the right focus. Jesus became my source in time of need.

As His Word teaches, we must: "Trust in the LORD with all thine heart; and lean not unto thine own understanding. In all thy ways acknowledge Him, and He shall direct thy paths" Proverbs 3:5-6 (KJV).

Dear Lord, it is my prayer _____
Irene Aultman
Mitchellville, Maryland

AHA Moment

Jesus is our defender!

IT JUST WON'T WORK

"No weapon formed against you will prosper. . ."
Isaiah 54:17 (KJV)

Jesus prayed for His disciples. Knowing they would face fierce opposition, He asked the Father to keep them while they were in the world. We can rest in His promise that although the weapons may form, they will not accomplish the evil intended.

My friend lost another son suddenly to a massive heart attack. Her grief was overwhelming. When I spoke to her on the phone, the mother's heart in her touched me. I remembered how she prayed for my daughters who were in a serious car accident just a year before. I had to go to support my friend. I knew it would be a financial sacrifice and use of precious leave. What I didn't know, was that an attack on my character and threats of AWOL would follow.

As I traveled to Mississippi, I received word of my supervisor's anger and plans for me. "The children are suffering. I am putting her on AWOL." I returned to my workplace and was given the leave slip I had submitted with the following note, ". . . leave requests are to be submitted three days prior to the days requested." My supervisor didn't have a conversation with me. Death doesn't always give three days prior notice.

I continued to fulfill my responsibilities, but was tempted to confront my supervisor. One evening after school, I spoke with a friend. She advised, "Wait. Don't do or say anything. Wait." Although I knew the word of God, I was in need of a reminder. "No weapon formed against thee shall proper; And every tongue that shall rise against thee in judgment thou shalt condemn." I waited a week. I wasn't placed on AWOL and found out that it is illegal to do so! My students had the most growth in their test scores; they weren't suffering academically. The weapons did not prosper!

Do not fear what man will do to you.

Dear Lord, it is my prayer _____
Geraldine Boddie Meredith
Washington, District of Columbia

AHA Moment

Blessed are they who believe in God!

WHOSE REPORT DO YOU BELIEVE?

"Let us therefore come boldly unto the throne of grace, that we may obtain mercy, and find grace to help in time of need."
(Hebrews 4:16 KJV)

One day during a conversation, a young mother told me her 14-year-old daughter had discovered a lump under her arm. Later, she shared that her daughter told her the lump had gotten larger and moved to her breast. Immediately, the mother thought cancer. With tears, the daughter looked in her mother's eyes and said, "It's on television and at school, a lump means cancer. I'm going to lose my hair, weight and eventually die!" The tears continue to stream down her face. Anxiety and fear had already set in.

The mother scheduled an appointment for her daughter with a cancer doctor the following week. I asked her, "Do you believe in God?" The mother said, "Yes I do." I asked, "Do you believe God can turn this around?" She said, "I hope so." Then, I quoted to her, "Now faith is the substance of things hoped for, the evidence of things not seen" (Hebrews 11:1 KJV). I asked her, "Do you remember the woman who had the blood disorder in the Bible?" She said "Yes." Well, what happened to that woman? She had to believe if she could just touch Jesus' garment, she would be whole. You also have to believe!

I told the mother I would take the cancer concern to the prayer warriors and we will pray to God. According to James 5:16b, "The effectual fervent prayer of a righteous man availeth much." The report from the mother indicated that they went to the doctor with certain expectations in their hearts. The report from the doctor revealed that the lump was not cancer. It was nothing but tissues.

Have you ever jumped to the wrong conclusion or doubted God? As prayer warriors, we must petition the throne of grace knowing God is ABLE!

Dear Lord, it is my prayer _____
Magdalene McNeil
Jackson, Mississippi

AHA Moment

God is always with is and is our help.

MY HELP

"My help cometh from the Lord, which made heaven and earth. He will not
suffer thy foot to be moved: he that keepeth thee will not slumber."
Psalm 121:2-3 (KJV)

As a 65-year-old woman who lives alone, I always felt that I could do things
alone; without help. It was an early evening in December when that notion was
tested. My sister was coming to spend Christmas with me after years of being
unable to travel due to illness. Preparing for her visit, I purchased a flat screen
television to replace the older model CTR tube that was mounted about seven
feet high. We called the older model "Big Boy".

I was anxious to set up the new television. With my stepstool between the
bed and the heavy TV, I stood on the step, lifted 'Big Boy', planted one foot on
the bed and attempted to move the other foot. I lost my balance and fell back-
wards. Praise God, He gave me the presence of mind to push away the old TV
as I began to fall.

It sounded like the thump of a coconut inside my head when it hit hard on
the dresser behind me. Disoriented and in pain, I said, "Thank you Lord! Please
don't let me go out like this."

I lay there for a moment then called my daughter who in turn called her
siblings. They came and scolded me for not realizing all the help I have access to.
Eventually, my son set up the new television set.

By God's providence, I have children and grandchildren; a gift and a reward,
according to Psalm 127:3. In God's perfect love, He continues to provide for
us; He never leaves us alone. If we trust the Lord and believe in Him, He will
be our help.

Dear Lord, it is my prayer _____
Lestine Drake
Los Angeles, California

AHA MOMENT

The Lord gives blessings and benefits to His children!

WHY LIVE FOR THE LORD?

"Bless the LORD, O my soul, and forget not all His benefits:"
Psalm 103:2 (KJV)

As a young girl, I remember struggling to walk from our house to the little church on the hill about four blocks away. My younger sister and mother walked ahead, and I followed behind, with long strides to keep up. There were no street lights on this dusty, country road which was hardly more than one lane wide. We couldn't see each other as we peered through the darkness. While we heard the rocks crunch under our shoes, we strained to hear the sound of any possible intruder, animal or human. I wondered if mother was afraid as I was and I whispered a prayer that we would be safe. Then she said, "Don't worry. God hears the prayers of His children." I was only 10 years old, but that made me want to give my life to Christ and I did.

Now I am older and years have passed since I made that commitment to Christ. Mother has gone to be with the Lord. The little church we attended is now a beautiful, modern edifice, and the road is a much-traveled, paved highway. Now instead of walking, we drive luxury cars to attend church.

Over the years, God has answered my prayers. He blessed me to walk away unharmed when my car pounced down the embankment, avoiding a head-on collision. By God's grace and mercy, I miraculously survived a blood clot in my lungs, resulting in only 9 days of hospital intensive care. Also, arthritis was debilitating until God delivered me from it by two successful knee replacements. In addition, the doctor's x-ray revealed the results of an internal injury, reportedly, making it impossible for me to conceive. However, the Lord blessed me to bring my son and later my daughter into this world.

Depend on God to receive your blessings and benefits.

Dear Lord, it is my prayer _____
Johnnie Phillips
Jackson, Mississippi

AHA MOMENT

Yield=surrender. If you surrender, then God provides.

LORD, I YIELD

"But thanks be to God, who gives us the victory through our Lord Jesus Christ."
I Corinthians 15:57 (KJV)

Pastor George Dillahunty said, "The only way to be totally and completely empowered to lead a victorious life in Christ Jesus is to yield totally and completely unto the Lord."

Why are we afraid to turn our lives over to the Lord completely? For me, I didn't want to lose control.

While preparing to speak to a group of women, "totally" and "completely" were scary words. Then the Lord reminded me, how He kept me when I was left as a child with strangers, and I never got hurt. He sent my grandparents to raise me when my mother couldn't, and when I said "no" to marijuana because the Holy Spirit said, "No!" Fortunately for me, I listened because it was laced with cocaine.

As an adult, He reminded me that my bills got paid with one income, even though we had purchased our home with two. He protected me when my sports utility vehicle spun out of control, and no cars were around.

What control? I realized during that quiet moment with God, that I had, and still have no control. I am victorious in all these life situations because of Christ. We are uncomfortable when yielding control totally and completely over to anyone, but when I read my Bible, Jesus is not just anyone. He *is* the risen Savior.

It is my prayer that I learn how to yield to your word. Teach me to lose control and claim the victory. Thank you for protection when I did not realize it was you in control. Make it personal. Surrender to God today.

Dear Lord, it is my prayer _____
Adrienne Miller
Markham, Illinois

AHA MOMENT

God will sustain you!

DON'T GIVE UP, KEEP GOING!

"And let us not grow weary of doing good, for in due season
we shall reap, if we do not give up."
Galatians 6:9 (ESV)

Our lives have become hectic and busy, and we sometimes feel overwhelmed and want to give up. It has been years, but I reached a moment when I wanted to give up. I was tired and wondered if it was worth even trying since it seemed that no one cared or appreciated my efforts.

After a long day at work, I walked to my car in the parking structure and found a very small piece of paper on my windshield. On the note was written this scripture: "And let us not be weary in well doing: for in due season we shall reap, if we faint not" Galatians 6:9 (KJV). I looked around to see who may have left the note, but no one was around. My first thought was, "Who put the note on my car?" Then I thought, "Who knew my car and where it was parked?" I prayed and thanked God for sending someone to encourage me to keep moving forward.

Instead of continuing with my "pity party," I was reminded that God supplies all of my needs. I did not need to be patted on the back for doing good, nor did I need to worry about being physically tired. Everything that I was doing was for HIS Glory!

When it seems that your days are long and your body is tired, don't give up! God has promised that He would never leave nor forsake us (Hebrews 13:5). He has done so much for us. It is worth it all—just keep going!

Dear Lord, it is my prayer _____
Arveal Keetch Johnson
San Diego, California

AHA Moment

Believing Him is the greater work.

STEP OVER AND MOVE AWAY

"Jesus said unto him, 'If you canst believe, all things are
possible to him that believeth."
Mark 9:23 (KJV)

Believing in God and His promises takes work, time, and daily practice. It takes reminding yourself by audibly repeating, hearing, and, listening to His word.

During my season of illness in 2010, and while waiting for complete healing in my body, God showed me a vision of a three-foot wire fence that I needed to step over. My healing was on the other side of it. I could see the beautiful green grass, rolling hills, and tall trees, and I desired to go there. God beckoned me to come. I gazed at the fence. I was tired, too sick to step over, but I wanted to live.

My sister had given me a CD with healing scriptures read by Pastor John Hagee. I listened to them continuously for many weeks; however, I was still unable to step over the fence. I trusted God, knowing He is the only one who can save me, and knowing also it was done back at Calvary.

During a women's prayer group, two sisters of strong faith laid their hands on me and prayed for me. Immediately, I could feel "cooling waters" running all over me, washing me, and tears flowing from my eyes. Without moving from my seat, I stepped over the fence into my healing, rejoicing! Moving with ease, there was no pain, and the swelling in my body was gone. I am healed! I slowly moved away but still looked back at the fence. The Sprit spoke to me and said, "Go! Move away from the fence, and stop looking back. Go live your life." I obeyed.

Jesus paid it all at Cavalry. Whatever it is that separates you from God, step over it!

Dear Lord, it is my prayer _____
Betty C. Brown
Monroe, Louisiana

AHA Moment

Mother knew best.

OBEY!

"Children, obey your parents in all things, for this is well pleasing to the Lord."
Colossians 3:20 (NKJV)

Every Wednesday after school, we walked 3 blocks to the home of Mrs. Ross for the Good News Bible Club. We would sing songs, have a Bible story, and then break up into groups by age and gender for further activity. At the end of each meeting, we were given a Bible verse to memorize and recite when we came back the following week. Prizes were given for learning the weekly verses. At the end of each semester, we could win a grand prize by reciting all of the verses at one time. I recited all of the verses and my prize was a silver cross necklace, with a small faux diamond in the middle. I cherished that necklace and still had it when I entered Junior High school a few months later.

"Don't wear your necklace to school today", my mom said. "You have gym and you might lose it." I responded, "But Mom, we have lockers in the locker room, my necklace will be perfectly safe." And so, I wore my necklace. I changed from my street clothes into my gym uniform, carefully hanging my necklace on a hook. I locked my locker and went to class.

Well, you guessed it. When I came back from gym class and opened my locker, the necklace was nowhere to be found. I looked all through my clothes and the locker. I asked my classmates and teacher, but no one admitted to having seen it. Immediately, I recalled that my mother told me not to wear it. I believe that God made it disappear just to teach me an important lesson in obedience.

As adults, we are instructed to obey God. We may be tempted to disobey in a certain area because we do not believe there are consequences. However, be sure that God can make strange things happen just to teach us a lesson.

Dear Lord, it is my prayer _____
Beverly Golden
Cleveland, Ohio

THE FAVOR OF GOD

"Blessed be God, which hath not turned away
my prayer, nor his mercy from me."
Psalm 66:20 (KJV)

I'm blessed going out and coming in. The Favor of God is upon me. I acknowledge the favor that God has over my life. I have no fear of stepping out on faith, because I have no doubt that God will see me through. "I cannot", is not a part of my vocabulary. When I start something, I like to go all the way until it is finished.

I love to travel. Once I decide where I'm going, I begin planning. For example, I knew that I would be attending a convention in July. Therefore, when we notified that reservations could be made a year early, I made them immediately so that I would arrive a day early and leave one day afterwards. In January, I began searching for the best air fares. The fares were low, so I purchased my ticket. To God be the glory!

I don't know if I will be alive in July. Only God knows. Some people may ask, "Are you rich?" My reply would be, "Yes, with the favor of God."

Proverbs 8:33-35 (KJV) reads, "Hear instruction, and be wise, and refuse it not. Blessed is the man that heareth me, watching daily at my gates, waiting at the post of my doors. For whoso findeth me findeth life, and shall obtain favour of the Lord."

Dear Lord, it is my prayer _____
Beverly Tate Latson
Temple Hills, Maryland

Stop worrying and believe that He will always take care of His children.

OUT OF WORK AND FULL OF FEAR

"I have been young, and now am old; yet I have not seen
the righteous forsaken, nor his descendants begging bread."
Psalm 37:25 (NKJV)

After working over 28 years for the same employer, on January 30, 2012, my entire team was given notification that we had 90 days left to work; our jobs would be sent overseas to Mumbai, India. This news was devastating to say the least. Each of my six teammates had over 20 years of service, and we all had plans to retire together. I quickly began to panic and became fearful about the unstable job market, and if I my skills were current enough to get another job. This was a very dark time in life; my faith was shattered. Some days I did not want to get up; I just wanted to sleep all day. My family and friends began to see a different me. I believe I had become somewhat depressed.

After church one Sunday, I felt God was speaking directly to me, reminding me that He would never see me forsaken or begging for bread. He also reminded me of the many instances He had watched over and taken care of me. Because He has promised in His Word not to leave me, I knew this time would not be different.

I stopped worrying and was determined make myself employable. I took some classes, updated my resume, and searched for a job. I was admitted to a Microsoft Training Program with over 75 applicants, yet only 15 were accepted. God gave me this time to regroup, refine my skills, and to render more service to my local church. Since that time, I have worked continuously and with increased earnings.

When you need answers in your situation, turn it over to the LORD! I have learned to trust God because He will never leave nor forsake you; He takes care of His children!

Dear Lord, it is my prayer _____
Bonita A. Brown
Wilmington, Delaware

AHA Moment

Suddenly, I was healed!

JUST PRAY

"Confess your faults one to another, and pray one for another, that ye may be healed. The effectual fervent prayer of a righteous man availeth much."
James 5:16 (KJV)

Several years ago, while visiting my mother, I was not feeling well. It was a Sunday morning, and I decided not to attend church because I was experiencing an onset of the flu. However, my mother went to morning service, and while being there asked the church to pray for me.

I felt horrible all morning, as is the case with the flu. Suddenly, I began to feel as though the sickness was being lifted from me. Naturally, I thought that was strange and had expected to be feeling bad for a few days.

After coming home, I told my mother how I suddenly felt better about an hour before. She said, "We prayed for you at church." Wow! As the saints were praying, it was at that moment that I was being healed. Years later, I realized two things: prayer is powerful and transcendent, and knowing that someone is praying for you is a very special feeling.

James 5:13-16 instructs us to pray for one another. Our prayers, when offered in faith to God, are powerful and effective. They can also help others who are in trouble, sick, in need of comfort, guidance, and more.

Before my mother and countless others prayed, Jesus prayed for me (John 17). Knowing this gives me confidence and encouragement. In fact, Jesus prayed for us. How much more then, should we do so for one another? What a privilege we have been given!

I hope the scriptures today remind and inspire you to pray for someone now—no matter where life finds them. I want to increasingly do the same for others. I pray that the Lord will help me bring the cares and concerns of others to Him, in faith, so that they may be edified, and He is glorified. How can I pray for you?

Dear Lord, it is my prayer _____
Candace Y. McRae
Jonesboro, Georgia

MY PROVIDER

*"Trust in the Lord with all your heart; do not depend on your own understanding.
Seek his will in all you do, and he will show you which path to take."*
Proverbs 3:5-6 (NLT)

I worked on a job for over eighteen years, progressing from Recruiter/ Trainer to District Manager. Subsequently, the company was bought, and my position was diversified. My pay and benefits were not altered, so I was fine with the changes.

In March of 2012, I was informed that my position was being eliminated. I experienced a sense of uneasiness, disappointment, and anger. Although I was offered a fair severance package, I thought to myself, "The nerve of them! After all the hard work and professionalism that I had exemplified daily, my qualities meant nothing. Well, adios amigos." I accepted the severance and left.

Then, uncertainty crept in. It is one thing to talk about faith, but it is entirely different to trust God in times of unemployment, disillusionment, and fear. As I doubted, I asked:

How do I begin this process all over again?

Lord, I haven't sent a resume in about twenty years.

What's going to set me apart from these younger applicants?

I've been faithful and obedient. Why me Lord?

I'm a witness that if you sincerely seek and trust Him, everything will work out for your good. Soon, I was interviewed for another full-time position. My salary was lower, but my benefits were better. I receive monthly bonuses, and God has blessed me by being able to attend church conventions, retreats, etc.

I trust that this experience will encourage you to trust Him, and spend more time reading the scriptures. Romans 10:17 (NKJV) reminds us that, ". . . faith *comes* by hearing, and hearing by the word of God." I am thankful *now* for the "test" that God allowed. He's preparing us for Kingdom work. Let's allow the Holy Spirit free course—even when we can't understand the reason.

Dear Lord, it is my prayer _____

Cynthia Broxton

Corona, New York

AHA Moment

God's got it, stop worrying!

THE PLAN

"In whom also we have obtained an inheritance, being predestinated according
to the purpose of him who worketh all things after the counsel of his own will."
Ephesians 1:11 (KJV)

My son and his wife were expecting their second child in May. We were all
excited because this was a girl! In February, she went for her checkup and was
diagnosed with preeclampsia. This meant that she may not carry the baby full-
term. I immediately started praying that she would complete the pregnancy and
I asked others to do the same.

One day, while at Bible study, as I was reading Ephesians 1:11, the word "predestinated" stood out to me. It was then that I realized this was not about what
I wanted, but what God had predestined for this child. God's plans for us are
totally different from what we plan. Jeremiah 29:11 (NIV) says, "For I know the
plans I have for you, declares the LORD, plans to prosper you and not to harm
you, plans to give you hope and a future."

Let us pray and ask God what His plan is for us, and wait for His answer. We
may not get the answer when we want it, but let us be patient as Sarah, Elizabeth,
and Hannah, who waited for the fulfillment of their dreams. Know that the plan
for each of our lives is not our own, but God's.

Have you asked Him to reveal His plan for you?

Dear Lord, it is my prayer _____
Deborah Judon
Starksville, Mississippi

AHA Moment

Life's circumstances bring tragedies, challenges, and opportunities.

SPARED TO BE A BLESSING

"For thou hast delivered my soul from death, mine eyes from tears,
and my feet from falling."
Psalm 116:8 (KJV)

On August 27, 1974, my mother, uncle, two brothers, cousin and I were returning from Louisiana after attending my grandmother's funeral. While driving through Wilcox, Arizona, we were involved in a tragic accident that took the lives of my mother, uncle, 8-year old brother, and cousin who had turned 12 that day. My 10-year old brother, David, and I were the only survivors of the accident.

We were on a deserted highway in the desert, and miles away from a major city. David jumped out of the car's window, yelled, and flagged for help as I was pinned in the back of the car, unable to move. A highway patrolman stopped to help. The vehicle's door had to be pried open with special equipment to remove me from the car.

I suffered major life-threatening injuries, including a broken femur and wrist. I was taken to a local hospital, treated, and then transported by ambulance 80 miles to another hospital. I was left all alone in Arizona for approximately 2 weeks and received medical treatment without family and friends. I was unable to be transported home, in California, because I was lying flat on my back in traction. Family members, there, were taking care of funeral arrangements and other urgencies. It was during my quiet, lonely hours, that God became real to me.

Psalm 116:6-7, 12, states, "The LORD preserveth the simple: I was brought low and he helped me. Return unto my rest, O my soul; for the LORD hath dealt bountifully with thee. What shall I render unto the LORD for all his benefits towards me?"

As I reflect on the song, "Showers of Blessing", written by Bishop Charles Price Jones, the lyrics remind me that, "There shall be showers of blessing; Glory to God they, are here! Souls are rejoicing in power, Jesus is answering prayer." I thank the Lord for sparing me so that I can be a blessing to others.

Dear Lord, it is my prayer _____
Donnetta Price
Carson, California

AHA Moment

I train but God completes the promise.

I AM THE TRAINER

"Train up a child in the way he should go: and when he is old,
he will not depart from it."
Proverbs 22:6 (NKJV)

I am a mother of three, an older sister in a family of five children, and have served as a Sunday School teacher since I was a young girl. Sometimes I've experienced great joy in seeing the fruit of my labor, but other times I'm saddened when students stray away and do not return. What happened to the training? God answered, "I fulfill my promises."

Training is the foundation for children to accept the gift of salvation through Jesus Christ. As a parent and teacher, my responsibility is to train in the "way they should go." God promises that when they are old, they will not depart from it. We are responsible for training those God has entrusted to us. He said to me, as you train, live a life before your students, speak encouraging words, and pray that what you sow will fall on good ground.

I gained insight from some of the things I learned while growing up, such as, memorization of the Word —"Do unto others as you would have them do unto you" (Luke 6:31). Even when I was not walking in the will of God, those teachings were with me and I could not cross "the line". AHA! His promises are true! He didn't let me fall so far in darkness that I could not call on Jesus.

When you get discouraged and begin to think, Lord, why are my children and students not following your teaching, remember, you are not the one who saves, nor are you able to keep them from falling.

Be encouraged by the parable in Luke 8, when some seed fell on good soil, it came up and yielded a crop a hundred times more than was sown. Pray for them, trust, and believe God for their salvation.

Dear Lord, it is my prayer _____
Elizabeth Izard
Conyers, Georgia

AHA MOMENT

No matter what changes in my life, God never changes.

GOD IS CONSTANT

"Be strong and courageous. Do not fear or be in dread of them, for it the
LORD your God who goes with you. He will not leave you or forsake you".
Deuteronomy 31:6 (ESV)

In the year following my graduation from college, I went through many
changes. The biggest change was starting graduate school. This was the first
time I moved to a city where I knew no one. I had no foundation, no church,
and no friends! On top of all of that, my workload doubled from undergrad.
Additionally, my apartment had an infestation of crickets that were everywhere;
and I was deathly afraid of bugs. This was a rough time for me! I knew of no one
I could call and there was no one there to hug me. I then realized that God was
there the entire time. He came to my rescue!

I began to understand that change happens. God has shown me that through
the ups, downs, lefts, and rights. He is the only thing constant in the world. God's
grace, mercy, kindness, gentleness, sacrifice, and love will never change or leave us.

Psalm 94:14 (NIV) reads, "For the LORD will not reject his people; he
will never forsake his inheritance." This is wonderful news! God, the creator of
everything, will not reject or forsake us!

Remember the hymn, "On Christ the solid Rock, I stand; All other ground
is sinking sand."

Think about God's consistency in your life. Has God proven himself constant in your life? If you cannot think of examples, ask him to remind you how
and when he has shown up for you. Lastly, ask God who you can show his consistency to today and in what ways.

Dear Lord, it is my prayer _____
Jasmine Wise
Monroe, Louisiana

AHA MOMENT

Just a tiny bit of faith brings a great yield.

TINY IS TO MAN AS LARGE IS TO GOD

"It is like a grain of mustard seed, which a man took, and cast into his garden;
and it grew, and waxed a great tree; and the fowls of the
air lodged in the branches of it."
Luke 13:19 (KJV)

One day I was doing one of the tasks I enjoy most in my life—gardening. I was in my vegetable garden planting squash, okra, corn, and a variety of greens, my favorite being mustard greens. As I opened the package of mustard green seeds, I discovered how tiny they are. These were the smallest of all the seeds I had planted that day, and my mind immediately reflected on the scripture in Luke 13:19. How can such a tiny seed produce such large mustard green leaves? As I continued with my gardening, God sent me a word. If we have faith the size of this tiny mustard seed, we can produce large things in Him. It takes trusting and believing.

The Lord will supply us with everything that we need in life, but we must work and have faith.

After all the hard-manual labor I performed that day in my vegetable garden, I was trusting God to bring the yield of vegetables I wanted. I completely trusted God for a large yield from the small seeds I planted that day. Guess what? It happened.

For further study read: Mark 4:31, John 4:1-33, Matthew 17:20, Luke 17:6

Dear Lord, it is my prayer _____
Equilla Miller
Louisville, Mississippi

AHA Moment

Not putting God in a box expands out spiritual view.

IN TUNE WITH GOD

"Prove all things; hold fast that which is good."
I Thessalonians 5:21 (KJV)

Not putting God in a box can be challenging. This is especially true if we have been conditioned to define God's speaking and working in limiting ways. We must remind ourselves of the unusual ways God manifested himself in the Old and New Testaments.

In 2015, I was going through two situations simultaneously; both required that I seek God's guidance. God had already impressed upon me that I needed to change my associations. I was having challenges reckoning with this, with respect to one association in particular. The other situation was a conflict of sorts, that I put myself in at a vulnerable moment.

Dealing with the person in the first situation became a major source of stress and distraction. Yet, because of the nature of our association, it was more than a notion to walk away. The second situation created an emotional conflict, which left me somewhat distressed.

I had to cry out to God. I made my request known, regarding the first situation, to my Bible study group that I attended. God repeatedly confirmed that he had already been speaking to me, through multiple posts on Facebook. He gave me the answer to the second dilemma while I was watching television. Am I suggesting that we seek answers from God through Facebook and television? No, I am not. Because I sought God so diligently and fervently on these matters, and I did not put limitations on the way God responds. I recognized the answers I was seeking and could not ignore them. When you are genuinely seeking God, you must be so in tuned with God so that you recognize Him speaking through things that might not otherwise speak to you.

Let us not hinder our own spiritual growth, because we put God in a box.

Dear Lord, it is my prayer _____
Monique H. May
Corona, California

AHA Moment

Forgive and experience freedom.

FORGIVE OR NOT TO FORGIVE, THAT IS THE QUESTION

"For if you forgive men their trespasses, your heavenly Father will also
forgive you. But if you do not forgive men their trespasses,
neither will your Father forgive your trespasses."
Matthew 6:14-15 (NKJV)

On our wedding anniversary in 2014, my husband and I received some pre-packaged amaryllis bulbs from well-meaning friends. The amaryllis bulbs were beautifully packaged, and because I do not have a green thumb, remained packaged and became a part of the decor in our living room. After several months, I decided to open the package and view its contents. Inside were instructions, two pots with prepared soil, and several pre-moistened flower bulbs. According to the instructions, if followed exactly, I should have flowers blooming in a few days. Well, because I allowed the package to sit several months without checking its contents, the flower bulbs inside were no longer moist, but very dry. I thought, "If only I had opened the package earlier." At this point I decided to follow the instructions—after all, what could it hurt. So I watered the prepared soil, planted the dry flower bulbs in the pots provided and placed them in the sunlight as directed. In a few days, much to my surprise, I had flowers blooming.

God taught me a valuable lesson that day about forgiveness. Much like the dried-up flower bulbs, if I withhold forgiveness, my heart becomes hard and dry just like those neglected flower bulbs. However, if I extend forgiveness, my heart becomes soft and flourishes just like the flower bulbs after they had been properly nourished.

Forgiveness is not for the offending party, but for the person who has been offended. We forgive not because we want to, but because GOD has said that we must forgive in order to be forgiven (Matthew 6:14-15).

If you are struggling with forgiving someone, "Stop it!" Extend forgiveness today and be set free!

Dear Lord, it is my prayer _____
Elma R. Smith
Decatur, Georgia

AHA Moment
God is alive in the small area of our lives.

GIFTS OF PEARLS FOR WISDOM

"... I have learned to be content whatever the circumstance."
Philippians 4:11b (NIV)

As Christians we readily recognize God in the grand occurrences of our lives, but for many it's the small things that God does daily we tend to overlook. Those things are where He's so real!! We are waiting for this great bolt of light or miraculous healing. Our God *can* do everything.

This became evident to me after returning home from a national convention in Berkley, California. In the rush to pack and get to the airport the meticulous packing done beforehand is no longer a priority. You just want to get home.

My husband had given me a 17-inch strand of pearls for our 17th wedding anniversary and a 25-inch strand for our 25th anniversary. I hurriedly stuck them in the jewelry box and threw them in the bag carrying shoes. When we arrived in Houston and went to retrieve luggage, one bag was missing. No shoes. No jewelry. With sentimental attachment tugging, immediately I talked to God to calm my emotions. Things can be replaced. I decided to leave this dilemma in God's hands. He would hear my prayer. Arriving home, I purposely decided to busy myself and get the loss off my mind. I distinctly remember letting go. At that very moment the doorbell rang, and the carrier handed the loss piece of luggage to me. Everything was there!

I've rehearsed that moment in my mind many times since then, to remind myself of God's answer to prayer and a real expression of God's love to me. I've told this story to others about God's goodness in the small things of my life and how He will come through in *all* things.

"Let us give up our work, our thoughts, our plans, ourselves, our loved one, our all—right into His hands and then there will be nothing left to be troubled about".
J. Hudson Taylor

Dear Lord, it is my prayer _____
Deborah Florence
Houston, Texas

AHA MOMENT
God uses the older servant.

NOT TOO OLD!

"Moses my servant is dead. Now then . . . GET READY to cross . . . into the land I am about to give them. . . .. Be strong and courageous. . . .. BE STRONG AND VERY COURAGEOUS. Be careful to obey all the law my servant Moses gave you; do not turn from it to the right or to the left. . . .. Keep this Book of the Law always on your lips; meditate on it. . . .. BE STRONG AND COURAGEOUS. Do not be afraid; do not be discouraged. . . .."
Joshua 1:2-9 (NIV)

Joshua may have been *my age* when he received this call from God! Now, he's to GET READY. In his sixties, he is to START on his life's biggest challenge. Isn't this kind of calling and commissioning best for the young? Did God possibly forget that Joshua had some years on him? Had He forgotten that Joshua was now retirement age?

God, what am I—at my age—supposed to GET READY for? What new conquests lie ahead for me that I am to answer the call to serve? Am I to:

✓ Teach Sunday school?
✓ Help a ministry that impacts my church or community with the Gospel?
✓ Join a mission trip—even though it sounds scary?
✓ Mentor a young woman who's struggling with her kids, marriage, or finances?
✓ Start a ministry in my church, or re-kindle one that is on life support?
✓ Intercede relentlessly (in lieu of favorite TV shows) for my pastor, church, family, or friends?

REMEMBER, you cannot dismiss older people because they still have something to offer. They may not have your energy, but they continue to have passion, drive, and creativity. If they have breath, God is not finished with them yet. So, if God is using them, see what He may offer YOU— *through* THEM!

Age will never be an excuse when you have a calling to fulfill.

Dear Lord, it is my prayer _____
Ethelyn Taylor
Chicago, Illinois

AHA MOMENT

Look to the past then move forward!

UNCONDITIONAL PROMISES—NO MATTER YOUR AGE PART II

"Moses my servant is dead. Now then . . . GET READY to cross . . . into the land
I am about to give to them. . . .. Be strong and courageous. . . .. BE STRONG AND
VERY COURAGEOUS. Be careful to obey all the law my servant Moses gave
you; do not turn from it to the right or to the left... Keep this Book of the Law
always on your lips; meditate on it. . . .. BE STRONG AND COURAGEOUS.
Do not be afraid; do not be discouraged. . . .."
Joshua 1: 2-9 (NIV)

"Be strong"

How, when strength and stamina are decreasing? Reminder to my (old) self:
When I am weak, HE is strong.

"Be courageous"

How? That's not exactly my nature. In the passage, God reminded Joshua of his
experiences under Moses' leadership. Reminder: I also have a personal history
with God which reminds me that I need not fear.

"Be careful to obey"

Don't I already? Reminder to my "I've been a Christian for a long time" self:
Don't let arrogance make me presumptuous.

"Meditate on it (the Book of the Law)"

Don't just read, checking off a few answers at the end of the Sunday school
lesson or Bible study. MEDITATE; chew on it. Get new meat off the bone.

"Do not be discouraged"

Implies that things will not be simple without challenges and disappointments.

God's unconditional promises:

- "You WILL inherit the land"—i.e., you will accomplish what God has laid
  out for you—IF you are strong and courageous.
- "You WILL be successful wherever you go"—i.e., God will take you to new
  territories, ventures, roles in your old age, and make you successful.
- "You WILL be prosperous and successful"—IF you meditate on the Word.
- "The Lord your God WILL be with you wherever you go."

I will be strong when I feel weak, courageous when I feel afraid, obediently following You into the Promised Land.

Dear Lord, it is my prayer _____

Ethelyn Taylor

Chicago, Illinois

AHA Moment

A Crown of Glory awaits you.

FINISH THE RACE WELL

"Do you not know that those who run in a race all run, but one receives the prize? Run in such a way that you may obtain it."
1 Corinthians 9:24 (NKJV)

I remember a time when I was late to catch the train to work. I started running to make sure I got there on time. When I saw the train coming, I thought to myself, "I'm not going to make it". So, I stopped running. I gave up! Soon thereafter, I watched the train as it came to a stop and picked up passengers. It seemed to take forever to depart. As I continued watching, I thought, "Wow, I could have made that train, if I would have just kept running!"

I was reminded quickly of the Christian walk and how important it is to never stop running the race. Yes, there are times when you will slow down to get some water, stumble because you are weary, or even fall. But our God is faithful and He is with you the entire way. You can't stop! The goal is to finish the race well and receive a glorious crown.

My friend, don't let the daily struggles of life hinder you from staying on course and finishing the race well! Stay connected, continue in prayer, and be encouraged by the word of God. He will give you the strength, endurance, and tenacity to do His will. Be still and let the Holy Spirit speak to your heart, and wait patiently for answered prayers. Be sure to thank Him for guiding you on the straight and narrow path and providing His grace when you fall short.

It is my goal to finish the race well and help others along the way. I know with the Lord; all things are possible!

Dear Lord, it is my prayer _____
Felissa Lynn Waynick
Los Angeles, California

His Word is the only map I'll ever need.

HIS WORD IS A COMPASS

"Your word is a lamp to my feet and a light to my path."
Psalm 119:105 NKJV

As a mother of three young children, ages five, four and three, I often find myself questioning whether or not I am making sound parenting choices. More than that, as they grow and enter new seasons of life, I frequently wonder if I am even prepared to parent and guide them through their next phase of life. One thing that keeps me grounded, is knowing that God will always see to it that I make the right decisions. I remind myself to seek His counsel, even with the little things, for He will provide me with the guidance, strength and wisdom to do what is best for them.

My loving God has charged me with the care of His blessed little creations, and I rest assured that His Word will always shine bright upon my path. By looking to God for guidance, I have found that He helps me when I ask. By seeking Him and reading His Word, God has opened doors for me that I would have never opened on my own. Many of those doors have led to amazing opportunities to grow as a woman, mother and wife. My God surely is an awesome God!

If like me, you are wondering if you are making the right choices, whether it be as a parent, a spouse, an employee, a friend or whatever position you may hold right now, know that God's Word is an ever-present light guiding you in the right direction. He will never leave you nor forsake you. I challenge you, the next time you feel unsure and do not know which way to turn, rather than fret or stress, simply reach out to our dear Lord in prayer. He will provide a lamp for you on the path of His will and His ever-ready compass will never steer you wrong!

Dear Lord, it is my prayer _____
Gabriella Marigold Lindsay
Lansing, Illinois

AHA Moment
Trusting God is a great thing!

TRUST GOD

"Trust in the LORD with all your heart; do not depend
on your own understanding."
Proverbs 3:5 (NLT)

I was thinking of the time that our family moved from Los Angeles to Houston where my husband, Pastor Drake, accepted his first pastorate. He drove a vehicle and pulled a trailer while I followed him with the other trailer. As we drove through San Antonio, the weather was extremely violent, and the rain was so fierce that I could hardly see his vehicle ahead of me. I just watched his taillights, and we kept driving. We continued driving through the storm in an effort to carry out the directions of our bishop. We had to trust the guidance of the Holy Spirit in this endeavor.

We even lost our dog, Socks, in the storm. This verse of the hymn, "Tis So Sweet to Trust in Jesus" by Louisa Stead, became our testimony.

"I'm so glad I learned to trust Thee,
Precious Jesus, Savior, Friend;
And I know that Thou art with me,
Wilt be with me to the end.
Jesus, Jesus, how I trust Him,
How I've proved Him o'er and o'er,
Jesus, Jesus, Precious Jesus!
O for grace to trust Him more."

We had neither a cell phone nor a Global Positioning System (GPS) at that time. God was truly with us as we trusted Him. Thanks be to God for our safe arrival in Houston!

I learned from this experience that anyone can make excuses, but it takes fervent trust in God to push through difficult circumstances. This is just one, example of how we trusted God. Experience has taught me to continue to trust Him and follow His directions. Trusting God gives us a greater faith and a deeper walk with Him.

Dear Lord, it is my prayer _____
Geraldine Drake
Franklinton, Louisiana

AHA Moment
Worship GOD even in your pain!

THE GREAT CREATOR – HEALER

"... and I praise you because of the wonderful way you created me. Everything you do is marvelous! Of this I have no doubt."
Psalm 139:14 (CEV)

It was on Monday, October 6, 2014, that I was scheduled for hip replacement surgery at Atlanta Medical Center so that I could get some relief from my pain. The surgery went well, and I only stayed in the hospital for a few days. However, something unexpected happened on the Sunday after getting home. I got out of bed, and I could hardly catch my breath. My daughter, Jamease, was there trying to help me but to no avail; she finally called 911. They came and immediately rushed me to the hospital.

After receiving a CT scan, the doctor soon discovered that there was a large blood clot in my left lung. I was not afraid because I knew that GOD had already promised HE was going to see me through the entire process. I know that GOD is the Great Creator-Healer and that I am fearfully and wonderfully made. I decided that I was going to trust and praise HIM during this storm according to Psalm 139:14. I was prescribed a blood thinner medication to be taken for one year, and the new CT scan showed no blood clot ANYWHERE ... **GOD IS A HEALER!**

Sometimes it may take a sickness or an injury to remind us of the masterfully designed bodies that the Great Creator – Healer has given us. So, if you are facing an unwanted interruption in your life, and it does not matter what it might be, focus on Jesus' wonderful love. Let HIM give you a grateful heart that is full of worship even in the midst of pain.

Dear Lord, it is my prayer _____
Jacqueline A. Gant
Atlanta, Georgia

AHA Moment

Man will hurt himself and others when he knows not God's truth.

FORGIVING ONE ANOTHER

"And be ye kind one to another, tenderhearted, **forgiving one another,**
even as God for Christ's sake hath forgiven you."
Ephesians 4:32 (KJV)

I grew up in Madison County, Mississippi in the early 50's when segregation was clearly defined by separatism and injustices. I was about 9 or 10 when I realized that there were racial differences. I was a teenager when I learned that the laws of Mississippi were designed to segregate the races. Whites, the dominant race, were the lawmakers. They were the privileged citizens with rights/freedoms that were denied to Blacks.

One day, I asked my dad why Blacks were so hated and mistreated. Calmly, he said, "Man will hurt himself and others when he knows not truth–God's truth". I could sense from my dad's words that man without God's truth can do evil and think of himself as good 'cause he's in darkness. That day, I made a commitment to seek and to teach God's truth.

I think the most difficult decision I've had to make after trusting Jesus as Lord and Savior was my decision to give up anger and bitterness toward the white man. That was not easy for me because I have experienced both, directly and indirectly, the injustices done to my people due to skin color. So, naturally, anger and bitterness were my emotions, and revenge was my thought. Yet, God commands us to be kind, tenderhearted, and forgiving to one another. I didn't want to be a hypocrite, so I asked God to create in me a forgiving heart and to renew my spirit. He gave me the capacity to love everybody, regardless.

Yes, I remember my past, but I am not angry or bitter anymore. I am free! You, too, can be free. Confess it to Jesus and let Him fix you within.

Dear Lord, we've been hurt and are hurting. Deliver us and give us clean hearts that we might worship and serve justly.

Dear Lord, it is my prayer _____
Jannie Johnson
Madison, Mississippi

AHA Moment

It's true: my discharge became my advancement.

GOD SAID PROMOTION

"There is a time for everything, and a season
for every activity under the heavens:"
Ecclesiastes 3:1 (NIV)

In November 2008, I received a note to report to the personnel director's office. I was alarmed because I felt I was going to be terminated. I quickly telephoned a friend who did ministry in Chicago and I asked her to pray. She said, "God said promotion." I said, "I don't think this is a promotion." When I went into the office, the director of personnel and two senior managers were present. They said we are terminating you. When I asked why, they responded "we want to go another way." Needless to say, I was devastated. I had worked there for13 years. There had been a recent change in management and many changes were occurring. When I called my friend again in Chicago with the news, she said once again, "God said promotion."

My season was up for that job. The new season He had for me has been so amazing. I started a publishing company with my son. I found I have a gift for writing which I never knew was there. I now have time to meditate and be with the Lord. He also showed me he had a better plan for me.

There are different seasons in life. When it is time to move to another level, sometimes the Lord abruptly pushes us to move on to the next season just as the mother eagle pushes her young out of the nest. Our prayer should be that the Lord will guide us in the changing seasons of our lives. When it is time to move to the next phase, may we hear His voice and be ready to obey.

Dear Lord, it is my prayer _____
Kathy Nash
Decatur, Georgia

AHA Moment

In the midst of the storm, call on the Master of the storm.

THE MASTER OF THE STORM

"And he arose, and rebuked the wind, and said unto the sea, Peace, be still. And the wind ceased, and there were a great calm."
Mark 4:39 (KJV)

Back-to-back storms! Maybe you have experienced storm after storm with no breathing room in between; health problems, financial woes, job concerns, family issues. The list could go on. It seems like the storms will never end. That is how I felt in the summer of 2012.

My son and I were flying from Houston, Texas to Washington, DC for a family function. We were experiencing extreme turbulence and a bumpy ride so powerful that I could not go to sleep. With every bump, I silently screeched and prayed. The pilot instructed everyone to sit down and buckle up. I looked two rows to my left and my son was asleep. How could he so peacefully sleep through this storm?

I am certain that the disciples also wondered how Jesus could sleep calmly through the raging storm in the Sea of Galilee. In desperation, the disciples woke Jesus and said to Him, "Teacher, do you not care that we are perishing?" Mark 4:38 (ESV)

Just as the disciples called on Jesus to calm the storm, I called on Jesus, He revealed His power, and He carefully guided the plane through the storm.

When we approached Reagan National Airport for landing, I heard the gasps from the passengers. I glanced out the window and saw how close we were to the Potomac River. I just wanted to get my feet on solid ground!

As we continued on our way by car, we encountered strong winds, heavy rain, and reduced visibility. I prayed my way through another storm. The sun did finally shine as we arrived at our destination.

In the midst of a storm, we can call on Jesus to bring calm and peace. He can calm the storms of your life because He promised, "I will never leave you nor forsake you" Hebrews 13:5 (NKJV).

Dear Lord, it is my prayer _____
June Bond
Houston, Texas

AHA Moment

Push forward, jump, and run!

THE BEST IS YET TO COME!

"But those who trust in the Lord will find new strength.
They will soar high on wings like eagles.
They will run and not grow weary. They will walk and not faint."
Isaiah 40:31 (NLT)

I was a 25-year-old single mother of a very energetic two-year-old little boy who required most of my attention. Being the provider, nurturer, and disciplinarian was overwhelming at times. I would always hear that voice speaking to my spirit saying, "DO NOT GIVE UP!"

Working as a Certified Nursing Assistant on a very limited income, I would find myself "robbing Peter to pay Paul"—an expression that I would often hear my grandparents say. I trusted, had faith, and believed in Philippians 4:19 (NLT) which reads, "And this same God who takes care of me will supply all your needs from his glorious riches, which have been given to us in Christ Jesus." God's word will never return void.

As the years passed, God always made a way for me to provide for my son. In 2003, I received my first degree in Health Science as a Respiratory Therapist. Working twelve-hour shifts in this profession was extremely challenging for the first two years. It was during my third year that God blessed me with an eight-hour shift. In addition, I was scheduled to work Monday through Friday, being off on weekends and holidays. As in Proverbs 3:5 (KJV), I placed my trust in the Lord: "Trust in the LORD with all thine heart; and lean not unto thine own understanding."

Through all of my trials and tribulations, I trusted in the Lord, and prayed day-in and day-out for a better life. Most importantly, I prayed over my son at night while he was asleep. Although life throws curve balls, never give up. PUSH FORWARD, JUMP, and RUN!

Dear Lord, it is my prayer _____
Latarsho Griffin
Atlanta, Georgia

AHA Moment

You can count on God!

LEANING AND DEPENDING ON GOD

"Be still, and know that I am God: I will be exalted among the heathen,
I will be exalted in the earth."
Psalm 46:10 (KJV)

As I go through life's journey and encounter various obstacles, Psalm 46:10 gives me the most peace and calmness.

When I was a child, I learned the Christian hymn, "Jesus Loves Me." Now, as an adult, I know that my God loves me!

My husband and I had been married for 24 years when he passed away unexpectedly. The suddenness of his death caused me to cry so many tears, and to ask my Lord for an understanding of why my husband had to leave this earth so soon.

We had plans. We were empty nesters and had planned to move to Mississippi, his heart's desire, when I retired. How quickly my life had changed. One day I was married, and the next day I was a widow. I found myself home alone and unable to sleep at night.

During those sleepless nights, I asked God to help me sleep and not be afraid. God gave me Psalm 4:8 (KJV), "I will both lay me down in peace, and sleep: for thou, LORD, only makest me dwell in safety." He also gave me this assurance in Proverbs 3:24 (NKJV), "When you lie down, you will not be afraid; yes, you will lie down and your sleep will be sweet." These two passages of scripture have become so precious to me. I quote them daily.

Yes, I still cry over the loss of my husband, but God has given me joy! I know that, "Weeping may endure for a night, but joy comes in the morning" Psalm 30:5 (NKJV).

During difficult times, remember that you can lean and depend on Him because "God is our refuge and strength, a very present help in trouble" Psalm 46:1 (KJV).

Thank you, God, for the privilege of being your child!

Dear Lord, it is my prayer _____
Laurie Johnson
Detroit, Michigan

AHA Moment
God's Grace is extended in the midst of trouble; look for it.

IT WAS GRACE

"It is good for me that I have been afflicted; that I might learn thy statutes."
Psalm 119:71 (KJV)

It was Saturday before Mother's Day, 2015. This was to be a day of catching up on household chores and running needed errands around town. After returning home, exhausted, I decided to rest a bit. Later, I woke up coughing uncontrollably. Thinking that this would pass, I mustered enough strength to get up. As I proceeded, I encountered shortness of breath and decided that it was time to get to the hospital. After being seen by the doctor and having tests, my visit resulted in being admitted to the hospital for three days and two nights!

It was God's grace that I allowed Him to turn a hospital stay into a time of refilling. "It [was] good **for me** that I have been afflicted" Psalm 119:71 (KJV). My caregivers knew Him and ministered to me with prayer and encouraging words. God designed this stay for me. It provided the needed time to get away from my busy life, to rest, and to be reminded of whom He is, His statutes, and His call on my life. He provided me with the opportunity to renew my zeal for Him.

Romans 8:28 (KJV) states that, "And we know that **all things** work together for good to them that love God, to them who are the called according to his purpose." Although being in the hospital on Mother's Day was not my idea, God used this time to refresh my body for the days that were ahead. In a few short weeks, my son was graduating and preparation was overwhelming. After my hospital stay, I was refreshed, able to rise early, and ready to take on the coming activities.

Therefore, what seems to be discouraging in the natural, and a frustration to your plans, does not mean that God is not working it out for your good by His grace.

Dear Lord, it is my prayer _____
Linda C. McDonald
Decatur, Georgia

AHA Moment

God's love is all we need. This great love changed me.

LOVE IS ALL WE NEED

"Because your steadfast love is better than life, my lips will praise you."
Psalm 63:3 (ESV)

Three years ago, I struggled with grasping God's love for me. I had always felt unlovable given what life had thrown at me. The idea that this Perfect Being had such deep love for someone like me was unreal.

One spring day in a time of deep worship with the Lord, Jesus Culture's song, "How He Loves", came on the radio. I had heard this song many times, but this time it felt different. I began to listen to the lyrics: "He is jealous for me, loves like a hurricane I am a tree." I could hear the voice of God clearly crying out to me, "Lynn, I have always loved you!"

The tears started pouring like rivers from my eyes. Hearing God say that He loved me was literally indescribable. I began to cry out to Him saying, "You love me? You love me?" Each time I cried those words; I was met with, "Lynn, I have always loved you!" At that moment, I could feel God's love overflowing my being as if He were drowning me in it. This is a moment that I cannot put into words because it was so overwhelming. From that day forward, I knew that I was loved.

As followers of Christ, we must never forget God's love for us, even when we feel unloved.

Lord, remind us that Your love for us is deeper than all the waves in the ocean, and greater than all the stars in the sky. Your love is all that we need.

Dear Lord, it is my prayer _____
Lynn Marie Brown
Decatur, Georgia

AHA Moment

There is nothing too hard for God.

I'M SAVED BY THE BLOOD OF THE CRUCIFIED ONE

"Call unto me, and I will answer thee, and shew thee great and mighty things,
which thou knowest not."
Jeremiah 33:3 (KJV)

"Delight thyself also in the Lord; and he shall give thee
the desires of thine heart."
Psalm 37:4 (KJV)

Upon acceptance of the Lord as my personal Savior, at the age of eight, living a dedicated life for Jesus Christ has been very rewarding. After completing high school at age of sixteen, I married very early, and from that union, three children were born.

At twenty-seven years old, I became ill with cancer, and the Lord healed me. To God be the glory! It was a blessing to raise my children to become healthy young men of worth, and the Lord blessed me to be of service in the church and community.

My treasured pleasure has always been going to the nursing homes to visit the sick and shut-in, and also teaching boys and girls with reading deficiencies. Many students have graduated from college because of the love, small group and individualized attention, parental support, and homework that was provided during tutoring.

From 2008 until 2014, I encountered four strokes, and now at the age 83, I can truly say that through the blessings of God, most days I am free of pain. In 2016, I had a knee replacement, and the Lord is continuing to heal me.

"I have been young, and *now* am old; yet have I not seen the righteous forsaken, nor his seed begging bread" Psalm 37:25 (KJV). To God be the Glory! Every good and perfect gift comes from His begotten Son, Jesus Christ.

Through experiences of fasting and praying, God will take care of you. Pray, pray, pray!

Dear Lord, it is my prayer _____
Mary Etta Myles-Sutton
Bloomfield Hills, Michigan

AHA Moment

You don't know if what you're doing as a parent will be enough.

THE BEST YOU KNOW—IS IT THE BEST?
A PARENT'S DILEMMA

"I will make thy name to be remembered in all generations"
Psalm 45:17 (KJV)

"Train up a child and when he is old, he will not depart from it."
Proverbs 22:6 (KJV)

"That's all I can do; that's all I know." Hopefully, the person observing grasps what is being taught. This is the scenario of the teacher and student and what happens with the parent and the child.

Parents are teachers; not in the classroom sense, but teachers just the same. They teach what they know and believe to be true. We are teaching learners, and they absorb what they are taught.

As I reflect on my "teaching" experiences, I must confess, some things that I thought were best were without knowledge and naïve, but it was all that I knew. Consequently, what I taught was what I understood; that's the parenting dilemma.

Parents often ask themselves, are we teaching the "right" things? Too often, society challenges our parental ability to teach. As a godly parent, you are giving tools for life. Teach tirelessly, holding back nothing. This is our God-given responsibility.

Do you know all the acceptable techniques for teaching? *No!* All we have is a mandate from God to teach them when they get up and lay down; when they come in and go out. Then, we can rely on His promise that when they are old, they will not depart from it.

To the learners under my tutelage, I gave you the "best I knew" so that you might know the way to the kingdom. Was it always accurate? I thought so, and for that I make no apology. Teachers, keep teaching. Anything that you don't know, seek God's direction. A learner can rejoice knowing that a teacher gave them what they needed to grow in Christ.

Dear Lord, it is my prayer _____
Mary Kennebrew
Little Rock, Arkansas

AHA Moment

Stop, listen, and follow.

FOLLOW THE CLOUD

"And the Lord went before them by day in a pillar of a cloud, to lead them the way; and by night in a pillar of fire, to give them light; to go by day and night:"
Exodus 13:21(KJV)

I'm amazed how our Heavenly Father knows the purpose for our lives. God knew I'd be the mother of nine children and that He would teach me many lessons from these precious ones. They arranged my schedule with what seemed like endless tons of laundry that needed washing, ironing, and folding. My washing machine was the most used and valuable appliance in our home.

I learned to be thankful for every piece of laundry, each little body that fit those outfits, and prayed for the child who wore them. While listening to Christian radio, I often prayed and meditated on the Scriptures as I folded laundry. God taught me valuable lessons using the Israelites' 40-year trek to the Promised Land. He gave Moses instructions that His Presence would be evidenced through a pillar of cloud by day, and a pillar of fire by night. Whenever the pillar of cloud stopped, the Israelites knew the Lord wanted them to stop. When it moved, they were free to move.

Constantly washing large loads of clothing caused my washing machine to malfunction. I'd become discouraged as I watched the mountains of soiled laundry grow until the machine could be repaired. I envisioned the cloud, God's Presence, leading the Israelites when it might have appeared inconvenient to stop, so it was with my broken washing machine. The Lord showed me this truth— His purpose for me that day was to do something else instead of washing. There was a need to find another project that required my attention.

For the mother who has tons of soiled laundry and a broken washing machine, the God who led the Israelites is still the same today. He wants you to stop, listen, depend on, and follow His lead. Follow the Cloud!

Dear Lord, it is my prayer _____
Mattie Winn
Vallejo, California

AHA Moment

I'm glad I realize the importance of prayer.

THANK GOD FOR PRAYER!

"Be careful for nothing; but in every thing by prayer and supplication with thanksgiving let your requests be made known unto God."
Philippians 4:6 (KJV)

It was during my morning meditation and studying God's word that I read John 17. The chapter was entitled, "Jesus prays." I immediately began to reflect on the many times throughout the Bible when prayer gauged the outcome of desperate situations. That morning, I realized the manner in which Jesus was praying, and it resonated in my spirit. It was humbling to read how He petitioned the Father, and it reminded me of the benefits and importance of prayer in the life of the believer.

I sat there and thanked God for being able to *release my heart* through prayer. It has brought me lightness of heart, given me joy, delivered me from bitterness, resentments, and pain. It has released me from strongholds and enabled me to forgive.

I began to *remember His words* in Psalm 23, "The Lord is my Shepherd . . .", and in the book of Esther when she sent word to all the Jews to fast and pray with her for three days and nights, and how the community joined together in prayer on behalf of Peter in the book of Acts.

Finally, I thanked God, while reading John 17, for *Jesus being our lifeline to eternity*. Just before Jesus was betrayed and His death was imminent, His farewell discourse concluded with this prayer: He prayed to be glorified by the Father, to sanctify the disciples by the truth, and that all believers are brought to complete unity. It concludes with the verse, "And I have declared unto them thy name, and will declare it: that the love wherewith thou hast loved me may be in them, and I in them" John 17:26 (KJV).

I thank you God for your love and for prayer! Think about what our lives would resemble if we didn't have prayer. Remember to thank God for prayer!

Dear Lord, it is my prayer _____
Monocia Connors
Jackson, Mississippi

AHA Moment

Don't sow bad seeds.

REAPING THE HARVEST OF YOUR SOWING

"Be not deceived; God is not mocked:
for whatsoever man soweth, that shall he also reap."
Galatians 6:7 (KJV)

Each year, a farmer had a beautiful, bountiful garden because he would plant seeds, water, and fertilize it daily. Every now and then, he noticed a bad weed would spring up. Each time this occurred, he would take the necessary measures to eliminate the flower of the weed, but never took the time to eliminate what caused the weed. Although he was fully aware that he was sowing the seed that produced the weed, he felt that because he cut down the flower, his garden would always produce the same bountiful fruit each year. Year after year, this same weed would spring up from time to time, and the farmer would cut down the weed's flower. He was still unable to get to the root of the problem because he continued sowing the same bad seeds.

One year, he noticed that his plants were not producing good fruit as they had done in the past. It was obvious that the weed was appearing more often. Eventually, the roots of the weed took over the beautiful garden. He still had some beautiful, good fruit every now and then, but never the bountiful supply he had previously enjoyed. He failed to realize that he was continually sowing bad seeds and reaping what he had sown.

If you are not reaping the fruit of the Spirit (love, joy, peace, longsuffering, gentleness, goodness, faith, meekness, and temperance) in your life, examine the seeds that you are sowing. Be careful that you are not holding on to bad seeds in your heart that you need to surrender to God. Allow God to cultivate your garden, so he will remove the roots of all the weeds and give you seeds that will produce the fruit of the Spirit.

Dear Lord, it is my prayer _____
O'ka Duren
Jackson, Mississippi

AHA Moment
God has always had caller ID!

THANK GOD FOR "CALLER ID"

"When Jesus heard him, he stopped and ordered
that the man be brought to him. . .."
Luke 18:40 (NLT)

Nowadays we are continuously bombarded with annoying phone calls from telemarketers. You put your number on the "Do not call" list, but those annoying calls continue to flood your line. THANK GOD FOR CALLER ID! When I see an unfamiliar area code, telephone number, or hear an unfamiliar caller's name announced by speakerphone, I have stopped running to answer those calls and just ignore them. But when a familiar number or name is announced, I hasten to answer that call.

It has occurred to me that "*God has always had Caller ID.*" He knows when one of His saints is on the prayer line. He can identify every individual's voice. We can bombard His prayer line any time, and He welcomes our calls. In fact, He welcomes us to "...come boldly unto the throne of grace that we may obtain mercy, and find grace to help in time of need" Hebrews 4:16 (KJV). We can be confident that the line will never be busy; there will never be a dropped call, no "dead zones," or any access codes to remember. God's prayer line is always open with maximum transmission.

When Jesus heard the blind beggar's call, "Jesus, thou Son of David, have mercy on me," He immediately stopped and ministered to the man's needs. This is the same loving and caring Jesus whom we worship and serve today.

Are you confident that Jesus knows your voice? When we trust and obey God, we can have the assurance that He hears us. Jesus is the Good Shepherd; He knows our voice. He is our provider, protector, and Savior who leads us in the way of holiness. We, who believe in Jesus, are His sheep. His sheep know His voice, and they follow Him.

Call Him—He's waiting for your call!

Dear Lord, it is my prayer _____
Rosemary Tate
Franklinton, Louisiana

AHA MOMENT

Be thankful in all circumstances.

IN EVERYTHING GIVE THANKS

"In every thing give thanks: for this is the will of
God in Christ Jesus concerning you."
1 Thessalonians 5:18 (KJV)

On Sunday, June 3, 2007, my life took a drastic change as I attended service at New Lake Church in Jackson, Mississippi. We had just begun our Spring Revival. I had directed the choir that day, and then we had come down from the choir stand for communion.

I went outside to put something in my vehicle. While approaching it, I felt something like a drumroll from the top of my head to the tip of my toes on the left side of my body. I began to feel very weak at that point. Thankfully, there were several people outside, and I was able to get their attention. They came to my aid, sat me down on the sidewalk, and dialed 911. I felt as if I were having a stroke!

I thought about my thirteen-year-old granddaughter, who was inside of the church, and I was also thinking about my son. So, I prayed to the Lord requesting that He please not let me die because I wasn't ready to leave.

Meanwhile, my pastor came to pray for me while the congregation was praying inside. The paramedics arrived and worked on me for about forty-five minutes before transporting me to the hospital. The doctors stated, "You have a blood clot in the back of your head that is preventing the blood from flowing freely and causing a stroke." I was left with a feeling of heaviness on the left side of my body, but again, the Lord saw fit to leave me here. For that, I am truly thankful. I believe that it is the Lord's will concerning me and what I went through. To God be the glory!

Dear Lord, it is my prayer _____
Sandrea Myles
Jackson, Mississippi

AHA Moment

I won't complain. God is in control.

I AM CONTENT WHERE GOD HAS ME

"Be still and know that I am God, I will be exalted among the heathen,
I will be exalted among the earth."
Psalm 46:10 (KJV)

We all go through storms of life; everyone you meet is in a storm, coming out of or heading into one. Just know God is with you. He promised to never leave us nor forsake us and He is a promise keeper. God never fails.

Seven years ago, I was ill and was hospitalized for three months. My family was called in and the doctors had given up. But God had His own agenda; my work here wasn't finished. I am a miracle! Saints were praying; God heard and He answered. I know a man and His name is Jesus! He has all power in His hands. God has continued to bless me. I am confined but have been given a wonderful ministry to reach out to the sick, shut-in, elderly and, to prisoners. I know God has me where He wants me to be. I am content with His plan for my life, and until He says otherwise, I will serve Him with my whole heart.

God made no two people alike. We each have a different job. The harvest is plentiful and the laborers are few, so be content in the job God has allowed you to do. Do it to honor Him. Stay prayed up and focused on God. "Thou wilt keep him in perfect peace, whose mind is stayed on thee: because he trusteth in thee" Isaiah 26: 3 (KJV).

Let us not complain, but rather be content wherever the Lord has us today.

Dear Lord, it is my prayer _____
Sharon Bell
Seattle, Washington

AHA Moment

Trust God with your life!

TRUST GOD IN ALL THINGS

"Delight yourself also in the LORD, and He shall give you the
desires of your heart. Commit your way to the LORD, trust also in Him,
and He shall bring it to pass."
Psalm 37:4-5 (NKJV)

Trusting God in all things require intentional effort. We tend to seek Him for the big or difficult things in life; however, we must learn to seek Him in ALL things.

Most women have their husband and marriage planned out before they graduate high school. I was one of those women. I knew I would be married by age 25 with 2 children and living happily ever after. It did not happen for me that way. I found myself 30 years old with no prospects. This caused me to feel insecure and compromising, which lead to relationships that failed; one was really toxic.

Finally, at age thirty-eight, I got to a point where I prayed to God saying, "If singleness is the life you have for me, please help me accept my singleness." God gave me such peace after I prayed, and I began to serve Him with all my heart wherever He led me.

Six months later, God brought my husband into my life. The quality of man God gave me exceeded my expectations for a spouse. I think about the years marriage was delayed because I had not surrendered every area of my life to the Lord.

God wants the best for us. Trust God in all things, and see how abundant your life will be.

Dear Lord, it is my prayer _____
Sharon Logan
Snellville, Georgia

AHA Moment

WANTED: A humble servant totally God dependent.

OPENED "EYE" – ILLUMINED SPIRIT

"Open thou mine eyes, that I may behold wondrous things out of thy law."
Psalm 119:18 (KJV)

This journey began August 2008, when I was diagnosed with Sarcoidosis. It caused permanent loss of sight in my left eye. The transition was difficult, but there was no time for self-pity because I was so thankful to have vision in my right eye. In May 2013, I awakened but was unable to see anything. I was completely blind! "My God! What now? How will I make it?" The answer, "Behold, I am with you!" The decision was clear; I would continue to walk with the Lord, trusting Him either for the return of my sight or living fully for Him in blindness. The decision was easy; the living was a lesson in humility.

Believe me; it was not easy to be guided by someone at nearly every turn. I thank God for his patience with me and that of my husband during this trying time. Losing my independence was devastating. I discovered I had a real problem with leaning, depending, and following. Through this trial, God taught me that I needed to be ". . . clothed with humility: for God resisteth the proud" 1Peter5:5 (KJV).

Was I too proud to be humble, to be dependent? Did I want to be resisted by God? God forbid! Step by step, I yielded myself to the Lord, the guidance of my husband and to those who lovingly assisted me. He opened my eyes that I could see the wondrous things in His law. When this work was done in me, my sight was restored in my right eye! Praise the Lord! He is so AWESOME!!! God listens to our prayers. ". . . ye have not, because ye ask not" James 4:2 (KJV). Let us go to Him in faith, believing!

"Dear Lord, open my eyes, that I may see, Glimpses of truth thou hast for me. . ..
Open my eyes illumine me, Spirit Divine." (Clara H. Scott, 1841)

Dear Lord, it is my prayer _____
Shirley McClendon
Jackson, Mississippi

AHA Moment

There is only one way—JESUS.

CAUGHT OFF GUARD

"And we know that the Son of God has come, and he has given us
understanding so that we can know the true God
... because we live in fellowship with his Son, Jesus Christ.
He is the only true God, and he is eternal life."
1 John 5:20 (NLT)

My husband and I were in a meeting with our daughter's teacher, and she explained that our daughter had been exhibiting disturbing behavior for several weeks. The behavior was completely out of character, and quite frankly shocking. Where did she learn these actions? How had we missed it?

I was embarrassed. After all, I monitor my children to the best of my ability. Limited TV, restricted technology, and a close network of friends describe our lifestyle.

However, a door had been left open, and there was one way to close it. Armed with the Word of God, I rose one morning and shook off the hurt and confusion that discouraged me by not knowing the source of the problem. We tried rationalizing and theorizing, but methodologies were not the way to a solution. Our answer was found in Jesus, the way, the truth and the life. His promise is that we will find Him when we seek Him with all of our heart. I prayed in the Spirit—I needed the Holy Spirit to shine the light on God's Word and give me understanding that morning. I was determined to stay right there and not let go except the Lord bless me.

In a moment, my understanding was enlightened! I could see the open door, the who, what and when. I immediately prepared to make changes in this unguarded area. After the adjustments, the behavior stopped.

There is no magic, wizardry, or quick-fix gimmicks in Christ. The guarantee of the Holy Spirit and His power to help us in the matchless name of Jesus is our promise. So, if you ever feel "caught off guard", remember that the solution is found in JESUS ONLY.

Dear Lord, it is my prayer _____
Shonda Hill
Jackson, Mississippi

AHA MOMENT
Trust God recklessly.

TRUSTING GOD IN THE MIDST OF CHAOS!

"Trust in the Lord with all your heart, and lean not on your own
understanding; in all your ways acknowledge Him,
and He shall direct your path."
Proverbs 3:5-6 (NKJV)

Stress disappears when we acknowledge our dependence on God and submit to His leadership. The hymn by Bishop C.P. Jones, "O Soul Beset" says, *"O let not Satan frighten you, Trust God and His Salvation see; He will not fail thee, trust Him still, He ev'ry promise will fulfill."* With God there is stability and without Him there is chaos.

During my hospital stay in Chicago, God was the only shoulder to lean on. Knowing nothing but pain, I trusted Him. Because of my faith and vulnerability, God never left me as He promised in His Word. For 2 years I was in pain, and the doctors didn't understand why. Early one Saturday, while eating a nutty breakfast bar in the emergency room, my pain worsened; but, it resulted in a diagnosis that began my twenty-seven-day hospital stay. I had three surgeries within six months. The doctors thought it was cancer, but God said," NO." HALLELUJAH!

While healing, God's people continued to pray, blessed my family with meals, cleaned our house, and met their needs. I envisioned the IV as Life Water. It was my symbol for the Holy Ghost living inside me. Because my trust is in God, He healed my body, and I thank Him daily.

Don't wait until life is chaotic, or when the chaos is over. Take time to know God, now! He won't fail. When we trust, we can relax. Leave the stress on the altar. Never let your circumstances interfere with your faith. Trust God with <u>everything</u>. If you trust Christ as your foundation, you will never regret your decision.

Trust God recklessly; He already knows the outcome of the situation.

Dear Lord, it is my prayer _____
Valetta J. Ross
Merrillville, Indiana

AHA Moment

We must always trust and depend on Him.

GOD'S GOT YOU

"Now to Him who is able to keep you from stumbling and to present you
faultless before the presence of His glory with exceeding joy. . .."
Jude 1:24 (NKJV)

When my child was younger, I used to play games with him; one of them
was tossing him high in the air and catching him in my loving arms on his way
down. From time to time, I would toss him a little higher than he was accustomed,
which would cause his face to show signs of fear. A game that was meant for fun
would end with him not wanting to play anymore.

When this would happen, I would remind him of a promise I made to him, "I
will always protect you and will never do anything to hurt you." This story always
reminds me of the ultimate Promise Keeper. God has promised He will always
keep us from falling. We serve a God who will protect us from the wiles of the
devil. He has also promised that, "No weapon formed against you shall prosper"
Isaiah 54:17(NKJV), and if you wait on the Lord, He will renew your strength!

God does not expect us to live in fear or uncertainty in the midst of these
trying times. That is good news! Despite the fact that the world is getting worse
daily, we can still praise God because we know that He will protect and perfect
us until the end of time. What is our job? All we have to do is hold to God's
unchanging hand.

When we don't understand, just hold on! When we feel life has "thrown
us up in the air", stay encouraged! When you become frustrated and are lonely,
remember that the Promise Keeper will always protect you and will never do
anything to hurt you.

Dear Lord, it is my prayer _____
Tavia Patterson
Houston, Texas

AHA Moment

God's way is always a miracle.

UNITY BRINGS MIRACLES

"The Lord said, 'If as one people . . . then nothing
they plan to do will be impossible for them.'"
Genesis 11:7 (NIV)

In Genesis 11:1-9, God affirms that if we are on one accord, nothing can stop us from doing what we set our minds to do. I can attest to this as I recall a life-changing event where we touched and agreed; the outcome was nothing less than miraculous!

In December 2014, my husband, a non-drinker, was diagnosed with cirrhosis of the liver. The doctors said he was not a good candidate for a liver transplant because his liver function was not acute enough.

Month after month we were constantly in the emergency room and/or hospital. My husband began praying, "God, I just need a new liver, and I will be okay." This was his proclamation to everyone he encountered. I prayed, too. However, I asked others to pray with me for a miraculous healing that would baffle the doctors. While I prayed for a "miraculous healing", my husband prayed for a liver transplant.

One day the Holy Spirit said to me, "One accord, you need to be speaking the same language." At that moment, I began to pray for a liver transplant and asked those praying with me to do the same. Although my husband had been told he was not a good candidate for a liver transplant, we were certain God was preparing him for a new liver. On August 7, he was placed on the liver transplant list.

As I was praying on October 21, 2015, I remember saying, "Angels, go and get that liver!" We received a telephone call the next day stating that there was a liver for him. Two days later, he received the liver transplant!

Once my husband and I were on one accord, praying the same prayer, and speaking the same language, the process moved quickly. God's Word works! We just need to line up with His Word.

Dear Lord, it is my prayer _____
Thajuana Rainey
Jonesboro, Georgia

AHA MOMENT

Would you allow the Holy Spirit to smooth those dry and rough edges?

JUST A DROP OF OIL

"I will give you a new heart and put a new spirit in you; I will remove from you
your heart of stone and give you a heart of flesh."
Ezekiel 36:26 (NIV)

Many of us "beauty-conscious" ladies have rough, dry skin on our elbows,
hands and feet, which can turn into calluses without the proper care.

I love a pedicure, and am so excited about the end results—the softening of
my feet. Before the positive results, I am a bit embarrassed at the roughness on
my heels as the pedicurist scrubs away the calluses that feel like stones. As the
technician massages my feet, a drop of oil is used that soothes and heals the hard
and cracked heels.

Although we may have physical calluses, our hearts, minds, and spirits can
sometimes form calluses. Our hearts can become discouraged because of broken
promises and/or relationships that have not experienced a drop of oil. We need
a heart that yearns and beats for God.

Our minds are so distracted that we are unable to think clearly and focus
on our relationship with Jesus Christ. It is difficult to read God's Word and pray
regularly when we are distracted. We need refreshing like the cool mint scent in
a foot spa. Spiritually, we may have walked so far from the Lord that His Word
is not enriching but more like a stinging antiseptic that burns when applied to
broken skin.

When we ask the Savior for forgiveness, He washes us with the "suds of
purity" from the Holy Spirit. He also gives us a new heart that beats only for Him,
and a new spirit that represents the aroma of sweet smelling oil.

The Holy Spirit will lavish our heart, mind, and spirit with a drop of His oil
that massages the areas of our lives that need more love, extra confidence and
sweet peace that only comes from our Pedicurist, Jesus Christ.

Dear Lord, it is my prayer _____
Tiffany Castilla
Fayetteville, Georgia

AHA Moment

Look exclusively to God for all Good things.

THE GOODNESS OF GOD

"But as for me, how good it is to be near God! I have made the Sovereign Lord
my shelter, and I will tell everyone about the wonderful things you do."
Psalm 73:28 (NLT)

We were likely taught from an early age, whether from our parents, grandparents, or teachers, that we need to be "good." This was not always easy as a child. After all, there were many adventurous things in the world to partake in if we so chose; however, like many worldly things, those adventures often relied on us doing things that did not reflect a spirit of goodness. To make matters more confusing, many of our childhood friends and associates did indeed participate in unfitting activities with seemingly little or no consequence. Furthermore, as we grew into adolescence and adulthood we surely witnessed peers seemingly joyful and prospering from living a lifestyle we were vehemently taught to avoid.

As we grow in the values taught to us as children, and more importantly, as we grow in Christ, some revelations will be put into place. Firstly, God is good; moreover, God **is our** good. Goodness, when it comes from God, is not the tedious act that it used to be. It's not slippery in our grasp, rather it's an abundant gift, packaged together with Christ's salvation. This gift is free, and comes with benefits that go far beyond worldly awards. Secondly, those who refuse His goodness may take on the appearance of being prosperous in the physical realm; but when all flesh and hearts ultimately fail, God will be with us, the faithful, forever (Psalm 73:26).

Focus on God and his nearness to you today. This is where our goodness is found. It's a new portion, fresh and just for you! God not only does good things—He **is** good.

Dear Lord, it is my prayer _____
Zelma Watkins
Monroe, Louisiana

AHA MOMENT

What God allows is making me better. Keep the faith.

IN THE MAKING

"And let us not grow weary while doing good, for in due season we shall reap if
we do not lose heart."
Galatians 6:9 (NKJV)

As a former dressmaker, I have made suits, bridesmaids' dresses, and curtains.
Dressmaking takes time, skills, and a personal commitment. Had I fainted in the
process of making these garments, the task would not have been completed and
available for its purpose.

Similar to dressmaking, God is molding you into what He has purposed
for your life. He has a clear future in mind for you if you remain focused in the
making process. Many times, this process will take you through difficult and challenging situations to make you wiser, humble, patient, loving, and stronger for
the new level that He has for you. I believe all of these experiences help to make
us who we are today, as well as who we will become in God's Kingdom. It is for
these reasons that we should not faint because the process is working together
for our good.

Difficult times are also a natural part of life. These are opportunities for tre-
mendous personal growth. When I look back over my life, I clearly recall one
incident that shaped me for another level. It was very hard, so I wanted to quit
and turn back. While going through this difficult situation was not easy, now I
can see how it made me stronger, better, and increased my faith in God. It was
during this difficult period that God's grace and mercy abounded more. "If thou
faint in the day of adversity, then thy strength is small" Proverbs 24:10 (KJV).

If you continue until the end, so much can be learned during the making
process. You will be better and blessed beyond measure.

Dear Lord, it is my prayer _____
Betty C. Brown
Monroe, Louisiana

AHA Moment

The small quiet voice said, "JUST LET IT GO!"

FORGIVE, AND LET IT GO!

"Remember ye not the former things, neither consider the things of old."
Isaiah 43:18 (KJV)

How many times have you prayed to God, asking Him to forgive you for something? How many times has He given you another chance to get it right? So, why can't we forgive?

As a child, my father was not a part of my life, and to me, he really didn't matter... *or so I thought.* My pastor preached a sermon on forgiveness and the entire time the Holy Spirit kept whispering, *"Let it go!* You have to forgive him." In my mind, I asked, forgive who? As clear as day, I heard the words, *your dad.* The Holy Spirit said, "You have not forgiven him in your heart." I replied, "Yes, I forgave him."
The Holy Spirit then showed me that I had not truly forgiven him. Immediately, I experienced a flashback:

> *"Remember when your dad would call, and you said, he just wants something. When your sister took you to visit him, you said, he should come see me. While visiting him, his wife said, he is a great guy and does all these things for her and her children. You said, so what!"*

By this time, although I'm an adult, I was pouting like a child. I thought I had forgiven him. The Holy Spirit told me to look in the mirror, and reminded me of the many times I had been forgiven. My God! I fell on my knees and cried out to God to forgive me.

If there is someone you have not forgiven, ask God to forgive you. As God leads, reach out to that person and ask for their forgiveness. Now you are free to leave the past behind and look positively to the future.

Dear Lord, it is my prayer _____
Adrienne Miller
Chicago, Illinois

AHA Moment

You do not have to get ready, if you stay ready.

STAY READY

"Watch therefore: for ye know not what hour your Lord doth come. But know this, that if the goodman of the house had known in what watch the thief would come, he would have watched, and would not have suffered his house to be broken up. Therefore be ye also ready: for in such an hour as ye think not the Son of man cometh."
Matthew 24:42-44 (KJV)

I felt blessed to move into a safe and affordable retirement community. Upon moving in, I signed an agreement to keep my apartment clean, and well-ordered at all times. If I fail to abide by these conditions, I could be subject to eviction.

The apartment management can conduct an inspection at any time during the day or night. Not knowing when this could take place, I keep my apartment ready. On the other hand, it puzzles me when my neighbors become uptight about the inspections. Always remain ready, and there will be nothing to worry about.

Just as residents in the retirement community must always be ready for inspections, it is more important that we, too, remain ready. Mark 13:32 lets us know that no one knows the day or the hour that Jesus will return. We must be ready twenty-four hours a day, seven days a week, and stay connected to Him—the true vine. His expected return gives us the determination to live for Him daily. Staying ready means, we are reading His Word every day and being obedient to what it says. We should please the Lord and continue to do His will. Jesus wants us to always be ready and with the expectation of His glorious return when all true believers go to live with Him eternally. Are you ready?

Dear Lord, it is my prayer _____
Mae Kendrick
Long Beach, California

AHA Moment

When in the valley, the "living bread"—the Word of God, gives you
strength to overcome life's mountains.

THE "LIVING BREAD" IN THE VALLEY

"I am the living bread which came down from heaven: if any man eat of this
bread, he shall live for ever: and the bread that I will give is my flesh,
which I will give for the life of the world."
John 6:51 (KJV)

After I received my foreclosure letter in 2006, I wrote this poem:
In the Valley I Am
Surrounded by high mountains towering over me—rugged and too
steep to climb.
The land is dry, cracked, and barren. There is no life, but my own.
I've been wandering to and fro trying to find a way out.
I'm praying for a Savior—someone stronger, to lift me up
high above the steep mountains,
Where I once was. I have no strength to climb.
Where is the sun? Hidden?
Don't want to shine on me. Why?
In the valley, I guess.
I can't see the moon or the twinkling stars.
Where is the exit?
How did I come to this place?
I thirst. Thirst only for the living bread—God's Word.
It is the only bread to eat in this dry place.
In the valley, I am.
Waiting for a Savior—someone stronger than me, to lift me up high above the
steep mountain, and take me out of this dry, barren, and thirsty place.

Always turn to the "living bread", the Word of God, for spiritual strength.
Jesus gave His flesh, which symbolizes our "living bread". We should thirst for
the Word of God when in our valley moments. We will find that he will send
nourishment to our spiritual souls and lift us up above the towering mountains
once again.

Dear Lord, it is my prayer _____
Ramona Stevens
Decatur, Georgia

AHA Moment
Listen before you speak.

OPEN IT, SHUT IT, AND CHECK IT

"Understand this, my dear brothers and sisters:
You must all be quick to listen, slow to speak, and slow to get angry."
James 1:19 (NLT)

Working in the front office of an elementary school has daily challenges. Parents who are upset with the principal or a teacher often take it out on me since I am often the first person they encounter. After working in this position for a while, I find that being "dumped on" gets to me. Though I know I am not the object of their anger, it still gets me riled up when they yell at me!

There are times when I find that I don't wait for them to complete their conversation, I see the look on their face, or hear the frustration in their voice on the phone, and I start mentally planning how I will "set them straight." Most times, when I respond, it is with as much venom and frustration as they had when they began speaking to me, which only adds fuel to the fire.

Do you find that you are easily angered? When you are being spoken to, is your focus on formulating a response rather than listening to the person's concerns? God's word reminds us that we need to shut our mouths, open our ears, and check our anger if we are to please the Lord and be effective witnesses.

Dear Lord, help us to be conscious of what we say, how we say it, and when we are reacting in anger. Show us daily how to become open to hear what others are saying, but most of all, what You are saying. In Jesus' name we pray, Amen.

Dear Lord, it is my prayer _____
Sylvia Riddick
Berkeley, California

Stay focused, obedient, and have faith that where God is, all is well.

KEEP BELIEVING! KEEP WORKING!

"Now faith is the substance of things hoped for, the evidence of things not seen."
Hebrews 11:1 (KJV)

What are we hoping for? What is our action plan in regard to our hope?

Some time ago, I had a health challenge that negatively affected my speech. I often knew what I wanted to say, but I could not say it. The words just would not come out. I tried different ways to make what I was having difficulty stating, be understood. Sometimes, I would try to describe things as best I could, or I would point to something that suggested that thing. At other times, I would ask someone to help by expressing it. When I would become frustrated, I would stop, and then start over by trying again, as I still had hope.

We, in the same manner as the body of Christ Jesus, must persevere by whatever it takes. Faith, according to James 2:17 (ESV) reads, ". . . if it does not have works, It's dead." Let us do the work of God as we know it.

As the Holy Spirit moves, we should obey when, where, and how He wants. We don't have to broadcast that we are doing the will of God. When we are operating under the unction of the Holy Ghost, it will be evident to whom it is meant. God sees all. Matthew 25:40 (KJV) reads, "And the King shall answer and say unto them, Verily I say unto you, Inasmuch as ye have done it unto one of the least of these my brethren, ye have done it unto me." Do not abandon your compassionate edge, and don't look for cheerleaders.

Dear Lord, it is my prayer _____
Lajean Jones
Marrero, Louisiana

AHA Moment

... But God!

OH, BUT FOR THE GRACE OF GOD

"Trust in the Lord with all thine heart; and lean not unto thine own
understanding. In all thy ways acknowledge him, and he shall direct thy paths."
Proverbs 3:5-6 (KJV)

In the autumn of 2014, and unbeknownst to me, I had an issue of internal
bleeding caused by my intestines being folded like an accordion. Early one
morning, as I went to the restroom, I began hemorrhaging. I immediately woke
my husband, and told him that, "I need to go to the hospital, NOW!" We got
dressed, left home, and arrived at the hospital's emergency room within fifteen
minutes. After explaining my dilemma to the admission staff, I was immediately
admitted. Although I had not been assigned a room, I remained in the emergency area to be monitored for about twelve hours because my blood pressure
was at stroke level.

Since I was heavily sedated, the events that followed are unclear. However,
upon awakening in a room the next morning, I was being transported to surgery!
An angel, who happened to be my daughter-in-law and the manager of the emergency room, came in and asked, "Where are you taking her?" The technicians
responded, "We're taking her to surgery." My daughter-in-law asked, "For what?
Who is the surgeon? Have you explained to her husband or her what is happening?" She then began explaining in layman's terms to us, my condition, and
what needed to be done. She was familiar with the hospital staff, and preferred
another surgeon to perform my procedure. Unfortunately, he was not available
at that time, my surgery was urgent, so we consented to the surgery.

When I awakened, on Monday, I realized that I had missed an entire day
being asleep and sedated. I was told that the surgery went well, and if I had waited
for another day, I possibly could have died.

I thank God for His grace and mercy, for I would not be here today.

Dear Lord, it is my prayer _____
Vernell Kennedy Smith
Decatur, Georgia

AHA Moment

God loves and protects you because He knows.

THE LORD IS OUR KEEPER

"Because thou hast made the LORD, which is my refuge, even the most High,
thy habitation; there shall no evil befall thee, neither shall any plague come
nigh thy dwelling. For he shall give his angels charge over thee,
to keep thee in all thy ways."
Psalm 91: 9-11 (KJV)

Progressing on this journey of living for Christ I did not know
On my way to work for HIS business I was trying to go.
It was a Christian bookstore opened recently
A disciple for Christ is what I was trying to be.
On the interstate I was driving, merrily traveling along
I hit something, could not steer, EVERYTHING seemed wrong.
There was absolutely no traffic which was amazing to see
Except, the blinking light pickup and the angel waiting for me.
He changed the torn up, chewed up tire in no time flat
Asked to follow him off the freeway and was gone just like that.
The torn up, chewed up tire was kept for a good little while,
As evidence of His goodness, grace, and a reason for a smile.
That was in the '90s and what is well recorded in my mind
No matter the circumstance or situation God is always on time.
Living for Christ is not to receive an earthly reward
But an opportunity to be an ambassador for our Lord.
Take an opportunity to ponder what He has done in your life
Your testimonies and times when He helped overcome strife.
What He's done for you, do you find opportunities to share?
A witness encouraging others to know He is always there.
Lord no matter the circumstances which Satan may throw my way, I pray.

Dear Lord, it is my prayer _____
Deitre Terrell
Douglasville, Georgia

AHA Moment

Our testimonies are delightful to God.

DON'T GIVE UP, DON'T GIVE IN

"... be ready always to give an answer to every man that asketh you
for a reason of the hope that is in you ..."
1 Peter 3:15 (KJV)

Almost every day we are faced with moments to exercise our faith in God and in biblical principles. These acts of faith please Him, and those who diligently seek Him are rewarded. During her illness, my mother experienced a break in her skin, which developed into an open wound on her leg. Physicians, nurses, and wound specialists worked untiringly to dress and heal the wide "hole" that had formed. Talk about pain—and what a horrible sight! After many attempts to fix the problem, blood circulation stopped functioning properly, and the doctor decided that it would be best to amputate her leg. In his opinion, the wound would never heal.

After explaining to my mom his professional treatment plan and solution, her immediate response was an emphatic, "NO!" With eyes closed and her characteristic sweet smile and tone, she explained she wanted to leave this world <u>with</u> her legs. The doctor glanced at me with a desperate look for support to approve the surgery. I seized the opportunity to share with him that our mother always listened to the Holy Spirit for His direction regarding her health. As he left looking perplexed, I prayed to the Lord to heal the wound before his next visit. A month later he returned. To his surprise, the "hole" had closed and swelling was greatly diminished! What a testimony to answered prayers and God's awesome healing power.

God responds when His people proclaim their faith in Him, and find the courage to believe and obey Him in all things. My prayer is, "Lord, help me to . . . walk by faith, and not by sight" 1 Corinthians 5:7 (KJV).

Dear Lord, it is my prayer _____
Nadine Luster-Poe
Seattle, Washington

AHA Moment

Don't let distractions keep you from giving God your all.

STAY FOCUSED ON GOD; DON'T BECOME DISTRACTED

"Restore unto me the joy of thy salvation; and uphold me with thy free spirit."
Psalm 51:12 (KJV)

There were two men who were partners in a business. They had become successful over the years. However, slowly one partner got off focus and began to associate with another businessman. He felt that he was doing no harm, because his partner did not know about the relationship.

Eventually, he was so wrapped-up with the other businessman that he was unaware that the relationship with his successful business partner was being lost. After all, this is the person who had helped him get where he was in life. Although his partner could see him drifting, he could not heed to the warnings. He kept holding on to what he felt was important, while at the same time, he was moving slowly away from his partner. He felt comfortable as long as he could see what his business partner was doing while continuing to work in the business.

Unfortunately, he refused to believe that his original partner was observing every move, and could therefore, clearly see that he had an outside partner that interfered with their business growth. He continued moving very slowly and cautiously (so he thought) in the same direction. However, one day he looked back and realized that he had moved so far away, he could vaguely see his partner.

This story reflects some Christian's relationship with the Savior. Sometimes we become distracted with the many things we encounter in our daily routine and gradually move away from serving God. We justify our actions by explaining what we are still doing, going to church periodically. Remember, God knows everything about us and is patiently waiting for us to return and surrender all to Him. We should be like David and ask God to restore the joy of our salvation.

Dear Lord, it is my prayer _____

O'ka Duren
Jackson, Mississippi

AHA Moment

Ultimate joy passes all understanding.

EMBRACING JOY

"Fulfill ye my joy, that ye be likeminded, having the same love, being of one accord, of one mind. Let nothing be done through strife or vainglory; but in lowliness of mind let each esteem other better than themselves."
Philippians 2:2-3 (KJV)

In this day and time, trying to embrace joy is a very challenging task with so much unrest in the world. It now seems to be seeping in the church at a rapid pace. I believe that if we find the joy that God has, we will be made complete.

Our emotions can trip us if we are not careful of with whom we keep company. We need to rally around positive thinking sisters and brothers who can encourage us, and help us to maintain our joy. I believe that joy completes and fulfills us, embraces our hearts with love, and helps us to be more sensitive to other feelings.

Join with me inviting Jesus to fill our hearts with joy that is contagious, and to place people around us that we can encourage. Also, ask Him to help us to see the areas in which we need to grow, so that we can become more effective with what He has charged us with doing. After all, the ultimate goal of this journey isn't about us. On the other hand, it's about finding peace that fills our hearts with ultimate joy.

"Embrace Jesus!
Let him be the ultimate joy.
Let his thoughts be our thoughts.
Let his ways be our ways.
Embrace others with love, joy and understanding."

Dear Lord, it is my prayer _____
Linda Campbell
Terry, Mississippi

AHA Moment

HE is worthy to be praised!

I WILL BLESS THE LORD

"I will bless the LORD at all times: His praise shall continually be in my mouth.
O magnify the LORD with me, and let us exalt his name together."
Psalm 34:1, 3 (KJV)

Psalm 34 is one of my favorite passages of scripture. When I think about praising God continually—regularly, without interruption, constantly—I'm reminded of how we will be worshipping and praising God in eternity. Until we get to eternity, what is our praise like here on earth? When things are going well, it is fairly easy to praise God continually. However, when faced with difficult situations, can you still praise God continually?

I walk many mornings, praying as I go. When I began this morning walk journey, I did not walk and pray. Instead, I used that time to schedule appointments, return phone calls or talk with family/friends. One morning I tried unsuccessfully to reach someone to talk with while I walked. God said to me, "Why don't you talk to me?" I immediately hung up the phone, and repented. Since then, I have been "talking to God" as I walk.

There are benefits that I have discovered while walking and talking to God:

1. The physical being, as well as spiritual, is nurtured.
2. God has the solution for any difficult circumstance. "The righteous cry out, and the Lord hears, and delivers them out of all their troubles" Psalm 34:17 (NKJV).
3. God will not repeat what you share with Him—it is confidential!
4. We can enjoy all that God has created for us—the beautiful flowers, birds flying in formation, the green grass, and blue skies. "The heavens declare the glory of God; the skies proclaim the work of His hands" Psalm 19:1 (NIV).

Our God is awesome and worthy to be praised. You can't help but praise Him continually—regularly, without interruption, constantly—for all that He has done!

I will bless the LORD at all times!

Dear Lord, it is my prayer _____
Elma R. Smith
Decatur, Georgia

AHA Moment
Jesus is Real!

MY LIFE REDEDICATED

"And be not conformed to this world: but be ye transformed by the r
enewing of your mind, that ye may prove what is that good,
and acceptable, and perfect, will of God."
Romans 12:2 (KJV)

As a child, I was raised in the church. My family and I attended church regularly—it felt like we were there all of the time! But it was in Sunday School that I learned about God. One day while praying, I asked God, "Who is Jesus?" I heard His voice for the first time when He replied, "Jesus Christ is God's Son." I believed Him and continued studying the Bible with excitement.

When I was age 13, I was diagnosed with Bi-Polar Disease requiring that I take twelve pills daily. This disease caused me to hear voices in my head, which resulted in my burning down our home. My cousin, who is also a pastor, prayed that God heal me. I believed, and God healed me of this disease.

As an adult, I found myself in a backslidden condition after being a victim of domestic abuse. You name it, and I did it. The Bible talks about an idle mind being the devil's workshop. Satan is cunning, and it is easy to fall into his traps when you're not following God. He tried to devour me!

One day my cousin invited me to attend his church. While there, I had great praise and worship experiences. I rededicated my life to God, and it was as if I had a blood transfusion. The Holy Spirit filled my heart, and I began thanking and praising God for giving me a second chance. Thank God for second chances. I was later baptized and am now serving Him with joy.

You too, can experience this joy. Give your life to Jesus Christ and begin experiencing the goodness of God.

Dear Lord, it is my prayer _____
Denise Henderson Thompson
Hyattsville, Maryland

AHA MOMENT

Trust God's Precious Son.

TRUST THE RIGHT GPS

"In all thy ways acknowledge Him, and He shall direct thy paths."
Proverbs 3:6 (KJV)

I was invited to attend a retirement celebration in very small rural area where I had never been before. I was compelled to attend, even though I did not know how to get to there. I put all my trust in this new man-made technology known as a *Global Positioning System (GPS)* to help me get there safely and on time. After entering the address, I began my journey, listened to, and followed the directions. The GPS also informed me of the distance and where to turn. It would re-route me if I made a wrong turn.

Finally, the system said, "You have arrived at your destination on the right." However, I saw only soybean fields on both sides. I knew this could not be the correct location, so I reached for my cell phone in hopes of getting better directions — but I had no service! I became very upset and frustrated, and began crying because I was lost. Then, a quiet small voice said to me, "Trust in the Lord with all thine heart; and lean not unto thine own understanding. In all thy ways acknowledge Him, and He shall direct thy paths" Proverbs 3:5-6 (KJV). I hear you, Lord.

I immediately drove in the opposite direction while saying, "Jesus please direct my path home or to this event." After driving about three miles, I saw the road sign. I turned and there was the house! I had arrived with the help of God's Precious Son.

The Lord gave us the best GPS system we can have when He gave us His Precious Son, Jesus. This experience taught me that man-made devises can only help us to a certain extent. We must put our trust in God for He will direct our path.

Dear Lord, it is my prayer _____
Equilla Miller
Louisville, Mississippi

AHA Moment

Jesus always keeps His promises.

JESUS WILL BE THERE WHEN YOUR LIFE TURNS UPSIDE DOWN

"... and, lo, I am with you alway, even unto the end of the world. Amen."
Matthew 28:20 (KJV)

It was a first Sunday morning driving to Sunday School, when a sudden impact with another car caused my car to spin, twirl, and flip over. As my car headed toward a nearby canal, my granddaughter cried out, "Granny, we are going into the canal!" My reply was, "Yes, we are, but Jesus will meet us there." As the car continued across the embankment down into the canal, we both cried out, "Jesus! Help us!" We landed and began struggling to get our seatbelts off before the water entered the car. Immediately, men appeared jumping into the canal to rescue us; first pulling Tayla out through the only escapable window, and then working to get my feet released from the immersed front end. Suddenly, we were standing on the banks (without a spot of dirt on my white suit) waiting for the emergency vehicles to arrive. The Spirit then spoke softly to me, "I promised to be with you always."

That first Sunday experience in 2014 was pivotal in Tayla's relationship with Jesus. It also reaffirmed the promise of His faithfulness to me. God's faithfulness does not depend on where we are, or what we are doing. It is solely based on the love and assurances to us as found in His Word.

As Jesus greeted his disciples, He gave them power, along with instructions to go, teach, and baptize in the name of the Father, Son and Holy Ghost. But more importantly, Jesus reassured them of His faithfulness to them saying, "... and, lo, I am with you alway, even unto the end of the world. Amen." As we go, teach, and baptize, we will encounter some upside-down experiences, but remember, Jesus will also be there!

Dear Lord, it is my prayer _____
Betty Ratcliff
New Orleans, Louisiana

AHA Moment

His grace allows us to endure our trials.

SQUIRRELLY MESS

"O Lord, my strength, and my fortress, and my refuge in time of distress."
Jeremiah 16:19 (KJV)

Everything seemed to go wrong at the same time. The water pipes had burst in the kitchen. The air conditioner had stopped working on a hot humid summer day. Just when I thought nothing else could go wrong, a mother squirrel and her family, without our knowledge, had taken up residency in our house. I realized there was an uninvited guest, when I went to the kitchen to get a pear. I saw a squirrel standing upright near the fruit bowl nibbling on a piece of fruit. It took three days of trap setting to catch the new residents, not one, but *three* squirrels. It was a "squirrely mess"! The mother squirrel caused more damage than one could imagine. Needless to say, I was neither "calm, cool, nor collected!"

When the challenges of life come our way, it's easy to let our circumstances overwhelm us. I cannot say that I quoted scriptures and offered prayers at the moment of the crisis. I had to purposely look for the positive, which did not seem possible at the time.

Even in our "squirrely mess", we can persevere with God's help. Our faith helps us to continue on, to seek, and to stand on His promises. We can remain faithful, steadfast, and grow from our experiences.

We can learn that grace is for the present from Hebrews 4:16 (ASV), "Let us therefore draw near with boldness unto the throne of grace, that we may receive mercy, and may find grace to help us in time of need."

I don't know what obstacles you may be facing today, but I do know you can overcome them. The trials in our lives can be used for our good to strengthen us if we hold on and allow God to complete His work in us.

Dear Lord, it is my prayer _____
June Bond
Houston, Texas

AHA Moment

Getting spiritually fit.

S.W.E.A.T.

"For the Lord is good. His unfailing love continues forever,
and his faithfulness continues to each generation."
Psalm 100:5 (NLT)

One day my co-worker and I were sharing our thoughts about working out in the mornings. I made the mistake of telling her that I do not sweat when I workout. Her immediate response to me was, "You haven't gotten a good workout unless you sweat. You even feel better sweating while you workout." That was for my physical body.

Then a few mornings later, I was reading Psalm 100 (NLT). God spoke to me and said, "Just as your physical body feels better when you workout and sweat, your spiritual body needs to do the same." I started sweating, giving my soul the spiritual workout that it needed in order for me to remain healthy in Him. This is how I **S.W.E.A.T.** during my spiritual workout:

S – Shout by expressing to God how glad I am to come before Him. (v. 1)

W – Worship by letting God know that I magnify and adore Him. (v. 2)

E – Enter by coming into His presence to glorify Him. (v. 4)

A – Acknowledge by letting God know that I am grateful to Him for being who He is. (v. 3)

T – Thank God by expressing gratitude for His many promises and bountiful blessings. (v. 4)

God inhabits the praises of His people. We can remain spiritually healthy by "sweating" and allowing God to give us a good workout while we are in His presence. We will feel better every time while getting spiritually fit serving Him.

Dear Lord, it is my prayer _____
Santa C. Jones
St. Louis, Missouri

AHA Moment

God is in the midst of the storm with you.

LEAN ON YOUR FAITH

"Knowing this, that the trying of your faith worketh patience."
James 1:3 (KJV)

In my life, I have been through numerous storms. Storms of life can be devastating, large or small. The storms in my life have been no exception. In December of 2012, I received news that rocked me to my core. My endocrinologist revealed that I had cancer.

Initially, I cried out and asked, "Why me?" I prayed, cried, and then asked for the strength to make it through. After drying my tears, I washed my face and began to walk in my faith. This was the faith I had leaned on so many times.

My pastor said, "Remember, you are just going through a storm. You will have the victory on the other side!" My children reminded me how many things I had gone through, and it was my faith in God that brought me through. I received many healing scriptures to read from my Sunday school teacher. My pastor and church family prayed for my healing, and I was praying, as well.

I have also been blessed with a doctor who is a believer in Jesus Christ. During this time, I reflected on my favorite songs: "Peace in the Midst of the Storm" and "God as the Final Say."

Because of my faith and daily affirmation, "GOD CAN AND WILL HEAL MY BODY." I am three years cancer-free—PRAISE GOD! Whatever your storm is, believe that in the midst of the storm, God is with you and will bring you through it.

Dear Lord, it is my prayer _____
Marilyn Pitts
Los Angeles, California

AHA Moment

Who are you singing to?

AN AUDIENCE OF ONE

"And whatever you do, do it heartily, as to the Lord and not to men."
Colossians 3:23 (NKJV)

I am a member of the Interdenominational Cleveland Community Choir. We come together weekly to fellowship, learn and rehearse songs, and to worship the Lord. The choir belongs to a National Choir Convention. Although there is no official competition, each choir wants to do their best at the convention.

One of our directors, Pastor Michael Dotson, penned a worship song. *"Holy, Holy. Lord you're holy. All creation declares your glory. Angels bow to hail your majesty. Holy,* holy, thou art God." During the rehearsal in which he first taught this song, the Holy Spirit came down and inhabited our praises! *"He is the King of Kings. He's the Lord of Lords. He's Holy, anointed. The one and only living God."* Each singer began to reflect on the goodness, greatness, and holiness of God. We moved from worship and praise through song, to spontaneous outbursts of worship and praise to God. We had our song for the convention!

At the convention, we eagerly awaited our turn to sing. The choir before us sang, *"No Weapon" (formed against me shall prosper),* and the Holy Spirit fell upon the room. People began to praise and worship the Lord for the promise of *"No Weapon".* I said to myself, "But wait convention, Cleveland has the song of the night! Hold your shout! Wait until we sing!" After the worship died down, and the service continued, we were called and sang *"Holy, Holy".* It went over well, but did not have the impact that we expected. Rarely, will an audience shout on two songs back to back! Secretly, we were disappointed. But I heard God say, "Who are you singing for? Your praise and worship should be directed towards Me, AN AUDIENCE OF ONE."

Dear Lord, please help us to remember that our praise and worship is to YOU, and YOU alone.

Dear Lord, it is my prayer _____
Beverly Golden
Cleveland, Ohio

AHA MOMENT

Peace comes with following the path God has for you.

PERFECT PEACE

"Thou wilt keep him in perfect peace, whose mind is stayed on thee:
because he trusteth in thee."
Isaiah 26:3 (KJV)

On an early fall evening, I was walking the trail in a local park, communing with God; enjoying the cool breeze and smells in the air; seeing changing colors on the trees; and feeling the warm sunshine on my face. My heart, spirit, mind, and body were rejoicing at the wondrous love of my God. God spoke into my spirit, and I began praising and worshiping Him in the park, while walking along the trail.

As I strolled along, I experienced the warmth of the sunshine peeping through the shade trees. Continuing up an incline raised my heart rate, so I sat down to rest. I felt the cool breeze on my face as I watched the birds. The splendor of nature caused me to pray, then, God gave me a message.

I compare this trail to life. We experience joy, peace, and meet many challenges and obstacles as we go about our journey. God provides us with enough sunshine to brighten our day and lighten our paths. When it gets hot, He sends a cool breeze so that we are able to cool down. If it gets too cool, keep going because the warm sun is going to shine, or just look up and see nature's beautiful colors. Sit and rest when you get tired.

People on the trail are focused and walking at their own pace. Sometimes, we may pass someone, and others may pass us as we journey through life.

Keep your mind on the trail as you walk. Enjoy your journey in perfect peace. God has already prepared and provided just what you need.

Dear Lord, it is my prayer _____
Betty C. Brown
Monroe, Louisiana

AHA MOMENT

Do we quit too soon? Do we "pray through?"
The watchman's job has no expiration/retirement date!

A FAITHFUL INTERCESSOR?

"I have posted watchmen on your walls, O Jerusalem; they will never be silent day or night. You who call on the Lord, give yourselves no rest, and give him no rest till he establishes Jerusalem and makes her the praise of the earth."
Isaiah 62:6-7 (NIV)

". . . always pray and not give up." Luke 18:1 (NIV)

I confess to growing weary; to becoming doubtful and fearful. I entered into a 40-day period of prayer, fervently stirring heaven's gates, expecting to see radical—IMMEDIATE—response. But it did not happen that way. I began to rationalize more than to trust and believe.

God forgive me! Allow me to take up the call to be a "watchman" once again. Re-kindle. Re-impassion. Set me higher on the wall so I can see farther.

You have placed me on the walls of my church, family, ministry, friends as a watchman, a sentinel. That means You are showing me lurking dangers that others may miss. You're giving me a broad perspective that does not just focus on close, immediate needs, but also foresees coming danger.

You expect me to give warnings relentlessly; to stay alert and not give in to boredom, weariness, or distractions; to persist in prayer and to continue to "bother" You with my concerns. I am to do this until those things that come against "unestablished Jerusalem" have been dealt with. You expect me to "pray and not lose heart" until:

(Insert your own list of things for which God is calling you to intercede)

1. _____
2. _____
3. _____

Isaiah 62:6-7 paraphrased, personalized: "I have posted <u>YOUR NAME</u> on your walls, O *(your church/family/community)*. *She* will never be silent day or night <u>YOUR NAME</u> you who call on the Lord, give *yourself* no rest, and give him no rest till he establishes *(your church/family/community)* and make them the praise of the earth." You must stay vigilant on your post!

Dear Lord, it is my prayer _____
Ethelyn Taylor
Chicago, Illinois

AHA MOMENT

Jesus offers salvation to all who will receive it.

WHAT IS ELITISM?

"... for God *sees* not as man sees, for man looks at the
outward appearance, but the Lord looks at the heart."
I Samuel 16:7b (NASB)

Today's social media affinity is deceiving many people. Why do we idolize celebrities, government officials and even pastors? Does the color of one's skin make one more important than others? What is most concerning lately is seeing more and more folks referring to themselves as gods and goddesses; turning away from Christ and idolizing race and themselves. This is *not* acceptable.

Jesus came to save sinners. Skin color, social status, tradition, cultural bans, and the opinions of people do not matter when a soul's eternal destiny is on the line. God does not show favoritism. The fact that Jesus saw the *heart* of the individual, not just their label, no doubt inspired the people to know Him better. They recognized Jesus as a righteous man of God—the miracles He performed bore witness to that—and they saw His compassion and sincerity.

Jesus did not allow social status or cultural norms to dictate His relationships with people. He sought the lost sheep and was not above spending time with the outcasts of society. When Matthew hosted a dinner party, Jesus gladly accepted the invitation. It was an opportunity to share the good news of the kingdom. Jesus was criticized for His actions. (Matthew 4:23)

Jesus did not require people to change before coming to Him. He met them where they were, spoke truth to them, and extended grace to them in their circumstances. Change would come to those who repented and accepted Christ. Jesus did not come to save the "good, self-righteous people", but He came to save those who knew they were *not* good and *admitted* freely that they needed salvation.

Each one of us should make it a personal mission to treat everyone as we would want to be treated; avoid putting people on pedestals or treating some better than others. And be ready to share the Gospel.

Dear Lord, it is my prayer _____
Brittany Byars Williams
Houston, Texas

AHA Moment

GOD KNOWS YOUR NAME

"For God is not unrighteous to forget your work and labour of love,
which ye have shewed toward his name, in that ye have ministered
to the saints, and do minister."
Hebrews 6:10 (KJV)

There are so many believers who came to walk with Christ after illness, bitter losses, incarceration, or injury; all as a result of sin. Basically, God had to sit them down and get their attention in order to use them. Then there are those who received Christ without needing to be convinced that He is the way, the truth and the life.

I joined a church. My faith grew and my walk got closer as God used me in numerous ministries for His glory. There came a time when I started feeling overlooked and unappreciated. I felt that even though I displayed a hunger for the Word and wanted to be fed and edified, that the grand displays of support and appreciation went to those whose habitual sin brought them to a place where they are clawing their way to a Savior. I started feeling resentful. This disturbed me so I prayed and asked for comfort, and someone shared Hebrew 6:10. God revealed to me that the devil is always trying to make us doubt our dedication to Christ. I was shown that many people need extra encouragement and assistance to stay with Him. It's amazing to want to stand in His marvelous light without needing to be first consumed by darkness and dragged through the fire. What a blessing to have almost gotten Him for free. Almost, because we all fall short at times, but if you just heed to the Holy Spirit's conviction, Satan will fail at tripping you up off your walk.

Keep giving the glory to God and he will stay faithful to comfort your spirit by quietly acknowledging you. Hallelujah!

Dear Lord, it is my prayer _____
Doni Mason
Long Beach, California

AHA Moment

He will light your path.

GUIDING LIGHT

"Thy word is a lamp unto my feet, and a light unto my path."
Psalm 119:105 (KJV)

Lighthouses are objects of fascination. With a bright light, they guide passing ships in the fog. I have never needed to use a lighthouse before, but I have certainly needed that guiding light.

One Christmas, my daughter and I left Louisiana to visit my youngest daughter in Chicago. During our visit, we got the news report that a big snowstorm was coming. In an effort to outrun the snow, we cut our trip short and headed back to Louisiana. Little did we know we would drive straight into the blizzard! The snow blanketed the highway and visibility was practically zero. This was our first time driving in the snow! I was praying for the snow to stop and my daughter was praying for a way out. I suggested we stop since she could barely see, but my daughter was afraid if we stopped, we would be covered in snow or worse, struck by another vehicle. We could not exit because we could hardly see exit signs, so we continued to drive at 10 mph; praying constantly. When things seemed the worst, a white SUV appeared alongside us. Its lights provided light for us! That SUV stayed by our side for miles giving us comfort that we were not alone on the highway.

All of a sudden, the snow stopped, and the SUV was gone! I believe God sent that SUV to be a guiding light for us through the blinding snow. The Lord answered both of our prayers. I am so thankful we had His word to trust in. I believe Proverbs 3:5-6 even more so now: "Trust in the Lord with all thine heart and lean not to thine own understanding. In all thy ways acknowledge Him and He shall direct thy paths."

I challenge you to trust God in every situation—He will send His "guiding light" to see you through.

Dear Lord, it is my prayer _____
Sybil Young
Franklinton, Louisiana

AHA Moment

God knows our every need.

TRUST IN HIM AND HE WILL DO IT

"This is the confidence we have in approaching God:
that if we ask anything according to His will, He hears us."
I John 5:14 (NIV)

Having faith is an exercise to trust God, believe in Him and know that He will do what He said He will do. He is going to fulfill every promise He made.

On January 18, 2016, as I settled down for the day, I received a phone call from my grandson in Tulsa, Oklahoma. This was his third call. He mentioned he felt nauseated and really sick. I told him to call 911 if he needed to. He agreed and our conversation ended. Thirty minutes later he called back and said he was driving himself to the hospital. I started praying on the phone with him as he drove.

He arrived at the hospital and proceeded to the emergency room. He noticed someone was following him and he thought this person was going to harm him; instead the person showed him where he needed to go and then disappeared. After about 3 hours, I received a call saying he was being admitted to the hospital. The doctor informed me they were running tests and his condition may require emergency surgery. I immediately notified our fellow church members to begin praying and also made phone calls to family members in Oklahoma. When we arrived in Tulsa the next morning, my grandson had already had surgery and was in recovery. My other concern was that he had family members with him in case we did not arrive in time. God saw him through; prayers answered.

If we know that He hears us—whatever we ask—we know that we have what we asked for.

Dear Lord, it is my prayer _____
Gladys D. King
Pasadena, California

AHA Moment

Jesus is the only way.

LOCKED OUT

"Jesus saith unto him, I am the way, the truth, and the life:
no man cometh unto the Father but by me."
John 14:6 (KJV)

On several occasions, I hate to admit, I have found myself locked out. Locked out of my car and locked out of my house. What happened? I unintentionally set the lock, closed the door and then remembered the key is on the inside. The key was not lost. I knew exactly where it was, but I just could not get to it. My immediate thoughts were how to quickly and safely gain entry. I could call my husband to bring his key, or look for an open window.

In this life it is easy to get a spare or duplicate key to almost anything. Jesus is saying in John 14:6 that He and He alone is the key to the door of heaven which leads to eternal life.

In so many instances, we see people among us who want to live their lives their own way, ignoring God's Word and only calling on the Lord when there is a major calamity. Ask yourself this question, "Have I ever intentionally locked God out of my life in any way?" If the answer is yes, then know that when you lock God out, you have placed yourself on the throne.

Jesus wants everyone to open the door to their heart. He will not force you to let Him inside. Jesus has freely made himself available. He is the key to everlasting life. When the door to heaven is finally shut, which side of the door will you be on?

Dear Lord, it is my prayer _____
Linda Martin
Memphis, Tennessee

AHA Moment

Serve the Lord with Gladness.

AT LEAST ONE

"For though I be free from all men, yet have I made myself servant unto all, that I might gain the more. To the weak became I as weak, that I might gain the weak: I am made all things to all men, that I might by all means save some."
1 Corinthians 9:19, 22 (KJV)

At times it is very easy to get discouraged when you feel as though no one is listening to you as you are sharing the gospel. But just as you are about to throw in the towel, you will find that you are actually reaching someone. 1 Corinthians 9:19 reminds us that we may be free from all, but we are still servants to everyone in order to bring souls into the kingdom of God. Is serving popular? Not always. Is serving easy? Not always. Is serving rewarding? Not always materially, but it is spiritually.

Serving God to win souls for the kingdom requires our ability to adapt to the current situation. Sometimes we must become weak (I Corinthians 9:22), as we serve the weak. However, in the end, when at least one soul comes into the fold because of your serving, you have gained a star in your incorruptible crown.

Ask the Lord to help you to serve as His Son Jesus Christ served others. Serve the Lord with a glad heart knowing that serving is what is required to bring others to Him.

Dear Lord, it is my prayer _____
Alicia Conerly
Jayess, Mississippi

AHA Moment

Our breakthrough is in our praise and worship.

TOUGH TIMES

"We are troubled on every side, yet not distressed; we are perplexed, but not in despair; Persecuted, but not forsaken; cast down, but not destroyed;"
2 Corinthians 4:8-9 (KJV)

Life sometimes has a way of knocking us down; making us feel like God has left us or forgotten about us. We know the bible says that God will never leave us nor forsake us, but life will cause us to doubt the *very* Word and the God that we say we so strongly believe in. Life's challenges do not play favorites. It crosses all barriers and does not care how rich or poor you are. Educated or uneducated, preacher or praise leader, Sunday School teacher or evangelist. Life will 'put you on blast'! It will challenge us to the point, in some cases, to turn our backs on this great God. Preachers preach about this great God, choirs sing about this great God, teachers teach about Him. Some of us are taught at an early age about Him, but life has *more to teach* us about Him. All that we have learned and shouted about eventually challenges our faithfulness to the One who has always been faithful to us. This is the time to draw closer and know Him more intimately.

There came a time for me to learn something that I thought I knew already; how to praise and worship. I was taught and learned how praise and worship can become my spiritual weapons through my storms. I then realized the breakthrough *was* in my act of praise and worship. God will never leave us, and the Holy Spirit will always lead us in the right direction. The joy of the Lord is my strength.

Dear Lord, it is my prayer _____
Brenda Hartwell
Los Angeles, California

AHA Moment

Despite my limitations, God still has a purpose.

HAVE FAITH IN GOD

"For with God nothing shall be impossible."
Luke 1:37(KJV)

In September 2012, while in a local hospital, I had a near death experience. As a result of either a medication error by the staff or a reaction to the medication, I was left with some brain damage. I went from being independent to total dependence on my dear husband and family for my care. However, through perseverance, determination and most of all trust in God, I can function independently today despite residual long and short-term memory loss.

One day, while having a 'pity party' and considering suicide because I had lost my job of 13 years and had to give up my nursing career which I loved dearly, God spoke to me, "I didn't bring you this far to leave you! Where is your faith?" Ever since that day, I have asked God to use me in His service and to let my testimony encourage others.

No matter what obstacles you face in this life, always remember that God loves you and His purpose in everything that happens is to make you more like Jesus Christ. Satan cannot defeat us if we believe that God is working for our good. I know, without a doubt that I am a living testimony. Ask God how you can be used in His service all of the days of your life.

Dear Lord, it is my prayer _____
Lillie M. Kendrick
Terry, Mississippi

AHA MOMENT

I attest to the power of God, that the Lord will restore,
support and strengthen you.

RESTORE, SUPPORT AND STRENGTHEN (RSS)

"In his kindness God called you to share in his eternal glory by means of Christ
Jesus. So **after you have suffered a little while** He will **restore**, **support**, and
strengthen you, and He will place you on a firm foundation."
1 Peter 5:10 (NLT)

Labor pains and delivery of my first child was horrific. I pushed so hard that
I burst a blood vessel in my eye. The doctor used forceps to remove the baby
and bruised both sides of his head; he had two large lumps on his head that
looked like Mickey Mouse ears. He was kept in the hospital for 10 days because
of jaundice.

I returned home from the hospital and fell into a deep depression. I began
to question God. I just didn't know how things would turn out. The baby and I
had to see specialists; he had fluid in his head, and I had to see an eye specialist.
I was sad, weary and spent after pumping breast milk and running it to the hospital day after day. I was a 'big mess'.

I recall my pastor coming to our apartment to pray and support us during
our suffering. Our brother-in-law also came and told us that our baby would be
all right. Although the depression had me thinking my son was cursed, God had
my loving husband reassure me that God would give us **strength.**

I will tell it anywhere I go that the Lord will **RSS** you. The Lord **restored**
my vision. My son is a healthy and smart young man who plays piano, having
taken no lessons. The Lord sent people my way to encourage, pray, and **support**
me. This **strengthened** my faith. Today I am a living witness that after this trial,
the Lord is my **RSS.**

Dear Lord, it is my prayer _____
Colleen Hendricks
Los Angeles, California

AHA MOMENT

Remember the rainbow; God keeps His promises.

RAINBOW PROMISE

"I have set my rainbow in the clouds, and it will be the sign
of the covenant between me and the earth."
Genesis 9:13 (NIV)

Driving is when some of my best times are spent with the Lord. The drive when I am not running late; no appointments, no traffic, **no back seat or side driver**, and no one asking for something to eat or drink. As a safety habit, I adjust the radio to my favorite talk radio station before I start.

On this day, I did not turn on the radio. I began to talk to the Lord regarding a concern that had been on my heart for a while. I asked Him for confirmation that the situation was going to work out. As I drove, I noticed the sky was blue, the sun beaming and some of the clouds seemed to be hanging from invisible strings. Over the clouds was a large colorful rainbow. I had never seen a rainbow so beautiful. It was picture perfect.

In awe of the rainbow, the Lord began to respond to me. He reminded me of the covenant He set in Genesis. The rainbow is a sign; a confirmation that He keeps His promises. One day instead of driving, I was walking with a bowed down head. This time, a beautiful rainbow was on the sidewalk. Jesus said to me, "Lift up your head and remember the rainbow promise." Now after each rainfall, I search for rainbows.

We do not get a chance to see the rainbow often, but remember that God is faithful in fulfilling His promises. He is a promise keeper. In the 5th stanza of the old hymn, "Standing on the Promises" by R. Kelso Carter, we sing... Standing on the promises that cannot fail, When the howling storms of doubt and fear assail, By the Living Word of God, I shall prevail, Standing on the Promises of God.

Let's continue to believe that God is faithful in fulfilling His promises.

Dear Lord, it is my prayer _____
Carolyn Pittman
Detroit, Michigan

AHA MOMENT

Only Christ can save us; we cannot save ourselves.

SUPERFICIAL CHRISTIANS AFFLICTED RESTRAINED AND STRICKEN

"But He was wounded for our transgressions, He was bruised for our iniquities:
the chastisement of our peace was upon Him;
and with His stripes we are healed."
Isaiah 53:5 (KJV)

Close your eyes and let's imagine for a second. You take a deep breath, you steady your feet, and you begin your breathtaking feat onto a 100-foot tight rope without a net. The crowd below is silent so that you may concentrate on making it to the other side . . . and you make it!

Now continue to imagine. You once again begin the same feat but this time on a 150-foot tight rope. You had people in the crowd before who were on your side but are now wishing you fail at this attempt. The crowd is screaming, yelling; a mere distraction. You lose your balance and fall but catch yourself and now have to pull yourself to the end using your *own* hands; no net, no rope. Finally, you reach the end. Your hands are bloody and scarred. You are scared and frustrated. "What was I thinking?" What if those thoughts were our Lord and Savior's? "What was I thinking carrying that cross?" "I should have listened to the crowd and gave up. My hands are worn out." Our Lord carried that cross alone; but not for himself. He carried it for you and me. He looked death in the face and didn't flinch. Because He embraced the company of the lowest, we are here today.

Let's take the time to embrace the reason why we have the right to everlasting life. Our Lord hung, bled, and died because He knew that we would be fragile. So, let's not forget where our healing originated.

Dear Lord, it is my prayer _____
Stephanie Ervin
Monroe, Louisiana

SING A SONG

"... Sing with grace in your hearts to the Lord"
Colossians 3:16 (KJV)

How many times have we found ourselves humming or singing commercials or popular tunes? Somewhere along life's way, I gradually became aware that the Holy Spirit can and will utilize whatever is in our memory bank to calm, comfort, compel and convict us to look to Him as the source of our well-being. Singing is a divine tool.

Biblical accounts testify to the power of singing. Note the singing shepherd warrior, King David, who sang until demons were subdued in his leader King Saul. What about the singing duo Paul and Silas, who sang until their chains of bondage were loosed in jail? Can we not be inspired by the singing women of God, Miriam sister of Moses, and Prophetess Judge Deborah, in thankfulness to God?

The music of numerous gospel song writers and hymnists can be of great inspiration to those who discover its value. In my darkest hours, I have remembered the words of divinely inspired messages in song. One most memorable moment was the recalling of the comforting song, "I'll Trust Him Just the Same," penned by Charles P. Jones. It was a selection that had been one of my least favorite hymns. Now I'm intentional about the songs that I plant in the garden of my mind, knowing that they can produce a harvest of blessings.

Why not sing a song of traditional praise like, "Blessed Assurance Jesus is Mine" when confronted with a world of uncertainties; contemporary hymn "Because He Lives I Can Face Tomorrow" by Gloria and Bill Gaither; songs of encouragement like "I Feel Like Going On" by Keith Pringle, and giving credit to the Almighty with "Every Praise Is To Our God" by Hezekiah Walker? Singing our way through life can become a powerful way to live... it's more than mere enjoyment or entertainment.

God rejoices over us with singing, and we should sing regardless the circumstance.

Dear Lord, it is my prayer _____
Sharon Collins
Seattle, Washington

AHA Moment

What does God require?

80/20

"He hath shewed thee, O man, what *is* good; and what doth the LORD require of thee, but to do justly, and to love mercy, and to walk humbly with thy God?"
Micah 6:8 (KJV)

Some time ago, I was in the doctor's office, telling her proudly of my workout regimen and the many miles on the track I had been logging. I thought my doctor was going to be so pleased if not impressed with my workout efforts. She let me finish and then said matter-of-factly; "Exercise is 20% of your health, nutrition is 80%." I had not been as dedicated in my eating patterns as the scale and blood work confirmed.

When the doctor said 80/20 it occurred to me, what else in my life had I been doing at 100% but was merely weighted at 20%? I was not as focused on the 80%, because that portion required more dedication; changing mindsets and patterns, doing what did not come easy and on and on.

It occurred to me to find out what God requires. God said for us to do what is morally right with all. He also said for us to love; to show compassion and forgiveness toward all whom is within one's power to do so. God advises us not to punish or harm, but to walk with Him in such a way that shows a low estimate of our importance. Today, we can read this scripture in many translations, but it tells us what God requires; there's no 80/20 to it.

Dear Lord, it is my prayer _____
Pearl Wise
Monroe, Louisiana

AHA MOMENT
God will not leave us.

THE HEALING ONLY GOD COULD PROVIDE

"Then Jesus answered and said unto her, O woman, great is thy faith: be it unto thee even as thou wilt. And her daughter was made whole from that very hour."
Matthew 15:28 (KJV)

Two weeks after my daughter Malia was born we received devastating news that Malia had Sickle Cell Anemia. This disease and blood disorder caused Malia so much pain and suffering during her early childhood. She accepted Jesus as her personal savior and was baptized. She prayed for God to cure her and take away her pain. Through tears, doctors' visits, pain, and numerous hospital stays, Malia's spirit and faith remained strong.

In May of 2015 Malia started to have strokes on her brain. This news did not shake our faith because we knew God would not leave us. We read in Hebrews 13:5, "let your conversation be without covetousness; and be content with such things as ye have: for he hath said, I will never leave thee, nor forsake thee."

Malia visited a Bone Marrow Transplant Specialist in October of the same year. We were praying for a cure and a bone marrow transplant was her only option. Although her Dad was fearful, Malia received a bone marrow transplant from him on December 15, 2015.

On January 27, 2016, Malia's blood test confirmed 100% healing of an illness we were told that she would battle for her entire life.

We thank our merciful God for being a God that will never leave us; a God that has the cure when there was no cure. My daughter is a living testimony of His Grace and Mercy.

Dear Lord, it is my prayer _____
Cortessa Wallace
Pearl, Mississippi

AHA MOMENT

Be ready and willing to receive Jesus as Lord.

HAVE YOU LEARNED TO TRUST GOD?

"Trust in the LORD with all thine heart; and lean not unto thine own
understanding. In all thy ways acknowledge him,
and he shall direct thy paths."
Proverbs 3:5-6 (KJV)

During my maturing season, I was married, had a child and unhappy. I was 'unevenly yoked'. I was working to provide for a home that was not really a home. We were not focused on God. Yes, we were married and in a church; but the principles of God's expectations were not taught. We did not stand a chance against the principalities of darkness that sought out to destroy God's strongest union, the family. It starts with those before us that prayed for us. This was the net that kept us bound and covered by His blood. The power of prayer was present but not prevalent in my household.

But one day, when I had almost given up due to the pains of miscarriage, a husband who could not console me, and another child who did not understand, God stepped in! He entered my body and I could not move. He started from the top of my head and by the time He moved downward, I could see a misty vapor. I had no idea what was happening to me, but I remained calm and still. When I felt it was safe to move, I looked around and nothing was there.

This was the day the Lord reminded me that I had not been forgotten. He loved me. The Lord knew that my heart would receive Him. This was the day I began sincerely hearing from God, then, my self-worth was renewed. God acknowledged that I had indeed been on the right path. I found me and my God in the midst of my storm. This was the day I learned to trust God. He saved me! Always keep your heart open to trust God and receive His love.

Dear Lord, it is my prayer _____
JoAnne Boykin
Washington, District of Columbia

AHA Moment

Shed the guilt by having a repenting heart!

GOD'S GREAT LOVE

"But God commendeth his love toward us, in that,
while we were yet sinners, Christ died for us."
Romans 5:8 (KJV)

How many times have I asked, "Lord, please forgive me, I won't do it anymore?" Then, I go back and commit the same trespass again. I've failed God too many times to count, yet He faithfully wakes me up each morning, with His breath to breathe, His energy to work, and His strength to continue each day. Each morning I wake up saying, "Good morning Father God, Holy Spirit, Lord Jesus, Creator of all, Giver of life, Savior, Comforter, and Deliverer of my soul. As my Teacher and Guide, help me to do what is pleasing in Your sight today."

Somehow, throughout the day, I did not hear His voice, or feel His gentle nudge to be patient, kind, or to keep my mouth shut. I felt ashamed that when I asked for peace, I didn't accept it when He offered it to me. I chose to fight my own battles. Some days, I listen well, and I rejoice in Him. On other days, I do not. However, in the midst of it all, the Holy Spirit gently reminds me that while I was yet a sinner, Christ died for me!

Today, I have a repenting heart. Tomorrow I may have my own selfish agenda, then, still have to repent. Either way, God's great love continues to sustain me. I have learned that if I could keep myself, Christ would not have had to die for my sins. I have also learned to shed the guilt of not having done it right and to embrace the peace and joy that comes with repentance. God forgave us before we realized we needed to be forgiven.

So repent and let God restore your peace and joy today!

Dear Lord, it is my prayer _____
Tracey Cleveland
Upper Marlboro, Maryland

AHA MOMENT

We all have been a broken crayon some time in our life.

BROKEN CRAYONS STILL COLOR

"And I will restore to you the years that the locust hath eaten, the cankerworm,
and the caterpillar, and the palmerworm, my great army
which I sent among you. "
Joel 2:25 (KJV)

Examine a new box of crayons and a bag of broken crayons on a table before children. Of course, the new box is ripped apart with excitement. Nobody used the broken crayons with no tips, paper worn off, or different pieces in a zip lock bag. Let's consider Rahab the harlot. She was hurt, disrespected, and wanted something more. She knew about the God who had parted the Red Sea. Could that same God use a broken piece of crayon like her? Yes, God used her to hide two spies that Joshua, a well-respected leader, sent to spy out the land. Rahab knew the power of God and had a conversation with the spies to ensure that her family would be saved once they took over the land. The desire of her heart was honored. She married Salmon and became the mother of Boaz and was in the lineage of Jesus Christ according to Matthew 1:5-16. You don't have to be broken with no tips or no vision for the future, burdened with the cares of your life which has not turned out the way you expected.

Crayons are made with paraffin wax and color pigment. So, could you imagine, God taking all the broken crayons in one bag, molded to create something spectacular? God will take all the brokenness in your life, put it all together and make something beautiful, full of color, the radiance of God, a rainbow fitly designed by Him for His glory, Hallelujah!

Allow God to use your broken crayons to color, and He will make something glorious out of your life.

Dear Lord, it is my prayer _____
Lisa Johnson
Bowie, Maryland

AHA Moment

Consider the stars! God created each of them.

HOW GREAT IS OUR GOD

"He telleth the number of the stars; he calleth them all by their names. Great is
our Lord, and of great power: his understanding is infinite."
Psalm 147:4-5 (KJV)

During the summer in 1958, my mother, sister and I spent a couple of weeks
on my grandparent's farm near Yazoo, Mississippi. I enjoyed every minute, freely
playing and chasing chickens. At night, after dinner, we all sat on the front porch,
humming old hymns, talking, and looking at the night sky ablaze with stars. The
stars were so bright and numerous that they almost blocked out the darkness of
the sky. I remember a huge spider web in a corner arch over the porch. I'd never
seen a spider that enormous. No one seemed disturbed by or afraid of it, so I
wasn't afraid either. Life was so simple and innocent then. A live and let live
mentality seemed to be a country-life norm.

So many times in life, we take for granted our everyday life experiences
and childhood memories. Each and every moment that we are alive is precious.
We were created in God's image and our lives should reflect and appreciate the
wonder and beauty of that creation.

I will always thank God for those memories and cherish a mother and family
that taught me right from wrong, a rich heritage of love, how to worship, and
the blessings of growing up in a Christian home.

Sometimes in the midst of sorrow, I can rest in the knowledge that I serve a
God who knows the number and name of each star in the heavens. His power is
great, and He will take care of me.

We serve a mighty God! So, look to the stars in heaven and remember the
God who created the heavens and the earth will take care of you.

Dear Lord, it is my prayer _____
Jacqueline Lee Moore
Inglewood, California

AHA Moment

My hopes are placed on high.

I'M TRUSTING JESUS, HE NEVER FAILS

"...The effectual fervent prayer of a righteous man availeth much."
James 5:16b (KJV)

In 2006, I was suffering extreme fatigue and went to the doctor to check to see if something was wrong with my heart. As a result, I was given an appointment with an oncologist who explained that I had Chronic Lymphatic Leukemia (CLL). At that time the doctor told me that I would literally be sick, and to get ready. I rejected that! CLL is a slow growing blood cancer. I stayed in a stage one, until today. When the doctor told me, I immediately started praying, and asking God for a miracle, and to take the cancer from me. I have a husband of forty years, eleven children, twenty-four grandchildren, and the last thing I needed was cancer.

Some ten years later, on March 10, 2016, my cancer is now in a stage three, and the doctor explains that I am at a high risk, and must start chemotherapy, as an attempt to bring the cancer into remission. At this point in my life I am one class short from attaining my master's degree, and about three months before my school will be out. I am a teacher, and I told my doctor I needed to wait until school is out. I told the doctor that I am going to be ok. My God is faithful. He will bring the cancer into remission or take my soul to heaven. As of October 2016, God choose to bring the cancer into remission.

My faith and trust is in God. I do not have to worry! I believe to be absent from the body is to be present with the Lord. I decided a long time ago to follow Jesus and there is no turning back. "My hopes are placed on high, All other hopes are vain; Yet though at times God seems not nigh, I will trust Him just the same" (A.J. Scarborough).

Dear Lord, it is my prayer _____
Kathleen Simmons
Compton, California

AHA Moment

God does care.

THE DAY MY LIFE WAS TURNED UPSIDE DOWN

"For I know the plans I have for you, declares the LORD, plans to prosper you
and not to harm you, plans to give you hope and a future."
Jeremiah 29:11 (NIV)

It was December 2009, I woke up and called my son Jeremy's cell phone, no success. I was able to reach my oldest son, Marion. He told me Jeremy took the car and said he was going home and would be right back. No one had been able to reach him. In all of our rushing, Marion missed his flight. This was in God's plan for him to miss his flight. We called the hospitals and Jeremy's friend went to the police department. The police put an 'APB' out on the car. We got a knock at the door and it was a police officer and the county coroner. That is when my life made a flip.

I stayed mad with God. I am one of his servants. Family and friends consoled me. My doctor gave me medication; it did not fill the void.

Two months later, my pastor's sermon was, "God Does Care?" I had to realize at that moment, God does care about us. This is all in His control. I still have moments of missing my son. In the midst of a difficult situation, God wanted me to know that He has a plan. He wants me to know as we submit to His plan, He desires to use us to bless the world.

Dear Lord, it is my prayer _____
Mary E. Kendrick-Caldwell
Jackson, Mississippi

AHA Moment

God has a plan for our Lives.

GOD HAD OTHER PLANS

"For that ye ought to say, If the Lord will, we shall live, and do this, or that."
James 4:15 (KJV)

As I was preparing to go for a walk, I got the most excruciating headache. On a scale of one to ten, it was definitely higher than a ten. Something said, "Go to the hospital now!" I know now it was the Holy Spirit speaking. As soon as I explained my condition to the doctors, they started working on me at once.

Prior to this, I had bought an airline ticket to fly into Houston, TX, and then drive to Beaumont for a meeting. My plan was to drive back to Houston, pick up my daughter, and continue to San Antonio for a getaway weekend. Although I had not sought the Lord's will for this plan, God had to show me He was in control.

I was admitted to the intensive care unit of the hospital. After testing, it was determined that I had suffered a mild stroke. The scripture, Deuteronomy 31:8 (KJV), "And the Lord He it is that doth go before thee; He will be with thee, He will not fail thee, neither forsake thee: fear not, neither be dismayed." kept coming back to me. This experience made me realize God has to be first in everything. Proverbs 16:9 (NKJV) tells us, "A man's heart plans his way, but the LORD directs his steps." Someone once said write your plans in pencil, and remember that God has the eraser. My prayer now is to always acknowledge God, first seeking His guidance and plans for my life, and I will always thank Him and give Him glory.

Dear Lord, it is my prayer _____
Brenda G. Washington
Seattle, Washington

AHA MOMENT

God truly does hear and answer our prayers.

THE POWER AND REWARDS OF FAITHFUL PRAYERS

"The effectual fervent prayer of a righteous man availeth much."
James 5:16b (KJV)

Let me introduce you to Linda, one of my younger sisters. Linda worked 26 years for a well-known corporation in this nation. She worked in one of those positions where she was asked, more than once, to train the new supervisor; however, she was overlooked for that position herself. (This is one of the things that repeatedly happens in the corporate world). Linda developed hypertension, diabetes, and a series of mini strokes causing her to lose mobility on the left side of her body. Linda's health continued to decline, and she was granted total disability.

In 2013, Linda suffered a major heart attack requiring her to be on a life support system. We were informed by the doctors that Linda probably wouldn't live past the next few days. We were asked to pull the plug. But, no, we informed the doctors that we were trusting and praying for Linda, and we wanted a miracle! One of the doctors told us she would probably be a vegetable if she survived. In spite of what the doctors told us, we held on to God's hand. A few days later, my brother stepped into Linda's room and touched her feet telling her to get up. Shout! Hallelujah! Linda tried to get out of bed and raised her leg. The doctors were shocked and agreed it was a miracle from God!

Later, Linda was moved to a convalescence facility near her son. Her church family is able to visit and pray with her. In addition, she attends church periodically. As a result of her healing, others have come to trust and depend on God. We thank God for the privilege to reflect His graces. We know that the effectual fervent prayer of a righteous man availeth much.

Let us be faithful in our prayers. God is faithful with His responses.

Dear Lord, it is my prayer _____
Gloria Jean White
Los Angeles, California

AHA Moment

In times of trouble, God is ready to protect.

DIVINE PROTECTION IN GOD'S HANDS

"Though I walk in the midst of trouble, thou wilt revive me: thou shalt stretch
forth thine hand against the wrath of mine enemies,
and thy right hand shall save me."
Psalm 138:7 (KJV)

One morning, at 4:30 a.m., while going to a mandatory church event, I stepped out of my driveway into the street and walked to my van. I had just looked in both directions, before stepping into the street. Suddenly, a car with no lights came speeding directly toward me, and I could hear the accelerator being pushed harder to make the car go faster. Trying to make it to my van, I walked as quickly as I could with my cane. As I reached the van and opened the door, I felt a "lift" pull me into the driver's seat as the speeding car passed right in front of me. It was so close, it could have hit and crushed me to death. But no, I felt God's presence and do believe in His Divine protection. According to Psalm 139:10, the Lord's hand shall lead me and His right hand shall hold me.

No matter where we are, God is ALWAYS there, to pull us to safety by His mighty hands. "For he shall give his angels charge over thee, to keep thee in all thy ways. They shall bear thee up in their hands, lest thou dash thy foot against a stone" Psalm 91:11-12 (KJV).

Remember Psalm 23:4, "Yea, though I walk through the valley of the shadow of death, I will fear no evil: for thou art with me; thy rod and thy staff they comfort me." Know that God is omnipresent–He is everywhere we go! Pray, in the Name of Jesus, that each of us lives a life so we can be assured that God is with us and a very present help in the time of a storm!

Dear Lord, it is my prayer _____
Cordean Fitzgerald
New Carrollton, Maryland

AHA MOMENT

Know God's Word. Be careful of lips that use flattering words.

DON'T TRUST FLATTERING LIPS

"The LORD shall cut off all flattering lips,
and the tongue that speaketh proud things:"
Psalm 12:3 (KJV)

Have you ever gone down a road that really wasn't for you? Did you listen to a voice that was not confirmed by God's Word? We all have at one point or another, but God came to our rescue!

During a season of transitioning (moving from one church to another), my husband and I were in a fasting and praying time. We had served in our home church for over 20 years and we knew the Lord was telling us, "It's time to move and serve with all the foundation that has been laid before you." We began to pray for guidance and believed James 5:16, "Confess your faults one to another, and pray one for another, that ye may be healed. The effectual fervent prayer of a righteous man availeth much." We trust God with everything. There were church members, who meant well, but started speaking to us with flattering lips. Some of their quotes were: "you should open a church" or "you should never leave your home church." These statements were made to flatter us into thinking more highly of ourselves to create in us a proud spirit or proud look, which God hates. See Proverbs 6:16-17. Our God is an awesome God. We put our trust in Him. With His hand, He led us to the place where we are nurtured, healed and taught the unadulterated Word of God, Hallelujah! Has God activated our gifts to be used? Absolutely, because His words are true. God's Word led and guided us to a place where we serve and grow. To God be all the glory!

If you are in a place of transitioning in your life, do not trust flattering lips. Stay in prayer and according to Hebrews 13:5, God will never leave or forsake you. Trust God!

Dear Lord, it is my prayer _____
Lisa Johnson
Bowie, Maryland

AHA MOMENT
He saved us!

WAITING TO IMPACT

"I will praise thee, O Lord, with my whole heart;
I will shew forth all thy marvellous works."
Psalm 9:1 (KJV)

On May 15, 1995, I was enroute to work with my son, who attended the school where I taught. Prior to leaving home that morning, I noticed that he hadn't put on his shoes, so I told him that he had to put them on in the car. While driving, I looked at him for a split second and noticed that his shoes still weren't on his feet. Again, I told him, "Put on your shoes." Then I looked up, and saw that there were three cars stopped in front of me on the two-lane highway. I had to react quickly. Should I hit the car in front, roll down the steep embankment, or hit the brick mailbox? My only option was to cross the double yellow lines in an attempt to pass the cars.

As I proceeded, I noticed that the driver of the first car was yielding to oncoming traffic before turning left. I'm grateful that he saw me to his left and didn't turn. As I continued, a truck came around a curve towards me. I couldn't get back over in the right lane, so a collision was inevitable. I shouted, "Jesus!", as I waited to impact. The sound of clashing metal was terrifying, as the truck's undercarriage drove on top of my car, and then flipped into a ditch. Since we both were driving at 55 miles per hour, the impact was at a speed of 110 mile per hour! This accident had traffic on the highway at a standstill in three cities!

Thankfully, the truck driver, although seriously injured due to his dashboard collapsing into the floorboard, was forgiving. His children also had minor injuries. My son and I were not injured.

Having our lives spared gives us more opportunities to witness to others and daily thank and serve Him in all circumstances.

As this incident was shared, I was told, "You are lucky!" On the contrary, we were blessed!

Dear Lord, it is my prayer _____
Verletta Thompson
Fayetteville, Georgia

AHA Moment

God provides shelter

MY REFUGE AND HIDING PLACE

He that dwelleth in the secret place of the most High shall abide under the
shadow of the Almighty. I will say of the LORD, He is my refuge
and my fortress: my God; in him will I trust.
Psalm 91: 1,2 (KJV)

My mother passed away when I was very young. When my daddy, who was
my anchor, passed away in 2003, my downward spiral in life began. I had always
trusted in my inner strength and knew that I was never alone, but I had never
lived on my own, ever. I really did not know the true meaning of love and found
myself blind-sided by drugs, alcoholism, mental abuse and physical abuse.

By July 2005, I was homeless! I was living between motel rooms and boarding
houses. I continued to be abused to the point that I was physically disfigured. I
looked so bad that one day a young child deliberately turned away from me three
times. It was then I realized I was about to lose my light; literally, I was about to
give it away. I cried out to the Lord for help. God heard my cry and stepped in. By
August 2006, I was provided with shelter. It was a room that gave me a place to
seek God's word, and in this place, I allowed him to teach me to trust Him. Psalm
91 carried me through the darkest times of my life. My journey to everlasting life
returned and my light is shining bright. I am grateful to God for being my refuge.

This life is full of choices, but we must put our trust in God and abide in him
and rest in his strength to see us through all of life's circumstances.

This is how I now read Psalm 91, "[She] who dwells in the secret place of the
most High shall abide under the shadow of the Almighty. I say of You my Lord,
[You] are my refuge and my fortress. My God in [You] I trust."

Dear Lord, it is my prayer _____
Lea Wright
Los Angeles, California

AHA Moment

Don't look at the circumstances, look to God.

TRUSTING GOD IN ALL SITUATIONS

"The Lord is my light and salvation; whom shall I fear?
The Lord is the strength of my life, of whom shall I be afraid?"
Psalm 27:1 (KJV)

This scripture helped me trust God and have faith in Him. My husband and I went through a difficult time when he was diagnosed with cancer. My sister died from this same type of cancer several years ago. I cared for her and took her to doctors' visits, chemotherapy and various treatments. I was so scared because I did not know what the outcome would be. The terrible news of my husband's condition hurt me so much. It shook my faith. I could not believe that God would take me through another terrible situation with cancer again. Although I was working at home and in the church, I was depressed.

My desire to commune with family and friends had left. I basically wanted to isolate myself to wallow freely in the dungeon of self-pity. Until one day, I looked past my circumstances and felt the healing touch of God. His Word ministered to my broken spirit. My depression left and my joy came back. My new resolve was whatever happens, God is in control. Freedom engorged my soul!

The verse from Psalm 27:1 comforted me and helped me to trust God through another horrifying experience. I was able to trust that God would heal my husband of cancer, and we would have an even closer walk with Him.

Our thought for every day should be to cast all our cares on Him and to trust Him in every situation we encounter.

Dear Lord, it is my prayer _____
Lorraine Colbert
Vallejo, California

AHA MOMENT
Don't Get Mad, Get Thankful.

WHY I'M NOT MAD AT GOD

"Giving thanks always for all things unto God and the
Father in the name of our Lord Jesus Christ"
Ephesians 5:20 (KJV)

In my formative years, the Chairman of my church's Deacon Board—a postman by occupation—was a big man with a beautiful, booming, bass voice. I can still see him–head thrown back, eyes closed, tears running down, and singing with all his might to the glory of God. Yet, more than his music, I recall that he often spoke of divine sovereignty: "God says to some, 'be sick,' and to others, 'be well'; to some, 'live,' and to others, 'die.'"

One Wednesday in July my father, mother (diagnosed with cancer earlier that year and pursuing natural remedies), sister, and I commenced a six-hour road trip home. We had attended a momentous church National Convention and the funeral of my mother's cousin. While driving, a reckless, non-licensed driver hit the front left corner of our car. We careened from our extreme right eastbound lane towards the shoulder and cement wall. Unexplainably, we wound up crossing several lanes of highway traffic, stopping parallel to the concrete barriers separating us from the westbound traffic. The car was totaled! We all walked away practically unharmed!

Twenty-one months later my mother succumbed to the cancer: my sister unexpectedly passed away seventy-six days afterwards. Seething, moping, or fuming that my loved ones survived the crash only to die a short time later, might have been natural. However, in that period, my family experienced two years of the saints' sustained prayers upholding my mom and us. My sister had moved back in with the family, to situate herself to purchase a home, and we were privileged to nurse my mom. Both ladies transitioned to heaven from our home.

I learned to trust God's decisions, receive His grace, and still, thankfully testify that He decided our bereavement would not be difficult.

Dear Lord, it is my prayer _____
Nedra V. Moore
East Cleveland, Ohio

AHA MOMENT
Be Patient, Persistent and Stay Focused.

A JOURNEY OF FAITH

"And shall not God avenge His own elect, which cry day and
night unto Him, though He bear long with them."
Luke 18:7 (KJV)

In some instances, God instantly answers prayers. Then again, there are times when perseverance is necessary to receive what we need from God. As a child, I experienced one severe asthma attack, but none as a young adult. However, during my senior years, this illness attacked worse than before. It relentlessly attacked my body and lingered for several years. Medication provided only temporary relief. I prayed daily for God to heal me of this unyielding illness; however, I had no idea that my healing would not be instantaneous. When I did not experience an immediate healing, I accepted that God's grace was sufficient for me. I knew that my healing would come, but in the meantime, I had to press my way and trust God. Knowing and believing that He had never failed me, gave me hope and confidence. There was no one else to depend on but God, so I stood on His promises.

No matter how I felt physically, I had to stay focused on my healer. I needed something from God, and I had to press and pray my way through. I remained steadfast in my prayer life. I continue to remind God of His promises during my prayer time. I thank God for a saved, praying family who was also praying for me. One of my daughters told me that a prophet informed her that God was healing her mother during their church services.

The Holy Spirit ministered to me through the scripture, Romans 8:28. This strengthened my faith. Gradually, my symptoms began to disappear. My healing did not come all at once, but it came in God's timing. I am rejoicing in the Lord for all of the miracles He has performed in my life. When praying, always remind God of His promises. Consistently pray and stand on God's Word and expect a miracle.

Dear Lord, it is my prayer _____
Wilma Staten
Monroe, Louisiana

AHA Moment

Jesus is always there even when we don't want to listen.

IF ONLY WE HAD LISTENED – THINK ABOUT IT

"Then Peter and the other apostles answered and said,
'We ought to obey God rather than men.'"
Acts 5:29 (KJV)

How many times have we been told not to do something by our parents or someone that had our best interest at heart and we did not listen? There is a saying, "A hard head makes a soft behind." I have found that to be true not only in my young life, but in my adult life, as well. As a result, I had to suffer the consequences of my actions. I mumbled to myself, "I should have listened."

It is amazing that God speaks to us in the same way and gave us the Book of Life with instructions! However, for the life of us, we will not listen nor take heed to His Written Word. If we read and study His Word, it tells us what will happen when we do not obey Him.

Life can be wonderful but the journey can be either hard or smooth depending on how you choose to follow God's instructions. The choice is yours. If we stumble, God is always there to pick us up. When we listen, and are obedient to the Holy Spirit, everything will be alright because the Lord watches and gives His angels charge over us.

Proverbs 3: 6 tells us, "In all thy ways acknowledge Him, and He shall direct thy paths."

Dear Lord, it is my prayer _____
Belinda Hubb
Washington, District of Columbia

AHA Moment

As a believer, we must be kind.

KINDNESS

"But the fruit of the Spirit is love, joy, peace, longsuffering, KINDNESS, goodness, faithfulness, gentleness, self control. Against such there is no law."
Galatians 5:22-23 (NKJV)

Kindness is the quality of being warmhearted and considerate, humane and sympathetic, and having a pleasant and godly concern for others. Kindness is the fifth fruit of the Spirit. It is an attribute of God, necessary, but not consistently found in all Christians. The fruit of the Spirit is the result of the Holy Spirit's presence in the life of a believer. Kindness can be felt and taught.

After reading a Sunday school lesson where Cain hated and murdered his brother Abel, my sister Joi revealed that while growing up she hated me. Of course, she got a whipping, had to apologize, and was told never to say that again to anyone. Our Mom then made us learn Ephesians 4:32 (KJV) which reads, "And be ye kind to one another, tenderhearted, forgiving one another, even as God for Christ's sake has forgiven you." We had to be able to quote this verse and use it in various ways during our family devotion. Now as helpers, teachers, and prayer warriors, God is using us to share His Good News of love to others in the grocery store, beauty salons, doctor's offices, or wherever it is needed.

Love and kindness go hand in hand, so I challenge you to be kind to others. It will teach you to be more loving and forgiving like Christ. Relationships will be healed, and those in your circle will want to be better.

Always remember that 1 Corinthians 13:4 (NLT) reads, "Love is patient and kind. Love is not jealous or boastful or proud." We need more KINDNESS in the world today.

Dear Lord, it is my prayer _____
Valetta J. Ross
Merrillville, Indiana

AHA MOMENT
God is our strength when we are weak.

IT'S MAKING YOU STRONG

"Dear brothers and sisters, when troubles of any kind come your way, consider it an opportunity for great joy. For you know that when your faith is tested, your endurance has a chance to grow."
James 1:2-3 (NLT)

My day started with me being awakened by the ringing of my cell phone. I was dreading this day. My youngest daughter was to board a plane and go all the way to Ghana, West Africa on a youth mission trip. Although I tried to hide it, I was not ready for her to go. I rolled over and answered the phone and heard my sister's voice on the other end, say, "Sis, mom's gone." I sat straight up in my bed. This could not be happening; but it was. My mother, who had been battling heart disease and diabetes for years, had lost her fight and gone home to be with the Lord.

What was I to do? I had to wake my baby girl, tell her that her grandmother was gone, and she had to choose whether she would still go to Africa. This was more than I could bear.

There is an old proverb that says, "When it rains it pours;" we may find ourselves drenched in troubles and trials from time to time. Just remember that as we pray and press our way through those tough times, we gain spiritual muscles that strengthen us so that we can endure even heavier loads. It may hurt, disappoint, or dishearten but as we go through it, it is making us strong.

Father, please help us to remember that Your strength is revealed in our weakest moments. Thank you for the assurance that if we remain prayerful, persistent, and patient during times of testing, we will become strong enough to face whatever life brings.

Dear Lord, it is my prayer _____
Sylvia Riddick
Berkeley, California

AHA Moment

He is an "on time" God

BELIEVE AND WAIT PATIENTLY ON THE LORD

"I waited patiently for the Lord; he turned to me and heard my cry."
Psalm 40:1 (NIV)

The Lord truly answers prayers just the way He wants to and only when He wants to. I can say this because He has never failed me yet.

Some years ago, I had an accident and I was left with a condition that was difficult for me to bear. While wrestling with this condition, I cried out in prayer to the Lord for deliverance. It's so easy to say and hear the expression, "Just give it to the Lord and leave it there," right?

Well, I finally gave it to the Lord. I believed that He would hear my cry and I trusted Him to deliver me because of His love for me. Well, "Bless the LORD, O my soul: and all that is within me, bless his holy name" Psalm 103:1. One day while doing a little job, the Holy Spirit spoke to me and made me notice that the condition was gone. I rejoiced and gave thanks because the Lord heard my cry!

So, I say to you, wait on the Lord. He may not come when we want him to but he is an "on time" God. Yes, HE is. I waited patiently and He delivered me. My prayer now is to encourage someone else to wait on Him and believe on Him and have patience because He will come through, right on time.

Dear Lord, it is my prayer _____
Flora May
Jayess, Mississippi

TOPICAL INDEX

LIST OF CONTRIBUTORS

Renay Allen
Sondra Arthur
Irene Aultman
Betty A. Avery
Rozanna "Roxy" Bayne
Yvonne Bayne
Natalie Bell
Sharon Bell
Jerri Bell- Yarbrough
Cheryl Bibb
Deborah Bickhem
Annie K. Bingham
June Bond
JoAnn Boykin
Janay Brinkley
Betty C. Brown
Bonita Brown
Lillian Brown
Lynn Marie Brown
Cynthia Broxton
Brittany Byars-Williams
Linda Campbell
Tiffany Castilla
Sharon Johnson Cherry
Tracy Cherry Cleveland
Lorraine Colbert
Sharon Collins
Alicia Conerly
Monocia Connors
Mary E. Crute
Dana Cudjoe
Dawn Cudjoe
Sarah Beechen Daily
Georgette Davis
Shirley Duncan Dillion
Christina Dixon
Geraldine Drake
Lestine Drake

O'ka Duren
Stephanie Ervin
Priscilla Fields
Cordean Fitzgerald
Nikkia Fletcher
Deborah Florence
Jacqueline Gant
Jessica Campbell Gant
Constance J. Garner
Aldoria Gilbert
Beverly Golden
Latarsho Griffin
Darlene Hancock
Jo Ann Hardy
Janice Harper
Mary Harris
Brenda Hartwell
Colleen Hendricks
Shonda Hill
Terri Hill
Mary Hooker
Belinda Hubb
Gwendolyn Hudson
Elizabeth Izard
Loretta Jackson
Prissie Jenkins
Arveal Keetch Johnson
Denice Johnson
Jannie Johnson
Laurie Johnson
Lillian Johnson
Lisa Johnson
Ernestine Jones
Lajean Jones
Monique O. Jones
Santa Jones
Sheila Bingham Jones
Vonn J. Jones

Deborah Judon
Lillie M. Kendrick
Mae Kendrick
Mary
Kendrick-Caldwell
Mary Kennebrew
Linda Kennedy
Gladys D. King
Linda Lacey
Beverly Tate Latson
Erica Lindsay
Pearl Lindsay
Gabriella
Marigold Lindsay
Pamela Lockett
Sharon Logan
Nadine Luster-Poe
Linda Martin
Doni Mason
Theresa Mata
Flora May
Monique H. May
Shirley McClendon
Linda C. McDonald
Magdalene McNeil
Candace Y. McRae
Geraldine
Boddie Meredith
Adrienne Miller
Equilla Miller
Olvetta Mitchell
Carolyn Moore
Jacqueline Moore
Nedra V. Moore
Sandrea Myles
Mary Etta Myles-Sutton
Kathy Nash
Brenda Newsome

Orelia A. Nicholson
Iness Panni
Tavia Patterson
Johnnie Phillips
Carolyn Pittman
Marilyn Pitts
Donetta Price
Shenitha Pridgen
Viola Purry
Thajuana Rainey
Betty Ratcliff
Annette Richardson
Syliva Riddick
Frances
Christine Robinson
Valetta J. Ross
Kathleen Simmons
Jandrea Brown Sims
Elma R. Smith
LaTonya Smith

Lillie Earlene Smith
Natalie Smith
Vernell Kennedy Smith
Wilma Staten
Ramona Stevens
Zakiya Summers
Connie Tate
Rosemary Tate
Ethelyn Taylor
Deitre Terrell
Pauline Thomas
Valerie Thomas
Denise
Henderson Thompson
Verletta
Myles Thompson
Datrice
Vanzant-Weathers
Cortessa Wallace
Barbara Wolfe Wardlow

Brenda Washington
Regina Washington
Valora Washington
Zelma Watkins
Barbara Waynick
Felissa Lynn Waynick
Portia Waynick
Gloria Jean White
Julemi White
Bettye Willis
Mattie Winn
Jasmine Wise
Pearl Wise
Verneice Wise
Louvenia Wolfe
Lea Wright
Sybil Young

ORGANIZATIONAL SKETCH

United Christian Women's Ministries
of the
Church of Christ (Holiness) USA

The *Church of Christ (Holiness) USA* has a history that dates back to 1896. The Church was organized in Jackson, Mississippi by Bishop Charles Price Jones. Today this national church is comprised of local churches throughout the United States and sponsors ministry work in Africa, Dominican Republic and Honduras. In the early 1900's the Women's Ministries of the Church of Christ (Holiness) USA was organized. Since that time, women's organizations have been a viable and integral part of the church both locally, nationally and internationally. This ministry has operated under the names: Christian Women Willing Workers and The Women's Auxiliary. In 1997, the Women's Ministries became the *United Christian Women's Ministries*.

The United Christian Women's Ministries consist of the following: Family Ministry, Missions Ministry, Senior Ministry, Youth and Children Ministry and Christian Education Ministry.

MISSION STATEMENT

The purpose of the *United Christian Women's Ministries* encourages women of all ages to cultivate their relationship with Christ, and to provide services that will challenge, train, and equip its members and future generations for ministry, evangelism, and spiritual growth.

VISION STATEMENT

The **United Christian Women's Ministries**, through faith and prayer, will:
Uplift the name of Jesus
Cultivate relationships with accountability
Work to train, educate, build and evangelize
Mentor women, new converts, youth and children

For additional information about our church, please visit www.cochusa.org

CPSIA information can be obtained
at www.ICGtesting.com
Printed in the USA
LVOW11s0557120418
573204LV00002B/19/P